ANHUA, CHINA
NOVEMBER, 1944

"After dark our group of seventeen men (who were to set the explosive charge under the railroad track) moved to a civilian's house two hundred yards from the railroad and waited until 21:30. During our wait here the commander sent for the mayor of Anhua village, which was about four hundred yards away. On his arrival he made it very clear that he was glad we were there to harm the Japanese. The commanding officer, trying to secure last-minute intelligence, asked the mayor as to the time schedule of the expected train. He gave a startling answer, 'I will tell you when the train is coming and will be killed tomorrow for doing it, but after I am dead the mayor that takes my place will help you in any way he can.' "

"The war in China in the 1940s has been glorified, distorted, used and misunderstood. . . . In this marvelous book John Horton brings a unique insight to this complicated and brutal war."

—JAMES R. LILLEY
American Ambassador to China
1989-1991

NINETY-DAY WONDER

WONDER

Flight to Guerrilla War

John Ryder Horton

IVY BOOKS • NEW YORK

Ivy Books
Published by Ballantine Books
Copyright © 1994 by John R. Horton

Library of Congress Catalog Card Number: 93-91734

ISBN 0-8041-0564-2

Manufactured in the United States of America

First Edition: March 1994

Remembering particularly two valiant officers,

Captain Andrew Willison Long, USN, and
Colonel Milton Arthur Hull, USMC

So the brain constructs and reconstructs information, creating a highly personal mental artifact and calling it a memory. If people remember best when they enrich information in their own way and remember least when they simplify experience, draining it of meaning, each act of memory must be special, even unique, to each person.

From JEREMY CAMPBELL
Grammatical Man:
Information, Entropy,
Language, and Life,
New York: Simon and Schuster, 1982.

ACKNOWLEDGMENTS

I am grateful to Grace Calhoun Horton for her suggestions. To my mother and father for teaching me a respect for books and writing. To Admiral Milton Miles, USN, for much, including his collection of documents from Naval Group China. To Kathleen Lloyd of the Naval Historical Center for sending me to that collection in the National Archives. To Richard Von Doenhoff and Barry Zerby of the National Archives.

To Paul Stillwell of the United States Naval Institute and his remarkable collection of oral histories. To the Naval Institute also for publishing my piece, "Going Back to Camp One" in *Naval History* for Fall 1989.

To Earl Colgrove, Doctor Jacob Siegrist, the late Milton A. Hull, for copies of photographs of Camp One, some of these taken by J. K. McCoy. I am especially grateful for the help in writing this of Robert Boger, Judge Albert Close, Earle Dane, James Rainey, Jake Siegrist, and the late Doctor Arthur Tucker, good comrades at Camp One with whom we returned there one day in 1986.

Finally, to Owen Lock at Random House who told me to write this account, the serious editor and scholar whose generosity put me into print.

Chapter 1

In June 1940, at the end of my sophomore year at Indiana University, I dragged myself home. I had not found a summer job. Home was where my mother and father now lived in picturesque hill country, some twenty miles east of the university.

The sharp valleys of Brown County, Indiana, were peopled by the same Scots and Scots-Irish, some border English, who settled the mountains of Virginia, North and South Carolina, Kentucky, and Tennessee. They had worked their way to this far edge where the hill country ran out at the abrupt moraine left by the last Wisconsin glacier. The glacier had scraped northern Indiana smooth and left the south rough with knobs and hollows, creeks and branches.

The people were too poor to keep slaves, but that did not prevent many of the rawboned yeomen from sympathizing with the South in the Civil War, from preferring peace to preserving the Union. The local paper was still called the *Brown County Democrat*.

In the 1930s, visitors staying at Nashville House, the old stage inn, were much taken by the Elizabethan speech of the inhabitants. The charm of wooded landscapes and the seemingly simple pioneer ways of the remote place—Nashville was then the only county seat in Indiana lacking a railroad—led outsiders to build vacation cabins up the rutted dirt roads. They collected stories about the quaint ways of those they called the natives. (Waiting tables at the Nashville House, a local girl I knew stepped from invisibil-

1

ity to interrupt one such conversation by declaring, "I ain't no native!")

Mother and Father first stopped at the Nashville House on the way back to Chicago from a fall visit to the Great Smokies in the early 1930s. They found the same sort of people in Brown County. The hills were like the Smokies, too, if smaller, the same blue haze in the lines of receding ridges. Haze and the cheap living had brought the painters in. They put up board-and-batten studios at one side of a log cabin. Mostly they painted landscapes in oils, with treed blue-gray slopes in the background. As the county became known for its fall colors, the paintings showed the brilliant autumn leaves. When Mother and Father visited that first time, enough painters and artisans were around to have started a gallery and to speak of themselves as an artists' colony.

A year or so after that visit, my mother, sister, the family dog, and I spent a summer in a log cabin in a meadow along Hobbs Branch. Father came weekends from Chicago. We had kerosene lamps for light and a wood privy out back. The pump in the kitchen sink and the larger pump outside gave hard, sulphur-tasting water. My mother and sister used the water in the rain barrel to wash their hair.

Our gentle saddle mare snuffled when she heard us coming up the slope to the low-roofed henhouse. Wasps set their wings, hunched on their gray nests, if you entered. The trick was to persuade the mare to come out the door without going in yourself. The dog resented our attention to the mare, her jealousy once leading her to try to eat the mare's hard kernels of feed corn from the metal bucket. As our father was a magnificent horseman, he saw to it my sister and I learned to ride and also that we knew the other side of horsemanship: chambermaids to the mare, as he put it.

At twelve, I had been given a Winchester single-shot .22 rifle. With nothing better to do in the midday heat, I'd lie belly down on a narrow footbridge to plink the fat, gray rats that swarmed in the slough of manure in the breezeway of the cow barn across the stream. There were so many rats they didn't notice their companions falling about them. On my limited allowance, I had to make the small cardboard box of .22 shots last, so I zeroed in the rifle and gave thought to each shot, able to hit a chosen rat in the head at sixty feet.

The barn, then home to a single cow and two mules, belonged to the Petro family—they said Peter-oh. They lived a quarter mile down the branch, overlooking the Bloomington road. Pigs and chickens had free access to their cabin. The two Petro sons were around eighteen and twenty and illiterate. They wore overalls, straw hats, the same shirt every day, and were barefoot much of the time. We spoke different dialects of English, but we got along all right once we got used to each others' pronunciations and learned the meaning of new words. "Hit" meant "it." "Ole maw" was a respectful term for our mother.

Sometimes they handed over the leather reins, and I would get to drive the team in the rattling, springless wagon. Both mules were called Kate. Once I scrambled up on the gee Kate when her traces were unfastened from the whiffletree, the long reins gathered on her back, and took her by the bridle reins. The harness jingled as we went off under the trees at a hard trot, Kate's ears back, the Petros shouting encouragement. She didn't like having me aboard, and I discovered the difference between her gait and the mare's. Up the road, I turned her about, and she bounced me back at a far faster clip than we had left.

On Saturday night, there were dances at Beech Grove—real square dances, not the sort of thing contrived later for tourists in fake cowboy outfits. The covered platform in the trees was lighted white by hissing lanterns. As the summer night wore on and the young men came back from the woods, their faces flushed, the fiddler, Mr. Percifield, played faster, and the work boots stomped louder. We might be allowed to form a square in one corner but were always taken home before the real fun started, couples going off into the woods, the fights we heard about the next week.

In 1938, when Father was rejected by the world of business, Father and Mother came down from Chicago to live. A painter friend of ours in Glencoe, our town outside of Chicago, apropos of their moving to an artists' colony told them, "Of all company, that of artists is the dullest you will find."

They bought a cabin of heavy squared logs at the end of a narrow valley formed by Jackson Branch and the steep, wooded hills on either side of that stream. A dirt road, the old stage road to Indianapolis a century before, ran below the stone wall of our garden before turning to climb the steep hill behind our green-painted barn and twist out of sight among shagbark hickories, beech, and oak. The deep black soil beneath the older trees in the deep woods was covered with a layer of reddish leaf mold. If you kicked at a rust-colored tree trunk, decaying softly on the forest floor, the black beetles would rush out. Take home a piece of rotten stump, and it would glow in the dark on your dresser that night.

The water in Jackson Branch ran clear over shelves of beige sandstone just across the road from the house, an abrupt sandstone cliff rising forty feet to woods on the other side of the stream. In the clay streambanks were fist-sized geodes like nuts in a cake. You pounded them open to crystal quartz cores traced with topaz and amethyst. There was a dusty exhibit of them lined on a ledge of our screened porch.

In the streams, especially in Greasy Creek, you looked for deposits of black sand washed down from the glacial moraine. You could swirl a gob of the sand with water in a pan and wipe a fingertip dry to pick up the flake of gold or tiny semiprecious stone glistening in the wet sand.

Our house looked down to where the valley opened toward the blue hills on the far side of the town of Nashville. My father maintained valley living was better—you can have your view up there on your hill—being out of the winter winds and cooler in summer. At the end of a hot August day, drafts of cold air flowed quietly from the far coves of the forest where the morels grew, rolled down through wooded hollows, crept along the mowed grass to the house. You waded in these thick currents like water, and there'd be a fire in the fireplace that night.

The central part of the house was made of large trunks, adzed square eighty-five years before, a bedroom above, and the living room below. The dining room, the library, the kitchen, and the other bedrooms were lean-tos behind and at one side of the log house. The wide floorboards were uneven and some floors sloped, the house having settled like a ship canted over at low tide. The ceiling beams of the living room and three walls were painted white inside, but the room stayed dark, even on a bright day, so thick were the log walls at the windows. The mantel and the wood paneling on the far wall around the smoke-blackened, sandstone fireplace were painted black, as though to match it.

Through a door was the lighter library, a long room with apple green walls and a ceiling you could touch above your head without straining. Lined with books in shelves of green-gold tulip wood, there was a good place to read on the cushion of the long window seat. A light-colored Chinese chest sat at one end of the seat, exhaling breaths of camphor. Most mornings, Father sat at his desk in a corner of the library, looking into space, searching for the apt word or the quotation fitting the thought he was typing into a letter. At another desk, Mother was scratching out one quick letter after another. If you asked what she was doing, she would say, "I'm doing the dishes," meaning she had just interrupted that to write. Or, "I'm making cottage cheese," meaning that she intended to do that later. I can't remember her ever saying, "I'm writing letters."

Once when the termites began swarming from a crack in the two steps down from the library into the dining room, Father declared that we had a termite problem. This small room was light and nearly filled by the leaves of a maple dining table set against the windows, room for chairs on three sides. A large chest stood against the wall across from the windows. Shelves along the walls held majolica plates, pewter pots, vases of fresh flowers, or a winter bouquet. On visits home, or when there were breakfast guests, we might sit around the table two or three hours—coffee and talk, history and politics, about or from books, most of it. During the long walk following breakfast, the talk would go on. These last years, always the talk turned to Europe. And at some point, Mother would ask Father, "What's Hitler going

to do?" I never heard him admit himself unqualified to answer.

Part of one earlier summer, I shoved about on my back
in the old dirt and spiderwebs beneath the house, smearing
creosote on the foundation against the termites. The other
part of that summer, I spent in the sun on the top of the
house, smearing a tarlike red paint on an endless roof with
a long-handled brush. When I could be spared from those
projects, I was set to hoeing weeds in the vegetable garden.
Mother did not trust me in her flowerbeds. In the fullness
of southern Indiana humidity, the spate of sweat gushing
from your forehead into the eye sockets made hoeing the
least pleasant of these chores.

That June 1940, my father did not want me another summer as his employee, nor did I want to work for him. Nor
did I want to be idle at home. Anything I did in Brown
County would only repeat the past.

I had passed through my rat-plinking phase, and the .22
rested in the shed, pulled out rarely to shoot the odd prowling cat, gone wild, that preyed on the quail.

The girl from Indianapolis, whose heart I had won forever two summers ago, was seeing someone else and
passed me, unseeing, in the village street.

On that other summer's mare, I had ridden over one
large section of county. Once, going bareback up an abandoned logging road, I came on a bonneted old woman who
stood at the door of her earth-floored cabin to greet me and
offer us water. The cabin was set in a clearing of a narrow
cove, the trees behind it marching thick up a slope to a high
ridge. She shielded her eyes to look up at me and say she
had never been as far as Nashville, no more than eight
miles away. A visitor was unusual, but there was nothing
strange in my being mounted. I later thought it unlikely she
had ever seen an automobile.

In hot overgrown fields, I'd walked warily up to spooky,
abandoned cabins, watching for copperheads in the weathered boards and the brown grass bunched dry on the hard
ground. I had climbed animal tracks on foot over wooded
ridges and followed a north-south Shawnee trail through the
rich light in a tunnel of autumn leaves.

Two friends and I, another summer, explored the roads in a Model T phaeton with no top and few floorboards. Because the low gear had gone, we turned around and backed up the hills. Where the roads ran out, we lurched over rocks in dry creek beds.

Working ten to twelve hours a day in the state park, I had gotten up before dawn to watch birds in thickets along the streams.

I had read scores of the books that lined the walls of our library, books that spilled out into the living room, that were piled three-deep on bedside tables, and gone through John Buchan and P. G. Wodehouse in the town library two or three times.

Panning for gold sounds romantic, but it's not a real job. In the worst of the depression, when no one came to buy their paintings and they had no money to buy paints, some of the young artists panned gold for bread. They would cork the thin flakes, one by one, in a glass vial of water, as big around as your finger and a third as long. With gold at thirty-five dollars an ounce, they might earn a dollar or two in a day.

Our family lived in this pleasant country, and it was home now, but we were not of it. We had friendly relations with a number of the natives—our family called them that, too—but most of our time was spent with other outsiders, the painters, the potters, other refugees from the cities, the summer and the weekend people. My contemporaries, native or foreign, seemed to want no other world than that one. Hardship for them would be leaving it—staying there for me. As much as we enjoyed coming home to Brown County, my sister's thoughts and mine were elsewhere. I did not understand why a person could be content to stay in this quiet place while I longed to get out of it. Despite my restlessness, I had no particular place in mind.

Having failed to get a summer job left me open to my father's persistent scheme that I take time off from college. He was not wrong in thinking my course of studies at university to be aimless. I worked at what appealed to me. The history of philosophy, geology, comparative anatomy, constitutional history. South American geography! "Greek and

Latin derivatives? What in God's name is that?" He had spent some seven years at Latin, two or three at Greek, and Mother had once taught Latin along with botany and biology. They looked at each other and back at me.

It was obvious, too, that I was enjoying fraternity life, and that enjoyment loomed large in his thinking. My response under interrogation about my career intentions was weak: possibly journalism or, well, law, maybe. Definitely not medicine, I added. Too much memorizing, I said.

I could have added that the embryology man lectured so fast in the medical auditorium that I could not take notes and watch his pointer at the same time. Or that it had taken months to realize that the rash covering both my hands was caused by formaldehyde. The entrails of my dogfish had floated about the tank like spaghetti, his innards floated independently away from my frog and could not be found, and the name label disappearing from the delicate tarsus of my white rat caused disputes concerning his or her identity and my title of ownership. The dissections of the other students, especially those of the hateful girls in the same lab session, were meritorious bundles of neat flesh.

Turning away from a career in medicine cost me the support of my mother, my only local ally—my sister being in New York. Mother had hoped I would somehow turn into a medical doctor like her father. She would have been a doctor herself had not her father felt strongly about hen doctors.

Sensing the effect on them of my answers to their questions, I had the tact to omit reporting that a roommate and I, just a week ago, had been talking of raising sheep in Tierra del Fuego, a result of the impulsive course in the geography of South America.

I had no objection to leaving college for a while, but my idea for passing that interlude was not like my father's. For many years he had been an executive in a small, reputable Chicago firm, doing good business. When the firm was taken over by a large corporation, the new management broke their promise and paid him off. He never recovered from this humiliation and from having to discover in his late fifties that no one else saw any use for him. Yet he continued to hold the world of business up to me as the essence of American accomplishment. This irritating prejudice of his now threatened me.

One aspect of his integrity—for I knew and venerated his honesty, assuming it to have been a handicap in the business world—was a dislike of asking favors of friends. But he was ready to sacrifice this principle to pry me into a position from which I could feel the thrill of commerce and the joy of industry. The current idea was to get me working as an apprentice on the factory floor of the manufacturer of Allison engines in Indianapolis. Here I would come to understand the genius of American production and, with the right sort of zip and stick-to-itive-ness, work my way up to a place in the American corporate structure.

At just this point, I had a letter from the Tierra del Fuego roommate. He was working on a gambling ship on Lake Michigan. Stationed near the slot machines, he wore an apron from which he made change for the clients. He was developing a sense, he said, for when a machine, sufficiently played, became impatient to pay off. He would step quietly up to play a few turns, occasionally adding a torrent of quarters to his supply—all clear profit. The only annoyance, he said, came from lonely women forcing themselves on him. He thought maybe he could find me something—or did I have a job?

I didn't believe him about the women, but I answered immediately, asking him to get me on.

Chapter 2

You wonder that some people can live quietly, untouched, through a time of troubles. They pass through life apart from history, as though living in a cabin far up a valley with no road to it. They don't care that Alexander and his army, Caesar or Napoleon, passed nearby, if they ever do hear of it. Only the bad luck of living in the path of an army, being conscripted, having a barn burnt or a horse taken, drags them into what others later on will call history.

The tripartite family discussions of my future were taking place during another of those times in history when the grand visions of a strong leader had seized the imaginations of more modest men as he led them to one victory after another. Hitler had ended the eerie months of waiting after conquering Poland in 1939 by invading Norway in April 1940, sending his armies into the Low Countries and France in May.

So my future was being weighed in something other than a petty personal context. We had never been encouraged to think that events far away did not concern us. Something in family discussions had led me, a ten-year-old schoolboy, to throw my weight behind the boycott of Japanese goods to punish Japan for her adventures in China in 1931. (Weakly, I excepted a rubber squirt gun remarkable for the amount of water it could carry—early recognizing and succumbing to superior Japanese manufactures.)

Before Brown County, we'd lived on Greenbay Road north of Chicago, a narrow road winding along the old Indian trail that ran from the southern end of Lake Michigan to Green Bay at its upper northwest end. The Daughters of the American Revolution put approving brass plaques on deformed oaks that had been tied down as saplings a century or two before to mark the trail. This forested corridor ran between the lake and the bogs of the Skokie marsh, the marsh a transit stop for waterfowl on the Mississippi flyway, summer home to sora and Virginia rails, coots and gallinules. Islands of peat smoldered underground all year, breaking out in summer fires that turned the western sky red at night. Mosquitoes spawned there, too, until a mosquito abatement project was successful in draining the Skokie, getting rid of the habitat for mosquitoes and driving the water birds from their home.

Across the road from us, a dark brick house sat on a green lawn, behind red-berried barberry hedges. Behind that house, a green swath of park stretched to the tracks of the fast electric train to Milwaukee. Parallel to them ran the steam railway built by the British, that explaining why the heavy steam engines thundered down the left track of the Chicago and Northwestern on their way to the West. They left a brushstroke of smoke across the sky, a taste of sulphur in your nostrils. The smaller engine, pulling the green coaches filled with fathers coming back from Chicago at night, clacked slower along the same track from one suburban station to the next. The shined brass bell sitting among the domes on the engine's dorsum rang a clear evening Angelus.

Any one of the tracks was convenient for putting a copper penny down to be flattened. When the track began to vibrate with an approaching train, a winter trick was to persuade a new boy to put his tongue to the track. He'd find, as you had before him, that he could not pull his head away without leaving a patch of flesh behind.

Before going in for dinner on a winter's night, you could time a man's walk home from the station, set up a shivering ambush at a gap in a high snow-covered hawthorn hedge, mold a snowball, stomp your feet, heat pouring from your body through wet wool mittens. Waiting, you might wonder why the steam whistle of a locomotive left you with a different feeling in the blue twilight than did the same sound during the day.

The wheels of the morning ice wagon, pulled by two heavy bays, were exchanged for runners in the snow. Taciturn, dark-faced, shiny-haired Clancy wore a leather cap and a leather bib across one shoulder, over which he tossed the tonged blocks of ice to lug them to the house. He didn't seem to notice if boys got up behind, winter or summer, as long as they behaved themselves.

Around 1930, they replaced the metal tires on the white Bowman Dairy cart with rubber and shod the horse with rubber shoes. They even put rubber stops inside the metal basket the bottles fitted in. When the milkman went to leave milk at the back door and pick up the empty bottles, they no longer set up an early morning jingling. If you slipped out of bed on a summer morning, before anyone else was up, the milkman would let you step up into the milk-smelling cab. The horse rarely needed to be told anything, knowing to move off by the creak of the cart when the driver climbed back aboard. If the horse dozed between stops, head drooping, the driver flicked the reins along his back, and the horse would jerk awake in the shafts and clop along a few yards before slowing to a walk at the next house. When the driver could cut through a back yard from one house to the other, he would cluck at the horse as he swung to the ground, and the horse would pull along to the next stop to wait for him.

We had a maroon Chrysler with whitewall tires on chrome wire wheels, dove gray upholstery, a square trunk sitting on a platform in the back. One Saturday, my father drove to a place in Chicago near a railroad yard, not far from the stockyards, turning off the road onto an expanse of black cinders. He drove slowly past a wall of shacks so I could see the unsmiling faces of ragged black children peering shyly, fearfully, at us from one set of broken windows after another. He delivered no homily with this. He didn't have to, although I was not sure at the time why he felt I needed to see such things.

After their father died, he and his brother lived on in the Iowa town with their schoolteacher mother. The family was respected so they did not lose caste. Their poverty may have been genteel, but it still tasted bitter fifty years later. Usually, he would make a story out of it: how the cow would step on his foot and the pushing it took to get her to move, the way she switched her tail in his face while he milked her. My sister and I had a sense of being well-off in childhood—of being fortunate—but our family was not wealthy. We were not being brought up in luxury, certainly not, as it were, spoiled. Our father saw to that. It bothered him, my sister says, that we didn't know hardship.

I realized Father and Mother were peculiar. They were older, for one thing, than the parents of my contemporaries and interested in a curiously different set of objects and ideas. We went walking in the forest preserves west of Chicago instead of belonging to Skokie Country Club. They could name the birds and made us look at them through a pair of wobbly brass German opera glasses. My mother could identify plants. If she came on one she didn't know, she picked it apart with a needle and leafed through a tattered *Gray's Botany* until she classified it—she went through four of the Gray's in her lifetime. We went for winter picnics, gathering sticks for a fire in the snow of a sheltered swale in the Waukegan dunes, the dog racing about in a frenzy, stopping to gnaw the snow packed in her paws. We camped there in the summer, our tent solitary behind the deserted beach.

I began to notice that visiting friends would remark on a strangeness about us that I took for granted. Their wonder might come out as a compliment. More often, I was uneasy and defensive about it, wishing my parents could be more like the others. My sister says that it never occurred to them to worry about the expectations of those others. They kept up with no one. For my part, I began to wonder what kind of people we were.

Hard to pigeonhole. We certainly weren't old money— hardly money at all. Not the aristocrats or patricians in the books, but hardly common folk, either. Old families going back into time, pioneers, displaced landless gentry, trading the land for books, being raised with deep—exaggerated?— respect for the printed word, for nature and the outdoors, for learning, for science and the mind. Yet our family was by no means alone, nor lonely, and less unusual, less distinctive, less separate than I feared.

Shortly after Hitler came to power in 1933, we were still living in our Chicago suburb. One night at the dinner table, I reported that the father of a neighborhood playmate had come back from a visit to Germany to say that Hitler, among other promising accomplishments, was dealing with the Jewish problem. My father's anger on hearing this was directed not at me but at the neighbor, a public utilities lawyer whom he already disliked, aggravated by an earlier insult. Like a lot of other midwesterners, my father had lost the money he'd invested in the utilities empire of a speculator of the period, Samuel Insull, notable for his carelessness with other peoples' money. I had aroused his anger on an earlier occasion by racing home with the observation of this same neighbor to a remark of my father's, critical of Insull. My friend's father had loftily corrected me and, through me, the courier, my father: those who wanted Insull jailed were persecuting him. Insull was a scapegoat.

There was nothing fashionable in my father's anger of 1933. He went by his own standards in saying what was wrong with our neighbor's praise of Hitler. Father named people in our community he knew—some of their children were my classmates—men and women he had worked with on the school board or in charity drives. These were Jews, he said, people to be admired. He spoke of their community spirit, reminding me that one businessman I saw walking to the morning train when I was on my way to school had been a brigadier general in our army in France. For me, anyone who had fought in France was above criticism. My indiscriminate admiration included a young German immigrant, then our part-time gardener, who had been a machine gunner in the German army fifteen years before. He performed such breathtaking feats as spying a rabbit in our tulip border at the moment the rabbit spotted him. He ran the racing rabbit down and snatched him up at full tilt. Coming to a stop, he held the animal by both ears with one hand, rapped him dead with a blow behind the neck with the other, laid the limp rabbit on the ground, and went back to raking. Seeing us play war, he spoke against it, advice we ignored until it was frighteningly reinforced by the first filming of *All Quiet on the Western Front*.

Without his having to say so, it was apparent my father viewed the persons he had spoken of more favorably than a certain non-Jew living not far from us. Anti-Semitism was for him—this was years before Hitler's "final solution"—brutal, bullying, a European disease, what you could expect of the lower-class German, surely in bad taste for an American. A popular view then saw Hitler as the upstart, the Austrian corporal—he wasn't even German—a rabble-rouser riding a wave of anti-Bolshevik reaction, copying Mussolini's fascist perversion of socialism with his National Socialism in Germany. He couldn't last.

But Hitler kept moving from one outrage to the next against the Jews. When he called the Versailles Treaty unjust, he touched the bad conscience of the victors of the 1914–1918 war. When he moved troops into the demilitarized Rhineland, his generals held their breaths. Nothing happened. Each following success of Hitler's was a blow, discussed and deplored in our family, in their circle of friends. It would be an exaggeration to say that our lives hung on these distant events, that they ruled us. But they were close enough then to rise unbidden today, attached to other memories of that time. Swatches of the civil war in Spain cling to an exciting, laughing dip in Lake Michigan in a November snowstorm. The attack on Poland in September 1939 is an arm aching with the last stiff turns of the dasher in a canister of black walnut ice cream.

June of 1940 in the living room of the cabin on Jackson Branch, we strained to hear the BBC, piecing together the crackling phrases that howled through magnetic storms to our quiet room, my father gazing about the living room from his wing chair, cigarette smoke curling around his head, Mother looking worried, glancing from one to the other of us. The British Expeditionary Force and some French troops barely got out of the port of Dunkerque to England the first week of June. Paris was evacuated. Marshal Pétain took over the government and asked the Germans for the armistice, signed a few days later at

Compiègne. France had fallen, and only the English Channel kept Hitler's conquest from being complete.

At the end of one broadcast, my father, who loved France, looked at my mother, saying, "Well, that's it. We're in it now." "Just a matter of time, now," he told people all that year.

Those broadcasts ended with a band playing "Rule Britannia," the music wavering defiantly through the static, whistling through Atlantic clouds, sinking, struggling heroically back. That was all the motivation I needed. I couldn't imagine going back to college as though nothing had happened, as though it had to happen right here in Indiana to matter.

That school year of 1939–40, some seniors I knew at Indiana had signed up for flight training. That was the most noble calling I could imagine at the moment, but I was annoyed that both army air corps and navy required cadets to have a college degree. There wasn't time to waste earning that, now.

A fraternity brother put on sudden dignity with the uniform of a second lieutenant of infantry. Until then, he had been the butt of jokes for having a sword up his ass, a common derogation for anyone who took ROTC in any way but mockingly. I envied him, too, but not enough to spend two more years at ROTC, grateful the obligation for close-order drill and map-reading class was ending with my sophomore year. A couple of us in the house got briefly excited about joining a Scots regiment in Toronto, losing interest immediately on learning of the four-to-six-year term of enlistment. You'd be old by the time you got out. And what if the war suddenly ends on you?

So I was home, without a summer job, far less inspired by the idea of factory life than my father was for me. He thought the Allison engines scheme to be good in peace or in war. Allison was starting to produce in-line engines for fighter aircraft. You got to work in the bowels of American industry and help the British defeat Hitler at the same time. I never thought that either my mother, seeing me as an MD, or my father, seeing me as a lieutenant if not a captain of industry, was so insensitive as to hope to live again in me. They just found my lack of vocation disappointing.

I had not the wit to present an alternative. I couldn't argue that I belonged back at the university. Learning for its own sake was losing its appeal, and I didn't fancy marking two years' time at Indiana that might not in the end qualify me for flying, for the infantry—might as well take a vocational course in business administration, like some of my fraternity brothers, cheerfully looking forward to life in Spencer or Versailles, Greencastle or Valparaiso in the family business.

Then a letter came with an invitation in it.

"The enclosed copy of the telegram, just received, will be especially interesting to you as a university man.

"This is an opportunity that has not been available since the world war.

"If you are interested, it is suggested you promptly contact us at the Indianapolis Naval Armory. We will be open from 8:00 A.M. until 10:00 P.M. every day next week."

The letter was signed F.F. Knachel, Lt-Comdr, USNR.
Special Reserve Recruiting Officer

The telegram was from the Ninth Naval District at Great Lakes, Illinois, and informed Lieutenant Commander Knachel, for his "immediate information," of the navy's

DESIRE TO ENLIST NATIONAL TOTAL OF 5000 MEN RATING APPRENTICE SEAMAN IN NEW CLASS NAVAL RESERVE DESIGNATED V-7 FOR ONE MONTH TRAINING AFLOAT CORRESPONDING TO PRESENT NAVAL ROTC SUMMER CRUISE. CANDIDATES FOR ENLISTMENT MUST HAVE MINIMUM TWO YEARS COLLEGE CREDITS FROM UNIVERSITIES ACCREDITED BY NATIONAL BOARD OF EDUCATION. BE AMERICAN BORN BETWEEN 19 AND 26 YEARS OF AGE. BE UNMARRIED PASS PHYSICAL EXAMINATION REQUIRED FOR ENSIGN VOLUNTEER GENERAL SERVICE AND SUBMIT TWO LETTERS OF RECOMMENDATION FROM RESPONSIBLE CITIZENS. CANDIDATES UNDER 21 YEARS MUST PRESENT SIGNED CONSENT OF GUARDIAN (OR PARENTS). CANDIDATES WILL BE REQUIRED TO REQUEST ACTIVE DUTY TRAINING DUTY WITHOUT PAY BUT WILL BE FURNISHED TRANSPORTATION IN KIND RATIONS AND CLOTHING.

AFTER COMPLETION CRUISE SUCCESSFUL CANDIDATES WILL BE
ISSUED APPOINMENTS AS RESERVE MIDSHIPMEN AND DESIG-
NATED ELIGIBLE TO RECEIVE NINETY DAY COURSE OF IN-
STRUCTION WITH PAY LEADING TO COMMISSION AS ENSIGN,
UNITED STATES NAVAL RESERVE. CONTEMPLATE COMMENCING
FIRST CRUISE JULY 16 AT NEW YORK NECESSITATING COMPLE-
TION ENLISTMENTS AND REPORT OF TOTAL NUMBERS TO BU-
REAU OF NAVIGATION BY JULY 10.

The government's preparedness for war precisely coincided with mine. I was six months over nineteen. I had no
questions. The family colloquies that preceded an explor-
atory visit to the naval armory in Indianapolis that next
week are gone from memory. I do remember portly Mr.
Knachel in black-rimmed glasses sitting behind a government oak desk in a corner of the echoing space of the armory, a damp cigar end in a glass ashtray on a pile of
papers. He wore a bulging white shirt, black tie, and black
suspenders, his uniform jacket hanging on a hook behind
him. I remember staring at the two-and-a-half, gold-
tarnished-green stripes on the sleeve. I remember bouncing
out of our black Dodge sedan by the woodshed when we
drew up in our yard and the way my mother looked at my
father when she heard what I told her. For whatever
reasons—seeing how eager I was to join, surging with patriotism himself—he had consented to my enlistment.

The summer's weak uncertainty was wiped away by my
enlistment, by my instant and unreserved commitment to
the navy. Obviously, the term "successful candidates" in the
telegram implied that some might fail, but that couldn't ap-
ply to me. Maybe I was insufferably cocky. I've never
known why my father, at some point in the ensuing days,
looked me over and said, "They won't commission you a
naval officer."

Anyway, that was the end of the talk about the Allison
engine factory.

Chapter 3

One hot August morning, our draft of volunteers mustered on the train platform in Indianapolis, answering as our names were called, cocking our heads to hear what someone was saying in the center of the cluster, hardly audible in the hissing of steam and the chuffing of locomotives. This was a self-guided tour, someone—probably the tallest of the group—being handed orders with our names on a piece of paper, the rest of us straggling after him up the steps of a coach. We rattled across Ohio and Pennsylvania for a hot day or so, as dust and cinders blew in the open windows. We left the worn, green plush seats to smoke on the swaying platforms between the cars and talk about where we'd come from, how we happened to enlist. In any group of twenty or so men, at least one voice will speak with greater assurance than others. We'd gather about to listen to him until satisfied he knew little more about our future than did we.

In New York, we hustled directly to the subway, again following written instructions, somehow finding our way to where the battleships *Wyoming*, *Arkansas*, and *New York* lay in the Hudson River on Riverside Drive. Directed through a roofed-over hulk alongside the dock, we went down a gangway to a boat that took us to the foot of the gangway of the *Wyoming*. Once on the quarterdeck, we were pushed and pulled and ordered one way and then another, told to stand out of the way, finally sent down a ladder to a narrow passageway where sailors were hurrying

past each other in both directions. Someone shouted "Attention!" and the sailors stopped shoving past us to put their
backs against the bulkhead. Seeing this, we quickly did the
same. An officer, godlike in white service uniform, strolled
along the passage. All eyes went to the one gold stripe on
his shoulder boards—an ensign!

Sailors began hurrying again on their urgent errands as a
piercing whistle wavered through a loudspeaker, followed
by unintelligible shouting. No one seemed to pay it any attention. We barked our shins on the high portal of a water-
tight door to a compartment where storekeepers handed us
two white jumpers of cotton canvas, two pairs of white
bell-bottom trousers, a round, white sailor's cap each. Your
name and a number of no known significance were sten-
ciled on a white band sewn across the middle of the
jumper.

I was one of some twenty apprentice seamen berthed in
number four gun room, this room being one deck below the
port aircastle, sharing the space with number four gun. On
the outboard side of the gun room, a large port opened wide
to air and sea, allowing the long barrel of the five-inch gun
to be trained from one side to another as well as elevated
and depressed. The gun mount so sat that its breech pushed
a good way into the room. On one side was a curved metal
seat—the perforated kind you used to see on farm
equipment—for the pointer to sit on and a pair of small
wheels on a horizontal axis for the pointer to spin as he
raised or lowered the gun. On the other side was the same
arrangement for the trainer to move the gun from side to
side. Each had a telescopic sight to lean his head into,
keeping the crosshairs on the target as the ship pitched and
rolled. Local control, that would be; the laying and firing of
the gun could be also directed from central fire control.
Then the gun crew would be responsible only for rapid
loading and seeing to it that the barrel was clean before
loading again. The five inch was a bag gun. That is, the
crew jammed a five-inch projectile into the breech and
packed a white silk bag of powder in behind it before slamming the breech closed and locking it.

We didn't know any of that. We learned it later when

taught how to serve the gun. That afternoon, we simply stared at the machine of gray-painted metal. Unused to living with a gun in our room, we lurched painfully against its brass knobs and steel handles.

The white-painted room had a spotless deck of unpatterned red linoleum, lockers against the bulkheads for our belongings, hooks from which we would hang the hammocks we were then sent off to draw. Wooden mess tables on metal legs were folded and put up on the overhead, to be taken down by the mess attendants when we ate. We stuffed our civilian clothes into a seabag and, there being no mirror, looked each other over to get an idea of how we looked in our new clothes.

As no one seemed to care for a moment what we did, I found my way aft to the quarterdeck. A steady rain had begun to fall. The cars passing on Riverside Drive and buildings on shore began to light up as the ship's company came back aboard. I lurked under a white awning to watch each man stop at the top of the gangway, turn aft to salute the colors and then that imposing figure of authority, the officer of the deck. I took care to keep out of his sight.

Sailors were coming up the gangway in numbers now, fast, to get out of the rain. At the top of the gangway stood a petty officer wearing an armband, a club swinging loosely from a thong around his wrist, a person I would later identify as one of the masters-at-arms, the petty officers responsible for discipline aboard. As I watched, he took a small step toward the gangway and swung his club hard across a sailor's paunch. The sailor grunted, bending, arms clutching his stomach and the broken pint of whiskey he'd hidden under his jumper.

Not a word was spoken. The sailor reeled off. The master-at-arms took a step back to resume his position. The officer of the deck seemed to have seen none of this. Bringing liquor aboard was a court-martial offense. By his quickness, the master-at-arms had saved the sailor a blemish on his record and the ship from wasting time on litigation. I didn't work that out until later on—just then it seemed a brutal foretaste of life in the navy.

I started forward to astound my messmates with a report

of what I'd witnessed, vaguely aware of having to elbow through a moving column of large cardboard boxes. I found myself pressed into service in the working party carrying the boxes below to the galley. When relieved of this duty, I found my way to number four gun room, too late for dinner, soaking wet, my whites smutted from the job. One of our number, either for his height or for his earnest demeanor, had been named section leader. I told him where I had been.

"That's very good," he declared, stripping down to his skivvies. "You attracted favorable attention to yourself by doing so."

"You think so?" That seemed unlikely, but I saw nothing to be gained by disputing him, so I prepared also for bed.

The gun room was busy. None of us had thought hanging a hammock would call for any talent. But if you strung it too loose, it folded you up like a fetus. That was easy to fix provided you could find a second hook at the right span from your first hook, and provided no one had slung his hammock across that path. Then, it took a few hops to get into it, like mounting a tall horse. In the same way, leaping athwartships across the hammock, you kicked with your legs and grabbed with your arms until you could slump prone inside the canvas.

What surprised us was the unlikelihood of the hammock's staying up once hung. It was a matter of knots. A couple of our messmates had been to sea before and helped the rest of us. Even so, there was thumping and cursing as a line let go, spilling someone five feet to the deck below. After waking once in midair, flipping to the deck like a cat, I found myself hesitating to go back to sleep. By midnight, the metal of the bulkheads echoed the sound of snoring and the odd cry in the night as still another line parted.

The next morning dawned, shining. We rose early to discover that beans for breakfast, far from being a joke, were standard navy fare. We were left free to wander about on deck and watch the preparations for getting underway. We sailed with slow dignity down the Hudson to the Upper Harbor on our way to the Narrows, the exit to the Atlantic that lay beyond. New York harbor was busy, the great liners lying at their docks, lighters and tugs crisscrossing the blue water in front of us. Four or five sailors lined up on deck to tootle spirited sea chanteys as we slipped through the harbor waters. Physically, they were almost a caricature of a ship's band, each of their figures so different, one from the other—short, tall, skinny, fat—that they might have been combined as sardonic comment on the male condition.

A dark-hulled passenger ship, flying the Dutch flag, was standing in from sea. As our two ships passed, her passengers packed the main deck and the boat deck above, waving handkerchiefs. From five hundred yards away, the fresh breeze carried the sound of their cheering. We waved back. The Dutch ship dipped her colors—as etiquette prescribes a merchantman passing a man-of-war—to the Stars and Stripes fluttering at our aftermast. Inspired by the moment, our little band broke into "The Stars and Stripes Forever."

I suppose they were new refugees on that Dutch ship— the Nazis had invaded the Netherlands only three months earlier—a few of our fellow Americans coming home, excited by our bright ship after the darkness of the old world. Later, some of us confessed how proud that passage had made us feel. For those glad hearts, we represented hope— the New World—not an old training vessel with five hundred one-day sailors aboard.

There were no more episodes of glory from there on. We spent the next few days getting to know the names of unfamiliar objects and learning to call familiar objects by navy names rather than as we knew them. We passed fresh lore from one to another.

"You don't whistle aboard ship."

"You know you don't say 'all right' on the navigation bridge, don't you?"

"Get some saltwater soap. The regular kind doesn't work in salt water." (Aft, there were two saltwater showers for the five hundred of us.)

"Watch out for that loudmouth master-at-arms. Know who I mean? The fat, rat-faced one. He's a real son of a bitch."

We had a Marine complement aboard who had nothing to do with apprentice seamen if they could avoid us. Their field music—that's what they called it—obliged us with a good deal of intrusive bugle blowing at inappropriate times. You got the idea that the Marines didn't want to leave communications in the hands of the boatswain's mate who was—after all—nothing but a sailor. It helped that the boatswain's mate followed his piping with an exegesis, loudspeakers passing the word in English. Even then, the meaning might not be clear. You could see a member of the ship's company responding to whatever had been said, and you followed him around, begging an interpretation. Occasionally the ship itself would let out a bellow from the stack to warn that it was getting underway, backing down, turning left or right, or to remark that the sun had just crossed the meridian. There were other noises, gongs and bells, that you simply couldn't be bothered with just then.

We turned to at 0545, a time given over to swabbing down the teak deck in our section's work territory, aft of the port aircastle. The band showed up to play chanteys and songs, "A Life on the Ocean Wave," "Sailing, Sailing, Over the Bounding Main." The ship gathered an impressive amount of dirt in a day's time, considering we were at sea, mostly coming from the stack. It smeared your seat with its black residue if you had the time to sit down. Blobs of the stuff flew straight to a white blouse.

We polished and repolished the brightwork, chipped paint, repainted, and chipped it again. Sometimes we'd exchange the swab for a holystone to scour the teak. The small, noisy boatswain's mate, Casey—he of the graying red hair and the little potbelly—presided over us when we worked on deck. Casey tore the handle from my hands one morning as I was scrubbing with the holystone. "You couldn't push a sick whore off a pisspot," he told me, rasping the stone along the deck at a rate he could have kept up no longer than the three seconds he held it before handing it back. I did not include the metaphor in my letter home.

We were fond of Casey and told each other stories about him. Cursing us amiably, he pretended astonishment at our incompetence, demanding perfection but actually satisfied to keep us busy. A week or so later, Casey staggered back aboard at Guantánamo with a skinful and was sick over the side, projecting his upper and lower plates into the water. The next day he applied at sick bay for a new set of teeth, telling the surgeon he'd lost them while passing the word over the side. He and the regular seamen who worked with him referred to us as "college boys." They saw we were ignorant but there was no meanness in them.

At 0630, we'd go below. The black mess attendants would have set up mess tables in the gun room, a bench on either side. A metal pitcher held black coffee that you poured into a thick white mug with no handle. With a metal serving spoon, you served yourself a glob of navy beans from a thick white bowl onto a thick white plate, ate it with a metal soupspoon.

From 0700 until 0830, we turned to again carry out whatever task Casey had for us. At anchor in a heavy swell, he might put a gang of us on a heavy line, running back and forth as we were hauled along the deck by it, damping the frantic tossing of a whaleboat trying to come alongside. Or there'd be the command to air bedding, and we'd dash below to the hammock nettings and stumble back up the ladders to fasten hammock and bedding just so to the lifelines. Casey would strut along the line of hammocks, waving his arms as though enraged by the sight of a hammock ill lashed.

At 0830, we'd go to quarters, our section mustering on the port side of the forecastle, just under number two turret. Mr. Walker was a lean lieutenant, piratical looking with a thin black mustache and gold wings on the breast of his white service uniform. His head was cocked to one side from breaking his neck in an aircraft accident. He was strict but pleasant and just the kind of officer you'd like to be— even wishing you might come to look like him.

The son of the ship's commanding officer, Captain Patterson, was in our section. The captain would show up from time to time when we were at quarters and eye his son with affectionate contempt. The captain was a short, dark man with heavy eyebrows and the son much resembled him. The captain showed particular interest in our hair as he inspected our ranks, pointing out those who needed it cut again, finding anything longer than half an inch an unseamanlike affectation. The chief petty officer who mothered our section would remind you in case it slipped your mind. (The ship's company was allowed more freedom in hairstyle than were we.)

After quarters some days, there were emergency drills, every means of communication whirring, hooting, blaring, ringing or piping. "Man overboard!" "Abandon ship!" Or general quarters. We each had our stations at general quarters, racing to get below or to climb up to stand by a gun. Some ladders were up only, and some were one-way down. A marine with bayonet fixed stood at the bottom of each ladder. One of our group missed his footing, stopping himself as he fell down a ladder by putting a bayonet through his hand. The forgetful among us thought it unfair that these assignments were changed just when you had learned how to reach your station.

Instead of drills, we might be lectured until midday when the ship would send out a blast, bells ring, boatswains pipe, and bugles blow us to mess again until mustering at 1300, then more lectures, and to shower and wash clothes—get a haircut—from 1600 to 1800, mess again, up hammocks, and movies on the after deck until 2130.

We were running south, toward Florida and Cuba, at twelve knots now, the water a deep blue, the bow wave hissing white down the sides of the ship. Panicky flying fish skittered across the waves. Porpoises rolled friendly with us through the sea. Our noses peeled. The sight of a sunset was expected, but you were not prepared for the magnificence of a sunrise at sea. From the fantail, the wake boiled white and green astern to the horizon we were leaving behind.

"I'm just trying to let you know this is no joyride," I wrote my parents. I must have feared my letters showed an unsophisticated pleasure unseemly in a hardened salt. "They're working us terribly hard—just to break us down."

Chapter 4

We learned a descant on loyalty: "A messmate before a shipmate, a shipmate before a sailor, a sailor before a Marine, a Marine before a dog, and a dog before a soldier."

One of Casey's seamen solemnly assured us that regular doses of saltpeter were stirred into our food to quell our sexual urges, a piece of folklore said to be traceable to a boatswain in the Phoenician merchant marine circa 700 B.C.

We were told of a place called officers' country and warned to stay clear of it unless sent there on ship's business. If dispatched there as a messenger, you were to uncover, that is to say, take off your cap.

"But you're not supposed to salute uncovered, are you?"

"You don't salute below decks, anyway, dummy."

"Just pull your forelock," said a sardonic voice.

You discovered "scuttlebutt" to be the term for rumors passing through the ranks, and you soon learned to pay no attention to most of it.

The first day at sea we lined up in the aircastle, stripped to the buff, to run a gauntlet of vaccinating pharmacist's mates. They kept track of us by painting sprawling numerals on our chests with swabs of Merthiolate, circles on our upper arms to show where we'd been vaccinated. Some of them were still drunk from New York, their needles hitting bone and drawing blood. More than one of our number fainted away in line, not unusual during vaccinations, to the loud amusement of the pharmacist's mates.

No real physical harm came of this. Our arms were hotter and more swollen than they need have been, and a few became infected. As an early impression of life at sea, it lacked elegance. Most of us shrugged it off. A few others relished such atrocities, totting them up, grumbling about making the navy pay.

We had always to keep clean one of our two sets of blouse and bell-bottom trousers. Allotted a bucket of fresh water a day to keep clothes and bodies clean, we were allowed to launder from 1600 to 1800. These were the same hours we could stand in line for a haircut or go to the bathroom, clutching in a free hand a mimeographed sheet of names of the parts of a twelve-inch gun, or it might be the inside of a steam turbine, or the sequence of events at the hawsepipe for the Eldridge method of flying moor (with mooring swivel).

Unless dainty enough to keep soil from your whites, most afternoons, you knelt or squatted near the aftermast, with scores of others, scrubbing clothes on the soapy teak deck. Wet cotton skivvy shirts and shorts, duck jumpers and bell-bottoms, were pinned to lines that would be hoisted skyward. You then stood guard. The lines would not accommodate all the laundry, and unscrupulous shipmates would try to substitute their garments for yours. A line might be heaved aloft before you'd pinned your wet clothes to it. Or the engineering department might choose that hour to blow tubes, cleaning the stack by shooting compressed air through the system. If they timed it right, oily soot would splatter the suspended wash, another outrage to fuel anger and despair.

The sailors' latrine at a ship's bow was once called a headbeak. The term "head" derives from that, and the term stuck, no matter where in the ship the head wandered. On the *Wyoming*, the head had gone all the way aft to the fantail. During the two-hour period in late afternoon, several hundred of us swarmed about the horseshoe-shaped compartment. Covered over, just below the quarterdeck, it was otherwise open to the air. The two saltwater showers were there, a couple of sinks we crowded around to shave in cold water with a sliver of hand soap and a metal hand mirror. The head proper was a trough curved to follow the shape of the fantail stern, saltwater rushing through it, rude wooden seats spaced across it. You stationed yourself before the current occupant to reserve a place. It was considered humorous to light off a wad of toilet paper and send it blazing downstream.

The motives of the navy were the constant subject. We talked about them when messing down, when standing about on deck, smoking if the boatswain had announced that the smoking lamp was lit, or swaying in hammocks in the glow of the night-light in the gun room, arguing until the last opinion met with silence from the other hammocks. There were two distinct schools of thought. One described the navy as malicious bastards and the cruelties deliberate. The other took its pleasure from denouncing the navy as an inept bunch of bastards. The third, and probably the majority, view took satisfaction in declaring the navy to be both.

Their grievances seemed fresh to the analysts of naval turpitide. But their every resentment was known under Nelson's burgee or in Paul Jones's forecastle. Their words might have been duplicated that very moment aboard the battleship *Arkansas*, steaming in company not a thousand yards away, or half a day earlier on the deck of the gunboat *Luzon*, lying in the stream of the Whangpoo off the bund at Shanghai.

Few of us were openly contemptuous or insubordinate. At the other extreme, a few had so shamelessly gone over to the authorities that we regarded them much as the peoples of occupied Europe looked upon their quislings. The majority, as did I, showed a public face of fealty to the naval system and a vigorous disdain of authority in the privacy of the gun room. Inside, belying that attitude, despite our reservations about the navy, most of us were dedicated to becoming a part of the system.

Being busy, we had to save eloquent bitching for off-hours. A letter home says I was on communications watch on the signal bridge when war raced by us one black sea night. In a breath-stopping moment, a darkened British destroyer raced by, blinking her greeting from a shuttered searchlight on her own signal bridge. We blazed in the dark, our ensign brightly lighted at the peak of the after-mast.

I took my turn at the wheel on navigation bridge, learning how long a ponderous battleship will plow on through the seas before deigning to answer the rudder. And how contrary the ship could be, full of stately mischief, unwilling to turn when asked, but leaving a wavy wake behind her with your unskilled hand at the helm. You were very careful on the bridge, speaking when spoken to or when you had a rote to pronounce. "Steersman properly relieved, sir. Steering 185, checking 184, two-and-a-half degrees right rudder." (Don't ever whistle. Never say "all right.") The bridge was as quiet as a church, no words save those concerning the ship, still quiet when Captain Patterson strolled in to exchange remarks with the officer of the deck. The captain might rally one of us seamen if in good humor. I kept my eyes straight ahead, looking earnest with him there, as earnestly rehearsing replies lest a question from him expose a feckless lack of aptitude for the naval service: my file number, the hour in Greenwich mean time, my hometown, our course and speed, the displacement of the ship.

On the wing of the bridge, the chief quartermaster pointed out the working parts of a sextant, and we took turns keeping one mark on the horizon while measuring the sun's azimuth as the ship rolled through the long Caribbean swells. Stars were harder. You began to appreciate professional skills and pick up the tired professional jokes that go with them. Back in the gun room you'd refer, in an offhand way, to Betelgeuse as Beetlejuice, and those who'd not yet held a sextant would be impressed but refuse to show it.

"Went past San Salvador where Columbus landed at about 0900," said one of my letters. One aim of naval training was to eliminate such imprecisions. (As a time for his landing, nine in the morning could be about right. That the island of San Salvador was his first landfall remains in dispute.)

One Sunday in port, I stood a messenger watch, hanging about the officer of the deck's station on the quarterdeck, trying to look alert and helpful, springing forward like a

good hunting dog when called. There was nothing in between. You skulked behind something or, fearing a superior
eye might have stopped on you, looked lively. ("Look
lively, there!") I stood stiff as side boy at the head of the
gangway, mutely rendering honors when visiting officers
came aboard. I practiced the abracadabra of battleship etiquette, saluting and asking for, "Permission to strike six
bells, sir." That granted, I marched forward and up a ladder
to where hung the huge ship's bell, grasping the lanyard to
strike the bells in twos: bong-bong, bong-bong, bong-bong.
The worshipers in the aircastle directly below began divine
services in a catatonic state. When I came back, the officer
of the deck was still grinning. "Given the occasion, a gentle
tapping would have done," he said.

One time, I stood with friends in our own aircastle, waiting for number four gun to be fired. We had neglected to
unscrew the light bulb in the overhead directly above us
and were showered with shards of glass by the explosion.
Scoffing at being told to cover our ears against the bark of
the five-inch gun, we were deafened. And our hats blew
off.

We went ashore in Guantánamo in heavy fifty-foot
wooden launches with black hulls that we called liberty
boats. They were commanded by a coxswain, assisted by a
seaman line handler. Not allowed on the base proper, we
were herded into a sandy compound, where we milled
around, stripped to play softball, sat in the shade to talk or
nap, drank enough Hatuey beer to make us squint at the
sun, heads pounding. The boats made regular runs from the
landing back to the ships, and you had to be sure to get in
your own ship's boat. Shore patrolmen in yellow canvas
leggings grasped the baggy rear of the trousers of our un-
ruly colleagues and escorted them to the landing at a brisk
turkey trot, sticks drubbing a soft tattoo on their skulls, the
only correction of their exuberance.

At the end of August, we anchored in Panamá. Before
going ashore in Colón, we were warned to show no disre-
spect for the members of the *Guardia Nacional*. On seeing
them, we were not tempted to test them. On their heads the
Guardia wore narrow khaki topees, the sort you see in steel

engravings of British troops in Victorian India. They swung leather quirts in their hands and were said to be alert to opportunities to slash an American sailor across the face. The *Guardia* faces I saw—there were many of them on the streets—lacked tenderness.

We'd been told to avoid areas posted off-limits to servicemen. Before long, nevertheless, we were standing with a streetful of whores in their cribs. These boxlike rooms, a step or two up from the street, were hardly wider than the bed inside. The women showed every human shade of skin and as much of it as local regulations allowed, propped half-naked in the doors or clopping and swaying high-heeled to street level, inviting us in by word and gesture.

Almost immediately, a patrol of American Army military police, obviously chosen for their immense height, dimpled campaign hats square on their heads, whistles and chains hanging on their shirtfronts, stared down at us. Paying no attention to our protests that we were no more than visiting observers, they ordered us to march off with them. Before we had gone far, a pair of sailors with the armbands and leggings of the shore patrol blocked our way. The smaller of the two sailors looked up at the tallest soldier and announced that he would take charge of the prisoners. The military policeman grunted a refusal. The small sailor raised his club in front of the other's face and repeated his statement.

We now quickstepped off in silence, a sailor on either side of us. In sight of the docks, the spokesman stopped, looking at us without expression, and commanded, "Now, get back to your ship."

Lectures, engine-room watches, abandon-ship and fire drills, the ship's work, continued on the voyage home. More firing on the southern drill grounds, where the ship rolled at anchor, and a good many of us got sick. In a letter home, I wrote of being section leader on a night watch, running up and down ladders all over the ship to wake the right twelve men to relieve the dozen on watch. (Nothing grumpier than the hammock mistakenly shaken, especially when you ask that hammock to tell you, then, for Pete's sake, shining your flashlight on the watch list in your hand, where the proper hammock is to be found.) Then you had to trot to all twelve stations about the ship to be sure that your man at each place had properly relieved the former watch stander.

We still turned to on deck with Casey and company, the deck force, members of the oldest profession at sea. Had we been under sail instead of powered by steam, Casey would have been as much at home in that wooden hull as in steel. Most of the men aboard that wooden man-o'-war would have been much like him. By standing watches in the engine room, with radiomen, electricians, and gunner's mates in their working spaces, we saw the elaboration of specialties needed for a modern man-of-war.

In Norfolk, pulling boats were lowered from their davits with us in them. We strained at the oars to stay in one place, the tide was licking so fast past the hull of the *Wyoming*. In two hours' time, we could barely maintain our station near the gangway. The oars would tangle, and we'd roar with dismay as the boat spun off on the current. Ashore in Norfolk, the fifteen hundred of us apprentice seamen joined the mobs of sailors already on the streets. There was nothing to do but stand on the curb and regard other sailors across the street. We hadn't believed what we'd heard aboard ship but, indeed, there were the signs in the restaurant windows: "No sailors or dogs allowed." This in a city living off the sailor's dollar: the signs would come down after we were in the war and angry mothers of new sailors wrote their congressmen.

Not every moment in the old navy was manly fun. On the voyage home, there were games one night instead of movies. A few pairs of sailors took turns boxing respectably in a bright ring erected on top of a barbette. Then six or eight of the young black mess attendants were shoved into the ring, gloves hanging on their arms, and told to box each other. This they did reluctantly for some ten minutes to cheers and catcalls. Among these unwilling entertainers was the young black sailor who set up our table in the gun room, brought us our food, told us what to expect that day, how to get ready for inspection, who was strict and who unfair among the petty officers.

And "Jew Boy." I don't remember it's being said to a man's face—more often spoken behind a man's back, maybe so he could hear it.

The way we were packed together, the senseless demands to drop whatever we were doing to race about the ship to a new and puzzling task, the humiliating competition for such fundamental rights as a seat in the head, being awakened at midnight for a watch or a drill after hours of labor on deck, being scorned for not knowing something you'd not been taught, the loss of status or place we'd left in the world behind us, were insults profoundly hard on some of us. The younger among us took it all more lightly, I think, possibly having accumulated less self-esteem in our briefer lives.

Those of us who passed the physical examinations, and most of us did, were allowed to volunteer for further training. Defiance of the navy took precedence over both patriotism and resentment—we'll show the bastards. We signed up and went home to wait for the navy's next move.

Captain Patterson had the last word when he came by to see us at quarters, a day out of New York. It may have been the sight of his son in our ranks. Whatever the reason, he told the chief to see to it our heads were shaved before we were let ashore. I showed up shorn at my sister's apartment in Forest Hills, itching in a wrinkled tweed suit mildewed from being balled up for a month in a seabag in the *Wyoming* bilges. She changed her plan to have friends in to meet me.

I went to stay a day or two with our aunt and uncle in White Plains. I stood on the windowsill to blow cigarette smoke out the top of the bedroom window, so she wouldn't smell it in the curtains. She was indignant when I told her of the cruel floggings instantly administered on the *Wyoming* for the smallest infraction of discipline.

Chapter 5

General Foreword

"Neatness and percision (sic) will be stressed throughout this course, and adherence to form will be required." We took comfort from the fumbling austerity of this instruction from the navigation department of the U.S. Naval Reserve Midshipmen's School. At once arbitrary and erratic, it comported with our impression of the navy so far.

It was 16 December 1940. The six of us in room 716 of Tower Hall on East Pearson Street in Chicago had been waiting since mid-September to enter the school. On arrival this day, we had abandoned careers as apprentice seamen to take oaths of office as midshipmen of the volunteer reserve. While we unpacked, we were working through the sheaf of mimeographed instructions handed us on arrival.

The navigation department went on to define form so that we could adhere to it. "Form is chiefly a matter of using the vertical spacing on the paper in the intended maneuver, and having due regard to the vertical lines, which should separate symbols from numbers." That wasn't all. "The use of scratch paper for simple arithmetical computations, which can be done mentally should be avoided." A pause to read that sentence again, mentally inserting or deleting a comma.

We six discovered ourselves to be part of the 3d Section of the 1st Platoon of the 7th Company. There were some twenty of us in each of the three sections of a platoon. Each

35

of the seven companies had two platoons, so that we were more than eight hundred midshipmen in all. As roommates, we would come to be close comrades, the section our larger family, marching off together to classes during the next three months.

"Muster for all formations on your company deck." Mustering was accomplished by standing at attention against the near wall of the passageway immediately outside our room. The trick was to be there on time, in proper uniform, to answer when your name was called. "You will muster for breakfast at 0700, dinner 1205, supper 1815." We ate on the fourteenth floor of our building and met in navigation classes on the thirteenth.

We were issued thirteen volumes of textbooks plus such items as a navigator's case, parallel rulers, and something called a celestial coordinator. For navigation, good old Nathaniel Bowditch, LL.D. (1773–1838), *The American Practical Navigator*, Dutton's *Navigation and Nautical Astronomy*—our main text to which I took immediate dislike because of its finicky demands for meticulosity—a *Nautical Almanac, 1940, H.O. 214 - Tables of Computed Altitude and Azimuth*, a stunning product of the Works Progress Administration in the 1930's, and even more indecipherable compendia of information such as the *Red Azimuth Tables*; *Current Tables, Pacific 1941*; and *Tide Tables, Pacific, 1941*.

We drew uniforms. Our daily garb was a dark wool shirt with black tie, navy blue bellbottom trousers, black shoes, topped off with a sailor's cap, a broad dark band around it—a mode of little dignity. Slightly or a great deal better, depending on the fit, was a brass-buttoned, double-breasted navy uniform jacket with a brass anchor on either lapel, worn with white shirt and black tie, matching trousers, the legs of mine stopping far short of the shoetops. (Some of our sophisticates got a tailor to take in or let out their clothes.) A visored cap with a gold chinstrap and another brass anchor as cap emblem crowned the ensemble.

In another year, uniformed men would be common in the United States and a tolerance of servicemen officially encouraged. In 1940, a uniform was a rare sight in downtown

Chicago, and we were often stopped on the street and asked to explain ourselves. Once we did so, the invariable response was a mixture of surprise and praise. When war did come, Chicago would earn with servicemen a particular reputation for friendliness. As a native, in a sense, I was proud of the natural warmth of the people of Chicago on which my comrades constantly remarked—a long way from Norfolk. The counterpoise to the graciousness was the troupe of small boys trailing you down the street shrilling "Anchors aweigh, my boys, anchors aweigh."

For classes in ordnance and gunnery and in seamanship, our section marched from Tower Hall, along East Pearson Street, across North Michigan Avenue, past the 1869 water tower that survived the fire of 1871, to the buildings of the Chicago campus of Northwestern University. The traffic policeman whistled traffic to a stop for us to march across Michigan Avenue. Later in our time as midshipmen, when our formation moved with éclat, pedestrians on the corners would break into mild clapping.

Not for our first ragged formations. Early on, the four companies in Tower Hall straggled over to the armory on Pearson Street on the other side of Michigan Avenue. Once we were lined up on the packed earth of the armory floor, an instructor invited those of us in any way acquainted with close-order drill to step forward. No one in our company spoke or moved.

This lack of response revealed nothing of our military experience. I was not an unusual case with my three years of military training in high school, by the end of which I had moved up a notch from private to lance corporal. The faculty of military science at Indiana University was so little impressed by that record as to insist on my reviewing the material for another two years as a private. Thus, earlier instruction in the manual of arms, stacking arms, musketry, scouting and patrolling, map reading, cleaning a Springfield Model 1903, field stripping and reassembling a Browning automatic rifle while blindfolded, was repeated exactly according to the same rote and thus reinforced. Worse, after learning the intricacies of the elegant old eight-man-squad close-order drill, I had to lumber about the Bloomington campus for two years in the clumsy new drill.

There were others more experienced than I in the ranks that day who cagily volunteered nothing to authority. Our drill instructor fell back on a favorite and unreliable military solution by putting the tallest man in charge. The company paid immediately for our reticence. Our new leader had no idea at all how to get us moving around the armory. We stood dumb as cattle while he was introduced by the instructor to a few useful commands. When he had the phrases straight, he pronounced them with so improper an inflection, so uncertainly, that a number of us stayed where we were, another gaggle of us stepped off in front, and the rest marched away on a right oblique. In clouds of dust, coughing, complaining—"No talking in ranks, there!" bellowed the instructor skipping along on our flank—we angled into inevitable collisions with other formations in the manner traditional to our volunteer forces since the French and Indian War. As did those earlier comrades of ours, we got the knack of drill soon enough. We took turns at commanding the section, marching it to class and, once there, passing on such unnecessary advice as when to sit and when to rise.

In December 1940, the first draftees were reporting for duty; a dispirited bunch clustered around the doors of the armory as we marched past on our way to class. Not yet anonymous in olive drab, they draped themselves about the steps, ranging from natty in porkpie hats and peg-topped trousers to informal in sweaters, caps, and leather jackets. Out of their despair, they would hoot at us as we passed in review, neat in our navy blue cloth raincoats. The first time, we cackled back at them in an unseamanlike way. From there on, we rebuked them with coldness, dressing our ranks, the section leader picking up the cadence as we swung by, not looking at them, leaving their cries of invective in our wake.

Four of the six in our room happened to come from Indiana. Scott from Indianapolis was short, blond, looking well dressed even in uniform, quiet (compared to the rest of us), unflappable; Lauchner was younger, about my age, dark-haired, tall, full of bounce; Fitzsimmons, handsome, thoughtful, lithe. Reed was the older of two Virginians, lean, a teacher, the most learned of us, tart of wit; Pollard was lanky, open, excitable, inclined to be literal. We dealt with each other by surname.

From other rooms, we would occasionally hear quarreling. We six got along notably well, even Reed and Pollard, despite the appearance they gave. Rather than the two southerners standing back-to-back against us midwestern Yankees, they carried on a three-month-long argument between them, recessing only during drills or in the intense hush of our study periods. If one Virginian made a statement, the other would immediately challenge it. When they ran down, one of us would address a question to Reed or to Pollard. Whichever of them replied would come under attack from the other, and the jeering duel would resume.

Dominating the center of our room was a long knocked-together, brown-varnished, plywood table, three chairs on either side. The textbooks piled helter-skelter down the middle had to be arranged just so for Saturday morning inspection. The sheets and blankets on the three double-decked bunks had to be just so when we were not actually in them, top sheet folded back just so, the fold of the blanket making a forty-five–degree corner at the end of the bed. Getting the corner right and tucking the blanket so taut that a quarter would bounce in the air from it—another requirement put to the test at Saturday inspection—was as difficult for me as any other single part of the whole regimen.

All that was incidental to our studies. To claim that the content of four years of the naval academy was crammed into our three months would be excessive. Nevertheless, a minimum preparation of us as officers—even reserve officers, ninety-day wonders—meant covering all the basic material in navigation, ordnance and gunnery, and seamanship. I had come ashore from the *Wyoming* with a sense of panic about mathematics, spending my time before coming to midshipmen's school at a correspondence course in trigonometry. Although it did no harm to know a cosine from a logarithm and a tangent from a sine, figuring a ship's position on the earth required no original thinking and little mathematical talent. The hard part was getting the right data to begin with, an accurate reading on a sextant, say, and from there on being careful to follow defined steps in a mincingly proper sequence, a mental minuet. You had to know what page of what numerical tables in Bowditch or in *H.O. 214* to consult, and constantly remind yourself what you were trying to accomplish and what stage of the process you were dealing with at the moment. The unnecessary course in trig did give me a confidence I would have lacked otherwise. But the essence of solving a problem in navigation is concentration: a moment of woolgathering, and your ship is steaming across a prairie west of Lincoln, Nebraska. Getting the right solution to one of these problems in navigation was immensely satisfying—indeed, "adherence to form will be required."

In the second session of our class in navigation, Lauchner and I were called to our feet and informed publicly by the instructor that the two of us had shown ourselves deficient in arithmetic on our placement examinations. I thought nothing of being openly pilloried in a place where privacy was to be found only in one's own mind—the head in Tower Hall, for example, a palace of luxury compared to the head on the *Wyoming*, had no doors on the booths. I lay awake the night after that incident to stare at the bottom of the upper bunk, seeing too late I had failed myself irremediably some years before. The very next day, I was again told to stand, along with two others, and informed that we had made the highest grades in the exercise of determining latitudes on a Mercator projection. As pleasing as was this accolade for a comparatively mean accomplishment, I saw again, all things considered, the wisdom of escaping notice rather than attracting it.

The younger of us had the advantage in study of having been more recently at our books. Nevertheless, some of the material was hard to cram in, thick with new words and dense with arbitrary numbers. You suspected it would not remain with you long enough to be useful. The application of what we were learning in navigation classes was clear enough. In ordnance and gunnery studies, we had to depend on lectures and textbooks for learning what would better have been accompanied by practical work. As quick as we were to find fault, we couldn't fairly blame the navy for shortcomings in instruction in a time of low-budget peace and avoidance of foreign entanglements. Reading about a De Barge gas-check pad for naval bag guns—see figure K, that sort of thing—without having a gun to work was the essence of dullness. There were glimmers of light. The same mooring board on which we learned in navigation to lay out courses and bearings for maneuvering at sea was used as well for planning torpedo attacks, more fun than memorizing drawings of the three-inch semiautomatic breech mechanism, Mark V, modification 1.

Seamanship was anthology. Our texts were the comparatively sprightly *The Watch Officer's Guide*, the unrelievedly dull *Naval Administration*, and Knight's *Seamanship and Naval Tactics*. In these were concealed tasty gobbets of text able to hold your interest, sometimes weakly: honors and ceremonies—how many side boys you must scare up for a rear admiral of the lower half—ship handling, naval communications, rules of the road, watchkeeping, duties of the officer of the deck at sea and in port—everything, really, that wasn't covered elsewhere.

Generally, our classes ran from 0800 to late in the afternoon. We had a free period after returning from the last class before mustering for supper. Instead of lingering over a postmortem of the last puzzle propounded in ordnance class, you'd race to the elevators, spilling with others onto the street to rush to the Normandie restaurant nearby. Lined up on the counter were glasses of beer. You fought your way through a mob of midshipmen to throw down your money and pick up a glass, push your way back through the crowd to an open spot and peace to drink it. The story went around that some people on another deck had found complacent females in a handy apartment and spent the twenty or so afternoon minutes in bouts of lovemaking. Despite the currency of the story with its baroque elaborations, you never actually met anyone who had carried off one of these brief gallantries.

At muster, you could smell the beer and might have to encourage the man next to you to maintain himself more or less perpendicular during roll call. In serious cases, Sunday evening muster, say, the midshipmen on either side of a limp colleague would take him by the elbows, praying that the company officer would be charitable—you could hardly conceal the man's condition with his head lolling on his chest. His chances for survival were far better at muster than absent from it. After poking at him to rouse him before his name came up in the alphabet, you'd count on being excused for committing a false muster by answering "Here!" from one side of your mouth. For a moment, it might seem that two voices had answered.

The hour from 1520 to 1630 Wednesdays was devoted to athletics, the first couple of these periods being spent disconsolately bouncing a basketball about a smelly YMCA neighborhood gym. Someone brilliant—I think it was Reed—had seen an ice-skating rink a few blocks away and persuaded the navy to accredit skating as a recognized sport. The next Wednesday, in uniform rather than ragtag athletic costume, a select six or eight of us soul mates marched briskly off to the rink in a column of twos— marched, I emphasize. The suspicions of authority would have been aroused had we been observed enjoying a stroll. The determination of our quickstep hid our subversive intention.

On rented skates, we described tentative evolutions on the ice some of us more elegantly than others—it was the first time on skates for some in our party. An invisible organist alternated popular tunes with Strauss waltzes through pipes rising at one end of the arena. While pushing across the ice we saw two colleagues, making no pretense of skating, seated at a table on the edge of the rink. The rest of us glided over to them and clumped across a wooden platform on the points of our skates, to sit with them and order our own beers. Although there were few patrons at this hour, one gracefully bold fellow managed to waltz arm in arm with a girl. As we marched back to our quarters, he claimed to have made an assignation for the coming weekend.

We looked forward to Wednesday athletics, careful to say nothing of our sport to others, making some excuse if a fellow inquired about one's absence from basketball. Once word got out, we knew, our idyll would end. One of the company officers, a skater himself, wickedly chose to show up on our ice one Wednesday afternoon. He seemed more amused than otherwise to find us at the tables with our beer. But he was not generous about it. We found ourselves back at the YMCA, forced individually to invent falsehoods in order to be excused from athletics.

Authority encouraged us to get away Saturday midday after inspection until muster Sunday night. Even though it meant more stale hours with the textbooks, you'd sometimes stay in the room to study. One gray, midwinter, Saturday afternoon, as the snow whirled through the first evening lights I could stand the unaccustomed lonely silence no longer and dressed to go off on foot through the cold into the Chicago Loop. I found raucous comrades at our common practice of being treated to drinks by kindly Chicagoans. They were in the Brass Rail, where a musician of repute named Wingy Manone played a trumpet in the small space right behind the bar. We could hardly have inspired him, the dark-uniformed row of us confronting him, solemnly soaking up an antidote to naval customs and traditions.

We drank more than needed, ate fuzzily at a nearly empty Loop cafeteria, chairs stacked on the tables, a few lonely old people sitting separately at tables. The bitter wind rushed around corners to thump on the plate-glass window where we sat. We started home, late, coming out onto North Michigan Avenue into the blast of a nor'-westerly gale, heads down, twisting to turn our backs to it as the full force of it howled into us. We leaned into it to get across the bridge by the Wrigley Building, holding our hats to our heads with one hand, the wind going right through our light raincoats. We stumbled through snow piled deep along the sidewalks, falling, dragging each other out of the snowdrifts, chasing our hats, cursing, counting bodies to be sure no one had been forever lost. We spoke of this later as the retreat from Moscow, referring here, of course, to Napoleon's experience, having no idea of what was to come.

The persistent threat was the tree, so-called, and the fear

of seeing your name on it. The tree was a list of academic delinquents posted on a board at the duty office on the deck below ours. Friday afternoon, you shouldered your way into the clot of midshipmen, morbidly attracted to it, readying yourself for the shock of seeing your name there. By chance, I was mate of the deck on the Friday in mid-January when something more than a hundred midshipmen were dismissed for poor grades or bad attitude or—Lord knows what—saying the wrong thing to the wrong officer. (Drinking beer while dodging Wednesday athletics?) I'd be handed a list of names with room numbers and sent off to inform the unlucky ones. The word was out, and people huddled in their rooms. As I went down the passageway looking for room numbers, I could feel waiting eyes on me, and I'd sense the relief when I passed by. When I saw a room number on my list, I went into the stiff silence, as quickly as I could reading off the name, feeling shabby, a collaborator with authority. Why the names were parceled out this way, eight or ten at a time for all three decks, rather than all at once, I don't now remember. It surely made for suspense. With each new list, I glanced down to see if my name was on it.

Right in the midst of this harsh purging of our ranks, our roommate Fitzsimmons shocked us by saying he was going to resign. In and out of sick bay for the last weeks with a persistent fever, he felt it impossible to catch up. We in the room tried to persuade him to stay. Other members of the section came in to add their promises to coach him through. The department heads, the executive officer himself, in turn, called Fitzsimmons down to ask him to reconsider. We were struck by the way the authorities strove to keep one man on while arbitrarily banishing a hundred others. For once, we didn't grouse at the authorities. Their seeming inconsistency was a result of their having the same high estimate of Fitzsimmons's worth as did we.

Chapter 6

A friend of mine at eight years of age had been sent off, an American, to boarding school in England. "After that, the army was nothing." He was explaining his scorn for conscripts crying themselves to sleep their first night in an army barracks, perhaps their first night ever away from home.

None of us who rushed to the colors that summer of 1940 had gotten as far as midshipmen's school in Chicago in such tender state. The weeks we'd spent scrambling like rats about the *Wyoming* had winnowed those the navy thought unfitting. Others had withdrawn on their own. To survive this next level of testing, I decided to suppress doubts about my fitness and drop my easy cynicism about the navy. I suspected still that training as a midshipman would be nothing but a superior variation of the unpleasant side of life as an apprentice seaman. Maybe the navy was a short lifetime of tests. How you dealt with these doubts depended, crudely enough, on how much you wanted to be commissioned an officer. The navy didn't consider our sensibilities and left us no time for brooding.

In our studies, we moved from one subject to the next before mastering—even understanding—the earlier one. Stumbling over it sometime in the future, you might remember having had a look at it somewhere in the past. As vexing as that was, it was nothing like the terror of being examined on material that had been torn from you before you could grasp it. One Sunday in January 1941, I wrote a

45

postcard home: "Been studying all afternoon. Again escaped the tree." In February, another card transmitted my grades on a battery of exams:

Ordnance 3.18
Seamanship 3.43
Navigation 3.54

On the margin of the card there's still the scratching where my mother quickly divided these numbers by 4.0, the highest mark, to translate them into grades she could evaluate: 79.5, 85.7, 88.5, espying me lost back there in the academic pack, if to her disappointment, certainly not to her surprise. My lowest grade was in aptitude, 2.8 (a 70), unjustly harsh, I claimed, for being once put on report merely for talking in ranks. (But it made me careful.)

Regimentation requires conformity to a set of rules you had nothing to do with framing. You might respect the tradition that handed them on. Whether you did or did not, you had to obey them if you were to carry on to the end. This process of following navy rules, no matter whether you liked them, was beginning to change us from what we had been, separating us from the civilian world we'd left behind. It took me a while to see that. One Sunday that winter, the Tierra del Fuego roommate at Indiana University was in Chicago, and we had lunch together. It was good to see him. Right away he reproached me for joining up without telling him. He would have enlisted, too, had he known. He brought news of friends in the fraternity house and warm, if insolent, messages from some of them. I told him how close the midshipman duty officer had come to catching us after lights-out with the bottle of Chianti he and three others had sent me Christmastime.

We parted, as ever, fast friends, assuming, as you do at that age, we'd see each other one day. I doubt that he knew—I barely sensed it myself—how remote the Indiana campus was from midshipmen's school, how distant my recent past. If asked, I might have answered that life at Indiana University was reality and midshipmen's school the aberration. But walking back to Tower Hall Sunday after-

noon, it was navigation class the coming morning I thought
about rather than envying his riding the train back to
Bloomington.

I was lucky to have friends of the family twenty miles
north along the lake in Glencoe. Several times, I took the
train out for the weekend (as often refusing in order to
study instead) to stay overnight in houses I had known as
a child. On boyhood ground, I saw the gulf that was opening between me and elders respected from childhood. It
wasn't only the business of growing up—I knew about that.
These were people close to me for being in my parents' circle, courtesy aunts and uncles accepted from childhood
with the child's lack of reservation. Now, grateful as I was
for their kindness, I was made uneasy by the importance to
them of things that didn't really matter. I answered as well
as I could their polite questions about midshipmen's school.
I didn't try to explain what it was really like. They
wouldn't have understood.

They had turned into civilians.

One reason we weren't aware of changing until we were
set against outsiders is that there was no overt indoctrination, no fevered eulogies of the navy, no raging against our
obvious future enemies, nothing ideological, no pumping up
of spirits, no worry about our morale, not even a pep talk.
The navy correctly assumed that we'd brought our morale
with us, as shown by our being there. We did not need to
be motivated.

Aside from our being encouraged to get away on the
weekends, the only overt concern for our welfare I remember is from a Saturday morning inspection. The commanding officer himself, a dapper, white-mustached captain
called from retirement, marched out of the head on our seventh deck, grumping that there should be doors on the
booths "or these people are going to get constipated."

The ranks were purged again in February, and our numbers further reduced. The rumor was that the navy made
this latest cut for budgetary reasons, letting good men go so
there'd be enough money to commission the rest of us.
Maybe it was true, but so senseless that it caused more

grousing. We lapsed into a faultfinding mood, stale from the work, nervous, giddy from the pressure.

One Thursday afternoon late in February, when the week's clean linens had been passed out, Reed took advantage of the tendency of Pollard's mind to be elsewhere. We'd made our beds, all except Pollard who found he'd brought, along with his two sheets and one pillowcase, an extra pillowcase. He made up his bed with the first sheet, laid the second sheet and a pillowcase on top of it, leaving then to return the extra pillowcase. Reed immediately leapt to his feet and hid the sheet and pillowcase.

When Pollard came back, he looked about, cursed under his breath, and went back up the hall. He came back with a sheet and a pillowcase to find a folded sheet on his bed. He stared at it, put down the sheet and pillowcase, and went back to the end of the hall with the extra sheet. Pollard should have been alerted by the extraordinary stillness in which the rest of us, paralyzed by joy, were watching his every move.

When he returned, he found no sheet but two pillowcases. None of us was able to look at him. We knew him to be standing in silence. After a moment, he left again with a pillowcase. When he returned with a sheet to find no pillowcase, we could restrain ourselves no longer. Even knowing Reed to be his tormentor, Pollard was so rattled, he could only sit on his bed with his face in his hands and moan.

The next week brought confirmation that the class would graduate on 14 March, three months after we'd started as midshipmen. Another good omen: we were given time off to visit a military tailor in the Loop to be measured for uniforms. When we were told to put down our preferences for assignments, "Asiatic Fleet—destroyer" was my choice.

Physical examinations were scheduled, and those of us with infirmities—a surprising number—prepared for that examination as carefully as for a quiz on fire control. Just in our neighborhood on the seventh deck, Lauchner, for example, said that albumin in his urine was a symptom of some condition or other that doctors disapproved. A fellow across the hall was color-blind. I was anxious about my old inguinal hernia. Lauchner put himself on a week-long diet of bananas and water, a folk remedy for concealing albumin. Somehow a copy turned up of the black books with the diagrams used to test color perception, swirls of colored bubbles in which, for normal eyes, the proper number stands out of the mixture. We prepped our colleague until he knew the correct answer at any page, like one of those ponies trained to tap out answers to sums with one hoof. We had to warn him to show normal hesitation rather than instantly barking out the answer. To conceal my hernia, I practiced turning my head to cough according to a physician's requirement, deceptively loud, containing the effect within the bronchial system. Thus, I kept my intestine from popping guiltily out into the abdominal ring where the doctor waited for it. With a considerable minority of us afflicted and the nature of our afflictions a cause for hilarity on the seventh deck, it speaks well for the solidarity of our ranks that no colleague denounced us to the authorities as unfit.

A penny postcard home on 4 March: "Got through physicals okay. No trace of you-know-what."

At our nadir of morale, when it seemed it would never end, school was actually winding down. The remaining five of us in the room had run the race. The final proof for me was being granted two tickets to the graduation exercises for my parents. The navy could hardly avoid giving me a commission now.

Lauchner and I got orders to the Asiatic Fleet. We immediately began to wonder what was wrong with an assignment so readily granted by the authorities.

Our wardrobe trunks were delivered from the tailor's, typically containing two sets of service blues, two sets of service white dress, white shoes with felt soles (guaranteed not to slip on an oily deck), an officer's cap with the emblem of shield, crossed anchors, and eagle, done in gold-and-silver French lace, a raincoat, a sword with your name on the blade, a gold-lace sword knot, no less useful than the sword itself, to hang from the hilt on state occasions and to wrap around your wrist did you find yourself using the sword in hand-to-hand combat.

After ninety days—four months' time if you count the shakedown cruise on the *Wyoming*—the navy declared us ready for active-duty billets. Doctrine held that a naval officer was a generalist not a specialist and, above all, that the role of an officer is to command. Adm. Robert Dennison, USN, tells of being criticized by his fellow submariners, early in his career, for turning down the command of a newer and larger submarine than the one he was serving on. They thought he'd rejected a great opportunity. Instead, he'd chosen to broaden himself, asking to be assigned to a surface ship. Dennison said he wanted "an opportunity to practice my profession, which I believe is command, not specialization—in submarines or anything else."

Whatever had stuck from the hours of navigation, ordnance and gunnery, seamanship that we'd crammed into our heads, the real change in us was cultural. The months under discipline had changed us. We had acquired the habit of obedience that is said to be a requisite for him who would command. The uniform was the outward symbol of our one professional accomplishment. In the end we had taken on the minds of officers.

Once we were commissioned, the navy made it up to the twenty-five of us assigned to the Asiatic Fleet by sparing us the voyage across the Pacific in the usual dull gray navy transport. Instead, we were to cross on the maiden voyage of *President Hayes*, a one-class, hundred-passenger, American President Lines passenger ship.

Off duty, officers wore civilian clothes in those peace-time days, but our passports showed our occupation as "Naval Officer." When we went to the Japanese consulate, they looked from us to our passports and back, muttering under their breaths in a satisfactorily sinister manner. When the third or fourth batch of us presented our passports at the British consulate in San Francisco for Hong Kong visas, a young British vice-consul wryly asked if we were going to the Orient on a pilgrimage. Secretly, concealing romantic views of the Orient, I did think of myself as a pilgrim, although far more interested in the way stations—Honolulu, Kobe, Hong Kong—than journey's end at Manila.

In the storm of the first two days out of San Francisco,

even the blight of seasickness went toward fulfilling my hopes. A row of us new men of the sea sat in deck chairs, bundled in steamer rugs, waiting for the cart of bouillon and crackers, lemon and tea, to be rolled into sight by the overcheerful deck steward. Dully, we watched the gray sea rise toward us and the breaking crests fall away as the ship rolled through a seasonal storm. I was miserable but determinedly grateful for the experience.

We began to meet our fellow passengers, some of whom, less hardy than we'd been, had huddled in their staterooms, not appearing in the dining saloon until the seas calmed off Hawaii. Some equivocal French couples enroute to Saigon would not be drawn out concerning de Gaulle or Vichy. British colonials returning to Hong Kong and Singapore dismissed Far Eastern peoples with clipped clichés. They had sharp comments, too, for the neutrality of "you Americans," obtusely overlooking how unneutral we ensigns were. Merchants of obscure nationality were on their way back to Shanghai, some of them plausible, even commonplace; others standoffish, furtive, avoiding us and our innocent questions. These older passengers patronized or avoided us as best suited them. We adopted an Egyptian graduate in engineering of Purdue University, roughly our contemporary, who seemed not to mind being addressed as Omar the Boilermaker.

Lady Drummond Hay, a well-known traveler, joined the ship in Honolulu. (In those days, when far fewer people traveled, there was a recognized category of notable called traveler or world traveler, something short of explorer status.) We sailed from Honolulu at midnight as the moon hung over Diamond Head, a tourist's postcard. From the deck, a contingent of us cast our leis over the side, welcoming Drummond Hay aboard by singing, loudly, more than once, "Lady Drummond hey-hey-hey." Captain Collins, commanding the *Hayes*, himself a naval reserve officer, called a sheepish group together the next morning for a briefing on decorum. Those of our comrades who'd lain wakeful in their bunks the night before were lofty toward the guilty.

Our first block print was a monochrome seascape of violets and blues, some seventy fishing junks, sailing side-wise, dragging their nets off the coast of Honshu, outside Kobe. The boats were about forty feet long, bows pointed in the same direction, the square sails set alike, too, main-sail at the peak and the foresail halfway down the canted foremast. Still figures of fishermen came to life to wave at us, their arrangement of boats furrowing the sea as they parted to let us through.

After calling at Kobe we sailed for Shanghai. Before the low-lying land of the delta rose on our horizon, far out to sea the muddy Yangzi River stained me sea yellow. A brown stern wave curled behind us past Wusong, through delta country, green fields, and thatched houses the same mud color as the soil, our wake washing the low shores far astern. In a strong breeze, high-pooped sailing junks, with eyes painted on their bows, shaved our stern on their course upriver, tacking back under our bows, battened sails flutter-ing, the whistle of the *Hayes* roaring at their insolence.

As we came to commerce, oil tanks on the shore, foreign ships lying alongside or anchored in the stream—the hal-yards of a Soviet ship dressed for May Day, a huge red flag over her counter—one of the pursers told us of running up the river to Shanghai four years before. Then artillery shells whistled overhead—they'd holed the stack but luckily that was all. He pointed out the warship *Izumo*, a stiff antique, a prize of the 1905 Russo-Japanese war, sitting now in Shanghai as the Japanese station ship. Chinese planes, try-ing to destroy the *Izumo* at that time, had scattered death in the city streets, overshooting to drop their bombs in Shang-hai.

Just before we sailed from Shanghai, there was a scuffle at the gangway on the pontoon below us. A tall blonde woman, big boned, well dressed, respectable with a hat on, had demanded to be let aboard and was refused. Some of our comrades stepped out of her sight, snickering, aft to the bar. "I see you! I see you up there." She shook her fist, calling out names familiar to the rest of us. "Come down here immediately! You owe me money." At the bar, once underway, we learned she was the director of an establish-ment where our skulking comrades had become acquainted the night before with some young women who worked there under her supervision. Some fraudulent claim about a bill, some misunderstanding, was their offhand explanation. As we moved out into the stream, she was still there, waving her black purse at the ship.

The shoreline of Hong Kong looked like an ancient dead city, the arcades beneath the gray-and-white, two-story buildings hid the throngs milling along their walkways. At Repulse Bay, we had to walk around rolls of concertina wire on the sand, beach defenses against an enemy landing. We swam out to a large junk lying in the sun, the tide streaming past her, her woodwork varnished, brightwork shining. We took turns going up a stern line to peer over the railing of her poop—a portable radio playing classical music to no one in sight, colored cushions on her deck—before letting go to splash into the water so the next man could have a look. The smell of night soil in the nearby fishing village of Aberdeen was enriched by the smell of drying fish. Small sampans were packed close in regular lines. Beyond them, on the channel side, nets hung in drying festoons from the masts of great fishing junks—as large as some of the craft our ancestors had sailed in to the New World.

From the peak, Hong Kong harbor with the lights coming on across the water in Kowloon and below our feet on the Hong Kong side "beat San Francisco hollow," I wrote home. I resolved to go back home through China as soon as my Asiatic tour was up.

Two days later, the *Hayes* lay motionless at quarantine in Manila Bay. We stood on deck, looking gloomily down to the boat coming alongside the gangway. It was so hot, the sun not halfway up the morning sky, that my tweed suit began manufacturing prickly heat on my thighs. A small, thin man in an officer's cap, scrambled eggs on the visor, a short-sleeved white shirt, white shorts, white socks, and white shoes, the silver leaves of a navy commander on his collar, stepped aboard, smoking a cigarette in a long, black holder. He looked us over, amiably enough, and introduced himself as Commander MacGowan. A yeoman, standing behind him, handed him a sheaf of papers. The officer introduced himself and began to read off our names.

We were back in the navy.

Chapter 7

At the beginning, most of us who arrived on the *President Hayes* had been assigned billets ashore in Cavite, headquarters of the 16th Naval District. The navy didn't know quite what to do with all of us—not just the 16th Naval District or the Asiatic Fleet, the navy. Seeing what was coming, President Roosevelt was readying the army and navy for expansion in wartime, among other steps, pushing a cadre of new young officers into the navy framework. At the other end of the system, not all the regular officers were ready to welcome us tenderfoot reservists aboard. Our training had done little more than make us familiar with the navy and competent to fill no particular billet. Even with good will, a bare-bones, low-budget navy didn't find it easy to fit us in. We were still raw material for training.

Eight of our group were assigned to Radio Control, the fleet radio station in the Cavite navy yard that furnished communication to the Asiatic Fleet. So many of us were assigned to communications work that it was Commander MacGowan, the staff communications officer, who'd come aboard the *Hayes* to meet us. The navy put a large number of inexperienced reservists like us to work as communications watch officers. Working with words from the start, familiar material, we could be broken in faster and made useful sooner than in other technologies.

The yard was laid out in the Spanish days, the comfortable times before the automobile. So it was compact, easy to get around on foot or by bicycle. Every department in the yard had a bicycle rack. Noontime or in late afternoon, everyone in the yard seemed to be going somewhere. A bad time to be out walking. You were kept busy returning salutes of the knots of sailors streaming at you along the walks, worse yet having to return salutes on a bicycle, teetering through foot traffic with only one hand on the handlebars.

The day was filled with the sound of hammering and the flicker of welding torches from ships at Central Wharf. Filipino yard workers trooped by, carrying tools or lugging pieces of machinery from a yard shop to a ship. At the lunch break, the Filipinos would kick a small ball, woven of fiber, into the air, shouting, racing for it, leaping at it, keeping it in the air behind their heads. Even the waters were busy; yard craft, small single-funneled, heavy-hulled, their bows uncompromisingly straight and old-fashioned—680s, they were called—swished by, intent on errands, stirring the water into a chop.

The naval radio station—known by the call sign NPO—sat next to the docks where men-of-war lay for repair or refitting. (NPO was to be transplanted to Corregidor in December 1941, and the call sign would stay on the air until the final minutes of the last day when Corregidor fell to the Japanese in May of 1942.) The radio station was a barn-sized frame building painted white, antennae and cables looping from stanchions on top of its flat, graveled roof. We'd wait on that roof for the Pan American China Clipper to touch down in the bay waters, watch the plane taxi into the stretch of water between the yard and Sangley Point, bearing airmail from home.

Architecture in the navy yard was a victim of Admiral Dewey's defeat of the Spanish in Manila Bay in 1898. We took over the Spanish-colonial yard and added the American Navy utilitarian style. The white frame carpentry work of Radio Control, white-painted wooden galleries around the top, white wooden stairways angled up on the outside, typified it. The Spanish buildings, elegant, like the *comandancia* with its high ceilings and rooms paneled in mahogany, ancient, like the lichened walls of the Spanish fort around which our newer buildings sprawled, were cool, thick-walled, mildew-smelling structures, dark inside. The low arched roofs of cisterns, half-buried in the black sand, were scattered about the yard. Despite its utilitarian purpose, the yard was an attractive place. When we got there that May, the flame trees growing throughout the yard were in full bloom.

On the second story of NPO was a large room where radiomen on watch sat at tables, with radio receivers and typewriters in front of them, exchanging radio traffic with the ships of the Asiatic Fleet, with Honolulu, with Washington. At the bottom of a steep stairway sat the code room, where we communications watch officers worked. Many of the radio messages were sent in plain English. By the summer of 1941, an increasing amount of the radio traffic was in cipher to keep it from German and Japanese eyes. So we filled the need for more communications officers to encipher outgoing messages and to decipher the incoming ones.

We were nominally in charge when standing a night watch. Practically, a chief petty officer, a radioman, supervised the radiomen, the transmission and reception of traffic on the air. If he had to make an extraordinary decision in the night, he'd defer in a formal way to the communications watch officer. You would do your best to understand the technical points and then agree to whatever he recommended. If it was something really serious, he'd say, "I think we'd better call Commander MacGowan." You wouldn't dispute that either.

Usually, we were busy at our ciphering duties and seeing to it that the enciphered messages got to the proper addressee in the district command. Most of what we read was ordinary stuff, written in deadly navy prose, but it did give us a wide view of the navy. Enciphered dispatches from the chief of naval operations (CNO), from the commander in chief, Pacific Fleet (CINCPAC), or from the commander in chief, Asiatic Fleet (CINCAF) across the bay in Manila, might be worth reading a second time, an intelligence report on Japanese actions in China or a startling estimate of intentions in Southeast Asia.

Interesting, that, but work in the code room was excessively clerkish, not at all what I'd pictured myself doing. I wanted to get to sea, but the opportunities for that were restricted by the size of the so-called Asiatic Fleet. The command of Admiral Bemis, the 16th Naval District, took in the Philippine Islands. He flew his two-star flag at the *comandancia* in the Cavite navy yard. Just to the east, across the bottom of Manila Bay, the Marsman Building sat in the port area on the Manila waterfront. There CINCAF, Adm. Thomas C. Hart, flew his four-star flag. With his staff, he directed the ships and aircraft of the Asiatic Fleet.

The river gunboats on the Yangzi, the yachtlike vessels of the South China Patrol, harmless up against modern men-of-war, had no role beyond the diplomatic, showing the flag. The heavy cruiser *Houston* was a comparatively up-to-date surface ship, but the light cruiser *Marblehead* was of World War I vintage, as were the thirteen destroyers of Destroyer Squadron 29. There were twenty-three modern, fleet-class submarines and six old S-boats. With some minesweepers, tenders for the destroyers, the submarines, and the aircraft, oilers, a squadron of motor torpedo boats, and a miscellany of assorted vessels, including yard craft—that was the fleet. The aircraft were PBYs of Patrol Wing 10, slow, reliable seaplanes built for reconnaissance, incidentally armed. Not much of a fleet, really not a fleet at all. Flotilla, in the meaning of a little fleet, would have suited us better.

So I buckled down to learning what had been set before me and, before long, I was allowed to stand watch alone at night or on the weekend. The difference in time zones meant that an urgent message sent us at midday from Washington arrived in the small hours of the morning in the Philippines. You'd get out the proper cipher and break the message and waken the operations officer or the chief of staff, sometimes Admiral Bemis himself. (As we young officers stood in awe of Bemis, it was considered funny to phone the colleague on watch at night and say, "This is Admiral Bemis." Eventually, to the embarrassment of one or another of us inured to the tired joke, Bemis himself would be on the line.)

I came to enjoy walking through the navy yard on these midnight deliveries, no one else about. I'd telephone the addressee—wake up the admiral himself in the middle of the night if the message called for that—stick the message in a worn leather pouch, lock the door to the code room, strap on the Colt .45 automatic pistol that hung in its holster on the wall over the work table in the code room. That was the rule when venturing out alone at night with classified material—I can't recall the nature of the likely exigency against which we armed ourselves.

I'd stroll through the deserted yard in the soft night to the *comandancia*, the old Spanish headquarters where the admiral lived and had his office. The gangway lights on our ships resting at the docks reflected orange from the water. Where I walked in the tropical darkness under the branches of the mimosas, the only sounds were the hum of the ships' blowers and the clucking of lizards prowling for insects in the trees.

I'd push the bell on the wall under the carriage porch. The high mahogany door would swing open and the admiral's sleepy Chinese mess steward in white jacket and black trousers would blink at me, shuffle in black cloth shoes across the hall to a reception room, mumble again, and head back to wait in the pantry. Admiral Bemis sitting in a bathrobe, looking old under a harsh overhead light, would take the message and read it. He never questioned your judgment in waking him. And, for whatever it was worth, he learned your name.

Not long after we arrived, Admiral Bemis had us new ensigns for coffee at the *comandancia*. He spoke of the role—he could as well have said the fate—of the professional to carry out the task assigned him no matter how difficult. He said something appreciative about our coming to take part in whatever lay ahead of us. His remarks were gracious, including us, just as though we were regulars, making us feel welcome. Implicit in his words was a foreboding of what lay ahead. Admiral Bemis couldn't forecast the future, and he didn't try to, in his talk to us, anyway. The probability of a Japanese attack on the Philippines was not the issue. No matter how low the odds you gave it, what mattered was that, if they did attack, it would be disastrous.

Bemis developed an ulcer and went home that summer, relieved by Admiral Rockwell. Inevitably, his leaving elicited one of those questions framed in terms of: "What does Bemis know that the rest of us don't?"

The Asiatic Fleet was a bachelor post. With a good sense of what was coming, Admiral Hart ordered all dependents home in 1940. Three of us, Norm Lauchner, Bill Long, and I, set up housekeeping on the naval reservation at Sangley Point, across a narrow neck of water from the navy yard. The word Sangley is a corruption of a Chinese term referring to trade, perhaps from the Fujian dialect pronunciation of *shanglu*, meaning trade route. The sangleys, as the Spanish called the Chinese traders, sailed down from China with their goods in time to meet the Manila galleon on its annual trip from Acapulco, the Philippines then being administered by the viceroy of New Spain in Mexico. The Manila galleon anchored in Cañacao Bay, the water between Sangley Point and Cavite, as did the sangley's trading junks. The crews of both nations would have come ashore at what was the hospital landing of our time.

After we replaced the Spanish, Sangley Point was our navy's coaling station. On the flat sandy point in 1941, three high, metal towers carried the transmitting antennae of NPO. Below them sat white-painted buildings, the officers club, a few officers' quarters, the hospital, a chapel, a swimming pool, tennis courts. Duckboards ran across low spots where water gathered during the rains. A half dozen PBYs of Patrol Wing 10 squatted ashore on the seaplane ramp north of the hospital landing. Rows of lacy casuarinas and shiny-leaved shade trees, the white-bloomed barringtonia, common on tropic seashores, grew along the edge of Cañacao Bay. On the empty west side of the point, where you looked right across the bay to the hazy mountains of Bataan, there was good walking along the beach, if you didn't mind the heat.

Ours was one in the row of private houses facing the reservation along a narrow macadam road, mischievously named Cañacao Boulevard, running from the entrance gate, along the boundary of the reservation, to peter out at the bay shore. Each frame house had a one-car garage and servants' quarters below, kitchen and living quarters above, windows all round to let the air through. Shutters slid across to keep out blowing rain in storms. From the outside, light glowed through saucer-sized translucent shells set, instead of window glass, in the shutters. Between the housefront and the road, our patch of yard had a kalichuchi tree, the white-bloomed frangipani, a gardenia bush, a nipa palm, and salmon-colored bracts of a bougainvillea growing up the side of the house to the living room window, the fragrance of kalichuchi and gardenia drifting through the house at night. A two-hundred-yard walk to the left down the road toward the bay was the officers club, a roofed pavilion with flame trees set about it. Three hundred yards up the road the other way was the gate, manned by Marines in tight-fitting, creased khakis.

Loose strands of barbed wire marked the boundary behind the houses from gate to seashore—more a concept than a working fence—and separated us from the municipality of Cañacao. On the other side of a rich-smelling mud flat, a barrio of nipa-roofed houses stood on stilts above the mud and black sand, close enough to the water for the odd banca, nets drying on the outrigger, to sit beneath a house. Black Far Eastern pigs, jungle boar strong in the blood line, strolled in the mud with varicolored goats and small brown children whose shirts covered half their bellies. The pigs wandered on delicate feet, ears quivering with quick rage when they contested a piece of offal in the mud, other times standing quiet, small-eyed and thoughtful. Under tamarind trees around the houses, older children wielded bamboo poles with snares on the ends to pull the sticky-sweet seed pods from the branches. Barrio roosters competed for first crow, calling each morning for an earlier dawn.

The living-room window of the house next to us was no more than five feet away. We joined in the conversations of the three ensigns next door as often as they interrupted ours. Our house rented for fifty pesos a month—the peso was at half a dollar—we paid the cook twenty and the *lavandera*, who washed our clothes, ten. We'd have friends on ships in for dinner who envied our setup ashore while we envied their being at sea.

Outside the gate, a cluster of calesas waited for fares. The calesa is a high, two-wheeled chaise with a calash hood that could be lowered, but ordinarily was drawn over the two-passenger seat and the driver on his seat in front of the passengers. The calesa chassis is brightly painted, decorated with scrolling and stylized floral designs, the wheels and the spokes picked out in matching colors. (The grotesque designs of Manila's elaborately gaudy postwar taxis, the jeepneys, were a rococo corruption of the calesa style.) If the drivers felt any affection for the horses, the sad, skinny ponies between the shafts, they didn't let it show.

It was bad form to ride in a calesa in uniform, although I frequently did so. Like other proscribed activities, calesa riding might be forgiven if you were in mufti, when your deportment would be judged more charitably than if you were in uniform. That was one reason officers and the men rated first class and above wore civilian clothes off duty. (One of my first calls in the Philippines was on H. Hing, Tailor, Calle Trece Martires, Cavite, P.I., to order what turned out to be a clingingly hot, white linen suit.)

The driver switched the horse's tender belly with a long-handled whip and hurried him along with a sound that began guttural and ended impatient: "Yu-ee!" The horse trotted, head down, blinders on either side of the bridle, through the crowded Cañacao streets with little regard for the children dashing out from the edge of the street, no regard for the dogs resting in the middle of the road, none for the dusky pigs that chose the last moment to rocket under the calesa's wheels.

At an open spot on the black-sand beach between Cañacao and Cavite, about halfway to the navy yard, sordid in the daylight, sat a vast frame building known as Dreamland. At night, the floor was full of sailors and Marines dancing with Filipinas, Dreamland's dance girls, the so-called ballerinas. Custom decreed officers had to stay on a balcony above the dance floor. If you wanted to dance, you had to summon a ballerina to your table there.

An older one of the ballerinas, plump and round-faced, wearing a proper long dress with the puffed sleeves of an earlier time, was known as Dewey for her claim to have lost her maidenhood to the victor of the Battle of Manila Bay. She was sedately past middle age so her dates were right, the battle having been fought slightly more than forty years before—fought just off Sangley Point and Cavite, actually. Along the seawall on Dewey Boulevard in Manila, rusty boilers and bent stanchions poked out of the black sand where some of the surprisingly small ships of Admiral Montejo's squadron had run into the shallows, aflame and sinking.

On past Dreamland, the road curved into Cavite proper, Kawit in Tagalog, a town before the Spanish came, later capital of the Spanish province of Cavite. The Spanish put a fort there, and the Dutch dropped by to bombard it in 1647. At the gate to the yard you dismounted, paid off the calesa, and walked through to the flame trees that bloomed on into June. There was often a gang of prisoners from the brig in blue dungarees, kneeling among the trees just off the walk, breaking rocks with short-handled mauls, guarded by a Marine who warned you against getting between him and the prisoners.

Next was a thick-walled, rose-colored building, the disbursing office. One of my additional duties each month was verifying the paymaster's accounts by counting every last dollar, peso, and coin, right down to the copper centavos. It took me all afternoon to get the total right. I detested that day as much as the paymaster loathed me.

After one such episode, I ran into a colleague, made sympathetic himself through suffering some naval insult. We sat together at a table outside Ships Service over a cold San Miguel—from the common pronunciation, at first I thought the brand was "Sam McGill"—and sought purgative answers to eternal questions, exchanging hypotheses, for example, about the meaning of being a reserve ensign. People look back on those days, war clouds on the horizon, great things afoot—what it must have been like! What it was like was this: sweating over sums not coming out right, kicking yourself for leaving a key word out of a message heading, being held in your job while the guy praying to remain ashore goes off to sea. Then it was my turn to listen to my companion. He'd gotten aboard a destroyer, as he wanted. But the captain didn't like reserve officers and refused to trust him as officer of the deck underway. The navy was a capricious Old Testament deity, we agreed, overlooking great sins in order to chasten junior ensigns for minor errors.

Manila was half an hour or so by ferry, twice that by taxi, further than that from the navy—not that we ever really left. The road around the bottom of the bay ran through delta country, past square seaside flats where sea salt, brought in on the tide, was trapped, dried, and bagged. Across the road rice paddies, also framed by dikes, reflected the same sky and clouds as the salt pans. The scene of a carabao dragging a plow through paddy muck, mud dried gray on the buffalo's gunmetal flank, the legs of a straw-hatted farmer glistening with black paddy mud, was repeated along the road, even to the same background of coconut palms in a grassy plantation. Cavite mangoes—the best in the world if you listened to the Cavite people—grew on the dark trees regularly set about in bright groves, as in a child's drawing.

We'd stop for a San Miguel at the white-painted stone house where papaya grew scraggly in back. The children would leave off chasing each other to stand big-eyed in a row to look us over. The people there would roast you a pig in the ground—*lechón* with the crackly skin—if you sent word ahead. Closer to the city, nipa-roofed bamboo houses sat behind green hedges, half hidden by broad-leaved banana trees, a glimpse of footpaths running like tunnels straight under high forest trees to places you'd never see. The village centers were Romanesque stone churches, green with algae, creeping fig covering the walls, banyans spreading over the bare ground of schoolyards. Forty years before, our troops had been driving the insurrectos through these suburban bamboo thickets, civilizing Aguinaldo's white-clad men with a Krag rifle.

Or we took the ferry. On free evenings, we'd be up on the boat deck in the wicker armchairs, the engines throbbing as the ferry moved out from the dock. Manila Bay's specialty is breathtaking sunsets. In the afternoon, the sun threw amber light on the spun-soft columns of clouds piled high above the bay, reflecting milky white on the bay waters. From the churning, green ferry wake and the pale blue of the sky, the color ran through violet to a blue so deep it was almost black. Cerulean, aquamarine, violet, Prussian blue, zinc white, would take care of it—add an unexpected touch of alizarin crimson. If you were facing aft toward Cavite, a band of light under the destroyers rafted together outside the yard would grow larger, show pale yellow, and the ships shrink until they hung shimmering above the water.

Toward the end of that summer, I met a Basque girl with dark red hair. She lived in Manila with her parents in a massive four-story building, its weighty look relieved by elegant wrought-iron balconies that would be stripped for scrap in a year or so. Her four brothers had all fought for Franco, thus putting us in opposite camps politically. One night I went to pick her up, and one of the brothers opened the door. He stared at me coldly and turned without a word to leave me standing there. I was never asked in by María (not her name) to meet her family. Given the evident level of feeling, I thought this policy to be a wise one.

"He doesn't like you Americans," she explained that night, by no means apologizing for her brother. By leaving that subject alone, I could avoid giving offense—I figured it was, after all, her country, her civil war—and we had a fairly good time together. She had that hoarse voice you hear in Spanish women, like the soloist in "El Amor Brujo." The last time I saw her, we hadn't gotten on well, but if things had been normal, I suppose I'd have seen her again.

But things weren't to be normal.

What happened in December seems now to have been inevitable, although it was not obvious then, certainly not in the United States, not in Washington, not in the Philippines. But that doesn't mean we were foolish or oblivious to what was going on around us. Those of us in communications saw the secret warning messages from Washington in the summer and autumn of 1941, warnings so general that your access to secret information left you no wiser than anyone else. Also confidential were Patwing 10's reconnaissance flights across the South China Sea to look at the Japanese

naval buildup in Cam Ranh Bay. At the officers club, the
PBY pilots talked about their missions, about glimpsing
through cloud cover Japanese men-of-war spread on a pewter sea below. The gunboats of the Yangzi patrol had their
bulwarks built up for the voyage from Shanghai to the Philippines. The 4th Marine Regiment came down to Manila in
November. Admiral Hart, with the assent of the Navy Department, was preparing for the worst.

We three roommates talked as much that autumn about
travel as we did about the threat from the Japanese. We'd
done Tagaytay, Pagsanjan Falls, a jungle picnic in
Mariveles. We were expanding our horizons—talking about
the interisland steamer to Mindanao, a motor trip north to
the pine forests of Baguio in the Luzon highlands, annual
leave in China on one of the French or British liners. We
argued about whether to get a monkey or a pig for the
house. Long and I voted for a pig and Lauchner threatened
to move out.

In November, I got orders to report to CINCAF in Manila for duty. I never did get back to Sangley Point.

Chapter 8

Everyone remembers Pearl Harbor. They'll tell you about it, too. The family was at Sunday dinner when someone phoned with the news. The radio announcer interrupted the broadcast of the football game. What they remember is not Pearl Harbor. They remember what they were doing at the time.

Few of the people who remember Pearl Harbor were there. I wasn't at Pearl Harbor either. On December 8 (the date of Pearl Harbor in Manila), I was deep in sleep in my room at the Bayview Hotel on Dewey Boulevard. We'd been working all that Sunday at CINCAF, Admiral Hart's staff headquarters at the Marsman Building in the port area of Manila. When the telephone rang, it must have been around three in the morning. It took me a while to grasp that the phone was ringing for me and a second or two more to get out of the mosquito net around my bed. I can't remember who it was that called, an officer superior to me, as most anyone on the staff was. He told me to wake up other officers in the Bayview, one being my boss, Comdr. Walter Lineaweaver, the fleet communications officer. I'd been billeted at the Bayview since my transfer from Cavite. I knew their room numbers—the sort of list a junior officer is expected to keep in his head—and dressed while I called them, in a hurry to get down to the lobby before they did. Dressing was easy as I slept in my skivvy shorts and had only to pull on my trousers and shoes, my tunic, button it up, and put on my hat on the way downstairs. At the lobby entrance, a sailor was standing in shadow by the black, staff station wagon. I asked him if he knew what the trouble was, and he said he didn't. That's how those of us riding in the station wagon would remember Pearl Harbor—being driven half-asleep through dark streets to the port area nearby.

There was little conversation on the short drive from the hotel to the Marsman Building, some sleepy curiosity. "Didn't say why they wanted us, eh?" Lineaweaver asked.

"No, sir. Just said we're to come. That was all."

Mild grumbling, but no surprise. After all, Hart's staff had been poised, expectant, for months now. It looked as though finally something had happened. Even I, a feckless ensign, mind drifting away from thoughts of the future to the pleasures of the present, assumed that something was going to happen. There had been practice blackouts in Manila as well as in Cavite. The Navy Department in Washington had told Hart to get most of his ships south, get ready to work with the British, the Australians, and the Dutch when war came, ready himself to make a stand at the Malay barrier. Many of our ships, the two cruisers, most of the destroyers, the train of oilers and tenders, were operating as far south as Balikpapan and Tarakan in Borneo. Submarines were on patrol. Minefields had been laid in Manila Bay, and our ships were running darkened at night, drilling for wartime conditions. In late November, the Navy Department in Washington sent still another ominous but diffuse warning about Japanese intentions.

Just three days before December 8, Adm. Sir Tom Phillips of the Royal Navy, in command at Singapore, had flown back home from Manila in a hurry, breaking off talks with Hart and Gen. Douglas MacArthur, commander of U.S. Army Forces, Far East. Phillips, recently arrived from the United Kingdom, came to Manila to talk about Anglo-American cooperation when the fighting started. He'd left abruptly because of reports of a Japanese force in the South China Sea sailing toward Thailand and Malaya.

When we got upstairs in the Marsman Building, lights were burning. A few people were moving about quietly. Comdr. Robert Dennison was standing near a bulletin board, and a few feet away from him was the neat, erect figure of Adm. "Thos. C. Hart"—that's how he signed himself—in white uniform, with his back to us, at a high desk, reading dispatches. That's how I see Hart now when I think of him, from the back, his gray hair going white above the gold-and-silver shoulder boards of a four-star admiral. That image remains from the intensity of that moment. I saw him often enough in the following days from other angles, spoke with him face-to-face.

Dennison pointed to a plain-language dispatch tacked on the bulletin board. We went up to the bulletin board to read the famous message: "AIR RAID ON PEARL HARBOR. THIS IS NO DRILL." I read it twice and turned away without a word. Normally, I would have exclaimed, but not with Hart standing there, capable of inspiring a respect as great as the awful news on the board. Awful and exciting, what we'd been waiting for.

Such images, portraits, landscapes in color, stay with me and illustrate memory. When I try to examine them, to look for details, find other faces than those I remember, the pictures fail, blurring. Objects around the edges refuse to get into focus. Pearl Harbor, for me, is more than any one of the pictures in the frame of memory, more than standing there to read the famous message for the first time, more than holding the phone in my room at the Bayview, heavy with sleep, more than my impatience with the stolidity of the driver of the station wagon who didn't care why he'd been sent to get us at three in the morning. Pearl Harbor stands for a highly colored strip of time that began running that morning in the silence of the Manila streets and that came to a stop in the brightness of High Street in Perth when Corregidor fell six months later. I can see the still-young faces of friends, the faces of strangers seen just once. I can hear the voices, the shaking of the air when guns slam, and the sounds ships make as they go through the water. To me it is still the most vivid of times when I do think of it, but I don't think of it often.

The dawn of 8 December was itself vivid. I'd climbed the steel stairway to the roof of the Marsman Building to look west over the bay to the low Cavite shore. With the sun still below the horizon, first light showed the landscape gray, looking cold, which it may have been, for Manila. As the sun climbed, it shined rosy on clouds and water, sprucing up the buildings on the waterfront. I was bareheaded and could feel the tropic sun's heat on my neck right away. The city was still except for the roar of aircraft engines from Nichols Field, along the bay shore to our left, the field hidden by trees. As the pitch of the sound rose, the first of the P-40 pursuit planes came in sight above the trees, the engine noise dropping down the scale as the plane leveled off. They came up from behind the trees, one by one, forming into threes before climbing out of sight over the city behind me.

Watching them leave as the sun came up brought my first apprehension of the meaning of war, that they were armed, that they were actually going off to kill or to be killed. (More likely the latter. Few came back.)

We were busy with incoming and outgoing dispatch traffic all that morning, ships reporting in, orders going out, reports from all over, reports in plain language, reports official and unofficial, coming by radio, by hand, from the U.S. Army, from the Philippine Army, from post offices. Many of the reports did no more than relay rumors, misleading rumors, too, spawned instantly by the news of disaster at Pearl Harbor. People who had given little thought to the possibility of a Japanese attack now believed anything to be possible and passed every outlandish rumor on.

The three favored themes of bad information were reinforcements for our side, fifth-column activity, and sightings of the enemy. The civil warning system in Manila was the most noticeable subdepartment of misinformation under the heading of sightings, as appears to be normal in the first days of an air war. In the first Japanese air raid on the city, the sirens sounded only when the raid was over. The next time, the throaty grumble rose to a shriek when no enemy was in sight. When an abashed all clear sounded, the planes began bombing. In the next raid, the sirens started when the raid was half over, and so on, until the civil defense people got a grip on themselves and synchronized the fear they caused with the cause of the fear. As the days went on, Japanese planes roamed the skies above Manila so freely that they hardly knew whether to sound the alarm or to sound the all clear.

Reinforcement by aircraft carrier. That rumor started early, if not on the very first day, and had a long and popular run. One version converted the former French liner, *Normandie*, then lying in New York harbor, into an aircraft carrier and had her steaming into Asian waters with a deckload of fighter planes. Wishful rumors of that sort grew desperately creative as it became clear to all that we were not doing well against the Japanese. Word flashed around that the famous navy aircraft carrier, *Ranger*, actually had called the signal station in the port area—not your usual scuttlebutt. I read the message myself: RANGER STANDING IN FROM SEA, something like that. It was the *Ranger*, all right, the tug *Ranger* belonging to Luzon Stevedoring, a company operating in the port area. Her identity long lagged behind the report of her arrival.

The most common fifth-column story came by word of mouth. Did you know that one of the barbers at the Manila Hotel (the florist in the corner shop in Makati, that photographer outside the navy yard in Cavite) turns out all along to have been a lieutenant commander in Japanese naval intelligence? (He was always a lieutenant commander whatever his alleged cover occupation.)

That first morning, Japanese air activity was reported from the far north of Luzon at Vigan and Aparri. Reports made in good faith might be no more dependable than a careless rumor. The week before, an army air forces plane on patrol off Luzon had excitedly reported battleships moving toward us—"one black and one white," it said. They were our Yangzi patrol gunboats wallowing through the seas to a temporary haven in Manila Bay.

A report that morning from the *William B. Preston*, an aircraft tender lying in Davao in the southern Philippines, was reliable but disheartening. Early the morning of the eighth, she and her accompanying PBYs tied to buoys nearby were jumped by Japanese aircraft, the first death being one of the Patwing 10 pilots, an ensign we used to drink with at the club in Cañacao.

The naval base at Guam reported that a bird-class minesweeper had been sunk in the first Japanese attack, sitting on the bottom in shallow water, her superstructure sticking up above the water. One casualty was the ensign aboard her, a ninety-day wonder, still firing a machine gun at the Japanese planes as she sank, dying at the gun.

The next shock of the day was less personal, an inexplicable disaster, inexcusable, a lot of us thought then. I still do, but I've always thought his reputation inflated by his own bombast: Gen. Douglas MacArthur was excused for it. Army B-17 bombers and P-40 fighters were caught on the ground, lined up on the runway at Clark Field, peacetime style, when the Japanese attacked at midday, some ten hours after the word of the attack on Pearl Harbor reached the Philippines. Most were destroyed or so badly damaged as to be inoperable. At the same time at Iba airfield, the Japanese surprised P-40s returning from patrol and destroyed them.

The first night of the war, I jumped out of bed, taking the mosquito net right along with me to the window at the sound of explosions. The Japanese had bombed Nichols Field. On Wednesday, 10 December, fifty-four Japanese bombers with an escort of Zero fighters, effectively unopposed, flew back and forth across Cavite navy yard and Sangley Point, destroying the yard and several ships, damaging others. We stood on the roof of the Marsman Building to watch, the sullen roar of their engines in our ears. I stayed there, off and on, the rest of the day to see Cavite and Sangley burn, the fires orange at the bottom of a twisting pillar of smoke, flickering red, roiling black and yellow at the base, a dirty ocher color stretching to a wispy gray toward the top until the column wound out of sight in the sky.

Cavite burned for days in the windless weather, stinking smoke hanging over the bay, a dirty thick rope winding up as far as you could see into the sky. What happened at Cavite was bad enough, but it could have been worse. We had lost our naval base, people, and some ships, but most of our ships were not in Cavite when the Japanese attacked. We didn't have much of a fleet before that, and we had less of one now. If we'd had a fleet near Manila, there'd have been no base for it. Anyway, the Japanese owned the air.

The same day, again for lack of air cover, Japanese aircraft sank the British battleships *Repulse* and *Prince of Wales* off Malaya, Adm. Sir Tom Phillips going down with them. The loss of their large guns meant the Japanese dominated the sea as well as the air from the Indian Ocean to Hawaii.

The days and nights after December 8 flew by. We worked all day, staying on watch all night, going off to breakfast, getting called back from the shower before we could climb into bed. We communications watch officers had reinforcements, among them Ensigns Hugh Lawrence and Bill Hirst, friends from Cavite. We had a pretty cheerful time of it. Commander Lineaweaver had a high, carrying voice so you could hear him coming for a long way. He was always popping in on us where we were deciphering messages, rallying us, reading the messages we had broken. We usually had company as we worked, reading what we were transcribing, fascinated by the stream of the bad news.

The occasional visual memories are comparatively fresh, but my hold on the emotional memory of the first weeks of war is tenuous. Of course, we were all shocked. Here's the world you've known falling apart as you watch. Much worse for civilians, for Filipinos—I know I was grateful to be in uniform, that my family was far away in America's safehaven.

The Japanese were bombing Manila at will, including the port area where we worked. When the first stick of bombs fell in front of the Marsman Building, curious people—including sailors who should have known better—were standing out in the street, peering up at the planes. Some civilians took cover by standing in doorways. We hauled them out of the rubble, their blood running in rivulets through the cement dust that covered them. One of the sailors in our working party remarked sarcastically on the contrast between Japanese propaganda, fulsome in friendship for the Philippine people, and the dead and wounded, all Filipinos, mostly dock laborers by the looks of them.

Seeing what bombs did to people made me thoughtful,

and the Japanese planes made me apprehensive. I don't think I was any more jumpy than the next man, apparently less so than some. Your thoughts about what was happening counted for less than your ability to conceal them from others. You pretended that everything happening was, well, maybe not normal, actually, nor for the best, exactly, but, on the other hand, it was only to be expected and nothing to be greatly concerned about. Being young means you bear fatigue better than older men. Being inexperienced is another advantage. Between youth and inexperience, you can imagine yourself invulnerable.

My roommate in Cañacao, Bill Long, showed up homeless after the Cavite raid. He said our other roommate, Norm Lauchner, had survived. Long admitted he'd had an unpleasant time but didn't want to talk about what he'd seen in the navy yard. He did add a light note. When the Japanese planes left and people got up and began to help the wounded, he'd passed by Ships Service, the building in flames like the rest of the yard. He saw sailors milling around inside. He joined them and picked out a new wristwatch for himself, his having been smashed in the raid.

Long was the second of two officers in a degaussing unit. A barge of theirs had survived the raid and been towed to Manila. He conscientiously reported aboard the barge at the Manila waterfront every day. Degaussing is a method of protecting ships against magnetically fired mines. Business had slowed considerably with the departure of our ships, and the loss of Cavite put an end to it.

We got a mattress in and took turns using it when he was there. The advantage of the bed was the mosquito net, patched as it was after my midnight dash to the window. We went through an Alphonse/Gaston routine the first night he was there, insisting the other take the bed. Later we took turns.

The Japanese landed a major force at Lingayen Gulf, north of Manila, a few days before Christmas, hardly opposed from the sea and, strangely enough, allowed by MacArthur to land with little opposition. It was becoming apparent that Manila would not long stand. I met Long at the Bayview one night toward the end and we crept a few hundred yards down the street to dinner at an Indonesian restaurant we knew. We'd eaten *satés* there in preblackout peacetime. Those last days, American and Philippine soldiers wandered around unsupervised, so far as any authority could be seen, more vigilantes than disciplined troops. They carried out their role as air-raid wardens by shouting and shooting at exposed lights, putting an occasional .30 caliber ball into a room at the Bayview.

Long and I reached the restaurant, irritated by the sound of shots around the city, some close by. It was so senseless. Air raids were bad enough, we agreed, but our jumpy soldiery blazing away in the blackout was worse. The Indonesian restaurant was stuffy inside, the covered windows keeping in the heat generated by lamps on the tables. The food was good as ever, but we couldn't be comfortable. When the proprietress came by our table to ask us what was going to happen, we couldn't give her much cheer. What could you say? She wasn't the only one. If you were in uniform, you were an authority. People were frightened and wanted reassurances you could not honestly give.

The next morning was the twenty-third, and Long and I went down to the street early to make our separate ways to work. We agreed to run the gauntlet of friendly troops for a Christmas dinner at the Arcade, a favorite restaurant of ours in Intramuros, the old walled city. We used to gorge on something they called a steak à la rousseau, a huge piece of meat smothered in other rich edibles and surrounded by piquant fried rice. I don't know that either of us expected the dinner would work out.

That night, when I broke away from the Marsman Building, I went to the bar in back of the Bayview lobby to see if Long was there. There were some Americans, civilians, men and women drinking, laughing a lot, too loud, some of the women. Standing by the bar was a grinning American army private, a young blond fellow, bareheaded, with a rifle, a half-empty pack on his back, his tin hat slung on the back of that. The civilians were buying drinks for their mascot. It soured me, the way they were making a party out of our defeat. I took my San Miguel to a table by myself.

When I'd decided Bill Long wasn't going to show up, I went bad-tempered up to bed.

Midmorning the next day, Christmas Eve, I was sent to Fort Santiago in the walled city with a communication for General MacArthur's headquarters. As we bounced over the stones of the Intramuros streets, I was feeling as foolish as usual in the sidecar of a motorcycle, the only transportation available. The dispatch rider was an amiable boatswain's mate attached to the staff. He'd cultivated an impressive handlebar mustache and enjoyed motorcycling, more than I did, certainly, having gone off on errands with him before. In tin hat and mustache, he cut a dashing figure, while I bounced comically in the sidecar beside and below him, holding my helmet on with one hand.

The office I wanted in Fort Santiago was up a flight of dark stairs in a wooden warren perched on top of the walls of Intramuros. I had some trouble getting the attention of anyone in the operations element where I was to deliver the message for MacArthur—our ship dispositions, I think it was. Staff officers and potbellied sergeants were bustling around, stuffing papers into boxes and briefcases, speaking tersely and only to each other, glancing over at me but not pausing to see what I wanted.

"What's going on?" I asked when I cornered one of them. I was in a hurry to get on my way because the sirens had just gone, announcing a raid.

"Didn't you get the word? Manila's an open city at midnight."

I didn't know what that meant, but I did know it was the first I'd heard of it. I got him to sign for my envelope. He promptly threw it in a box without opening it, and I ran to find my boatswain's mate. "Air raid," he said, looking skyward. "Around the port area."

"I know." I climbed into the sidecar. "Let's try to get back there before they hit."

We skidded off, careening and bouncing through the walled city, roaring out through the postern toward the port area. We made it just as the bombs were falling in our street along the waterfront.

When I got upstairs, I passed on what I'd learned at Fort

Santiago. The first people I talked to had no better idea than I what was implied by the term of open city. But almost immediately, I was being interrogated by someone who did. There was consternation in the office. For the Japanese to honor Manila's status as an open city, all military activity must cease, meaning that we and all navy supplies had to be out of Manila by midnight. That was impossible. For example, Hart had been planning to operate out of Manila and had stored ashore torpedoes for the submarines among other essential items. His failure to discuss the matter with Admiral Hart was typical of General MacArthur's dealings with Hart. CINCAF staff spent the night racing around the building, out onto the dark street, over to Pier 7 in front, trying to figure how to move tons of navy supplies from Manila to Bataan.

To pack everything, we communicators needed a lot of canvas mailbags and to burn whatever we could do without, not that we hadn't burnt a good many papers already. For the staff to operate, we had to be able to communicate with all of our ships plus the Navy Department, the 16th Naval District, CINCPAC, the Australians, the British, the Dutch. We had to haul a number of different cipher systems with us. Beyond that was the radio gear, transmitters, receivers, generators. Someone stuck us with about fifty pounds of war plans—whatever they were worth now. It may be they couldn't get them to burn. We spent the afternoon and all night packing.

Christmas morning I walked to the Bayview to take a shower and pack. We were allowed a suitcase each. I stood staring at my wardrobe trunk with my blues. I'd worn them for graduation in March and one other time when my parents wanted to show me off. My sword: I'd feel silly taking it. I felt the sleeve of my favorite tweed suit: material soft in feel and in color—I haven't seen a cloth like it since. We had to catch a PT boat at noon, so I stopped poking around and packed skivvies, khakis, couple of sets of whites, and a pair of white shoes, not knowing what social demands might be made of us, shaving gear, and toothbrush. I locked the wardrobe trunk and stuck the key in my pocket—you never know. I found a small amount of pleasure in the freedom of traveling light as I started off on foot across the Luneta, an open green park, for the port area. It was about time for the morning raid on our street. Twenty-seven bombers in three flights of nine had been circling the port area, trying to find something worth hitting that the Japanese wouldn't want to use later. I slowed down, feeling like an obvious military objective, alone in the grand expanse of grass.

The open city arrangement was farcical. The Japanese weren't honoring it. But they weren't trying to destroy Manila, either. They had attacked Clark and Nichols and Iba and Cavite and Sangley and our port area. Now they were bombing Mariveles and Corregidor while their infantry advanced on the city. Killing civilians and destroying buildings were incidental, not an objective.

I walked slowly until the planes stopped droning around our neighborhood and then walked faster. I could see a lot of splashing out in the bay, as though some weekend nitwit was showing off in a speedboat, and realized it was our PT boat moving away from the port area, unwilling to be either a target or associated with one.

At the office, I joined Hugh Lawrence and Bill Hirst and a party of radiomen to haul the mailbags downstairs. The stiff canvas bags were heavy and awkward, hard on the fingernails, all corners and angles, sharp-edged files, lead-weighted cipher books, rigid war plans, coding machines, and their key parts. We bumped and cursed to the fleet landing just across the street on the sea wall. We piled the bags on the edge of the concrete landing and stood inside the waiting room. When the all clear went, the PT boat crept suspiciously in to the landing where we waited. We had about half the gear aboard when we heard what we had begun to describe as the sound of tires slicking on a wet pavement.

I found myself under a green metal bench inside the waiting room, having gotten under there considerably faster than I was able to get out. The bombs must have hit the pier and the street on the other side of Pier 7. The skipper of the PT was far more interested in saving his boat than hauling a lot of staff types and their gear to Corregidor. His crew was so rattled by their first personal bombing that they pitched in to help us load. On the landing, we ran around, grabbing gear and throwing it aboard, mailbags piled high in the cockpit and on what deck space there was. Once sure we had everyone, we jumped aboard.

"We must have been doing fifty knots out from the landing," someone said later. Whatever it was, we didn't slow down until we were halfway past Cavite and not much then. We passengers were huddled all over the boat, hanging on and trying to keep out of the wind. I was prone, outboard of a torpedo tube on the port side, with a chief radioman's feet in my face. Luckily the bay was smooth, the boat up on the step, skimming the water.

Lying where I was, I raised my head to look at Sangley Point as it flashed by to port, trying to see what was left of the row of houses along Cañacao Boulevard. Long said ours had not burned but had been looted. The chief was looking back at me, shouting something that the wind snatched away. He pointed—one of the three radio towers on Sangley was down—the last look at home. Across from Cañacao, Cavite still burned.

Chapter 9

In that time, a popular expression was, "No strain in Asia," and its variation, "No strain in the Asiatic Fleet." A widely used stock comment as well as a free-standing observation, the meanings were various: to express coolness under pressure, sardonic after a terrifying experience, or simply to acknowledge an observation by another person, willingness to perform a favor, thus: "No strain."

Hugh Lawrence was much given to using it. I may have said, for example, on arriving at North Dock on Corregidor, something banal, "Well, here we are," at which Hugh Lawrence may have said: "No strain in the Asiatic Fleet," thus pronouncing a benison on a safe trip and admitting relief at its completion.

As our PT boat came alongside the landing on the Rock, we saw a platoon of khaki-clad American infantry, young fellows, sprawling dustily in the sun with their rifles, bareheaded, waiting to go somewhere, no one appearing to be in charge. We ignored their personal comments on us as we unloaded the gear from the boat. I ignored them, anyway. Some of our men found silence insupportable under the provocation, as I went off to find a truck. The soldiers were getting up to go somewhere—everyone on the island seemed to be getting up from one place and going to another—when I came back in the cab of a navy truck, a cloud of dust rolling behind it. That was another feature of Corregidor: dust, grass baking dry, the air full of particles, nostril-parching, a straw taste in your mouth, the sun so bright your head ached. Other features were ruffled military feathers, people and vehicles moving around, stirring up the soil, rattling and banging, what an innocent observer might assume to be useful activity.

We loaded up and drove to Queen Tunnel, new home of the 16th Naval District people after their move to Corregidor from Cavite. The commodious tunnels, drilled into the side of the island, were made to work and live in, as many did during the Japanese siege. The regular living quarters, soon to be uninhabitable because of bombing and artillery fire, were higher up on top of Corregidor, Topside. Once we unloaded at Queen Tunnel, I waited outside on a hot, gritty concrete ramp by the pile of mailbags while the others went inside to look for billets for our party and a place to stow the gear. Lineaweaver had made it clear to me that the gear was my responsibility: "Horton, that gear's your pidgin." So I stayed close to it until we'd found a safe place for it.

Once we'd stowed the gear in the tunnel, I went about looking for someone on the staff to report to. In the course of that, I ran into a friend stationed on the Rock. He asked me to spend the night Topside, and I accepted right away, glad not to have to bed down in Queen Tunnel.

Later, when we'd driven up to his quarters, he offered me a chance to bathe, possibly noticing how badly I needed it. With a bath, a shave, a cold San Miguel, and clean clothes, I revived; although the beer and the fading daylight reminded me I hadn't slept for a good thirty-six hours. Insisting that I share leftovers from their midday Christmas dinner, he and his quarter's mates sat around the living room, asking me questions about Manila while I balanced a plate of turkey and cranberry sauce on my knees. Across the water in Mariveles, a French merchantman had been hit earlier Christmas Day in a bombing raid on Mariveles. When night fell, the flames from her burning threw flickering light on the hillside behind her, making a path on the water as orange as a harvest moon.

We were awakened to go, disgruntled, down to the tunnel for the midnight air raid. I cheered up immediately on finding radiomen from Cavite. We greeted each other as though it had been years rather than weeks since we were together at Radio Control.

In the morning, our party was again in the tunnel—like being in a long, narrow, damp, gray basement—standing around, talking, trying to keep out of the way of those who had work to do, restless, waiting for some word. The sirens went, and our antiaircraft artillery drummed and roared and shook outside. The bombers were working over the only two destroyers left in Manila Bay, rather than attacking the Rock itself. I managed to get out of the tunnel in time to see the destroyer *Peary* disappear behind a wall of water thrown up by a stick of bombs that straddled her. Talk about your heart sinking—it was a physical sensation—when out of the shower of water, her bow pushed on through.

The Japanese bombers were chasing the *Peary* (DD 226) and the *Pillsbury* (DD 227), of Destroyer Squadron 29, the other destroyers having gone south earlier to the Netherlands East Indies. These two had been in the Cavite navy yard for repair following a collision at sea before the war started. Both were damaged in the raid on 10 December, the *Peary* more seriously, crews of both ships suffering casualties. The pair had been kept around Manila Bay since then to run errands. During the present series of attacks, the ships' executive officers were handling the vessels, racing and turning, outguessing the attacking Japanese. The captains of *Peary* and *Pillsbury* had come ashore to ask permission to rejoin their squadron. They were presenting their case to the admiral when the bombing attacks on the ships interrupted them. Like all of us on that end of the Rock, they could do no more than stand watching the contest between the Japanese planes and their own ships.

The admiral gave permission for the ships to leave. Captain Pound of *Pillsbury* chose to run straight south. Lieutenant Commander John Bermingham of *Peary*, because of the damage to her, decided he'd take a furtive course, staying close to land, lying to occasionally to avoid the open sea.

When the Japanese planes left, I'd gone back to the tunnel to stand by the gear while Lawrence took a boat to Mariveles with a message. I suddenly realized I'd left my uniform cap at the house on Topside, having come down during the morning raid with my tin hat on. Before I could do anything about that, I saw Commander Dennison coming through the tunnel. He told us to sort our communications materials into two integral portions so that the loss of one would not render the other useless. "Fast!" he added. He said that we should split into two parties to run south on the two destroyers. No one should be forced to go who objected, he added. None of our party did. While hastily dividing the gear into two batches, Lawrence and I picked *Pillsbury*, while Hirst and another ensign who had joined us chose *Peary*. We picked *Pillsbury* because Len Sulkis, one of our classmates from Chicago, was aboard.

I can't remember whether others were asked to go, this all happened so quickly. I do remember some of the Cavite radiomen in the tunnel cheered us up by predicting we had little chance of getting past the Japanese forces in the southern Philippines, a point that had occurred to us already. A rational estimate of the chances of getting through was quite impossible. There was no recklessness in my being willing to take the chance rather than staying on Corregidor as a supernumerary. Most of the people I knew would have leapt at the chance. Sadly, the chance was given to only a few of us. Many officers and men were kept back there, far less use at Bataan and Corregidor than if they'd gotten back to the navy.

We hurried to the North Dock with our separate batches of baggage, not wanting to let our chance slip by. There we stood on one foot and then another, while again nothing happened. After a while, the siren sounded. Lawrence and I sent the others off to shelter while we searched the terrain around us for nearby depressions, even shallow ones, to flop into if the bombers reappeared. We stood there quite a while in the late afternoon sun, squinting at the sky, helmets on our heads, khakis dark with sweat, .45s hanging from our waists.

I remember noting that Lawrence had lost weight in the past few days. Of middle height, pale-skinned, with wavy blond hair and blue eyes, as he went into his late twenties he was inclined to stoutness. When I complimented him on his figure as we stood there, waiting, he snapped at me, unwilling to concede that he'd been portly.

Mostly, I fretted about leaving my hat behind.

After a while, the all clear went, and we saw the gray shape of *Pillsbury* slip into view, the *Peary* dark behind and outboard of her. With no navy boats to be had, we commandeered the Pan American Airways launch, loaded our gear aboard, and headed first for *Pillsbury*. By the time we came alongside, the ship's company was in high spirits, having gotten the word from Captain Pound that *Pillsbury* had permission to run south. From the boat, I saw Len Sulkis hobbling toward the gangway, grinning, half dancing, half limping. He'd taken a piece of shrapnel in his ankle during the Cavite raid. During the afternoon's attack, Len had been climbing the galley deckhouse ladder when a near miss threw him against it. The rungs had left a series of parallel bruises down his body, which he displayed on request.

Once aboard, we went first to the bridge to pay our respects to the captain and meet the other officers while the radiomen were taken to their quarters. Len Sulkis took me to his small cabin, moving files off the empty top bunk and cleaning out a locker. Hugh Lawrence and I got permission to keep our canvas sacks of cipher materials on the starboard wing of the bridge. Either Hugh or I, often both of us, would stand there by them on the rest of the voyage. The bridge of the *Pillsbury* was the center of intelligence, as ever, additionally now, the origin of good tidings or bad. Everyone knew things might go wrong in a hurry. Being up on the bridge meant you'd know of developments as soon as anyone. Sailors going by would glance up at the faces on the bridge to see if they showed calm. When you went below, you'd be asked, "Anything going on?" I remember how keyed up we all were. If you heard a loud voice or saw someone moving fast, you stopped what you were doing: What's the matter? Why's he running like that? Becoming aware of this, we joked about it with each other. Out of consideration for others, hoping that they would do the same, you tried to act with deliberation, avoiding jerky or noisy behavior.

As the sun set, *Pillsbury* got underway, still at general

quarters, and we ran through the straits past Corregidor's satellite forts to the open sea.

Lawrence and I stood by the bags during general quarters but left them alone occasionally, at mealtimes, say. It wasn't that anyone on the ship would bother them. It was what might occur with no warning that kept us near them. We knew exactly what to do in case of attack. Our one function was seeing to it the cipher materials got safely to the next stop—wherever that was to be—or, failing that, were not captured by the Japanese. We'd worked out procedures for the eventuality of Japanese attack, being only unsure how we'd know that we'd reached the point when we should perform the final act. Once we'd decided that question or it had been decided for us, we'd sail the cipher machine rotors—the most sensitive items—one by one into the sea around us, then the tables for setting the rotors, then the other cipher systems in their weighted folders, then the instructions for them and so on, depending on the time left at this point, jettisoning the remaining materials in their weighted covers. Any papers not weighted, we'd rip up and scatter. Burning was out of the question: our first aim being to get the materials through in usable form meant no preemptive burning. Once we made the fateful decision to destroy everything, there'd be no time to form a leisurely burning party.

This duty of ours, while serving a purpose, would contribute absolutely nothing to the well-being of the ship. Yet, having a drill of any sort to fall back on during distress helps to keep morbid thoughts from the mind. We'd like to have taken on some ship's work. The ship was short of officers, and I would have been flattered to stand a junior officer of the deck watch, if asked. I did take some communications work off Len Sulkis's hands.

But the atmosphere aboard was austere. Len was an ebullient fellow, full of life and enthusiasm, and it was clear he felt sat upon as the junior officer aboard, and a reserve at that. The *Pillsbury* was hardly unusual in giving naval life this vinegary taste. Varying, of course, from place to place throughout the navy, young reserve ensigns were restless at not being given more responsibility early on. Stiff regulars were ready to squelch novices, insisting they be patient about learning the ropes as they had been made to wait in their own time. The outbreak of war led to some loosening of attitudes, but the tone on *Pillsbury* was still constrained in late December, whether set by the captain or the executive officer, I cannot say.

Not that we weren't warmly received aboard. We were quickly on familiar terms with the junior officers and were made welcome in the wardroom. That compartment's decorations included a number of holes, repairs to the ship's skin having been confined to damage below the waterline. The larger holes came from the Cavite raid. Sharp twists of metal, newly glistening where the light came through, were the near misses of the bombing attacks the day after Christmas.

The cabin that Len shared with me was tiny. Everything was small on these ships compared to those that came later. I have only one memory of ever being in the upper bunk, although certainly I slept there at times. At one end of it was an electric fan, no larger in diameter than a saucer, and I managed to stick my foot into the blade one night.

All officers have a series of additional duties, jobs like laundry officer or keeping the mess accounts often handed a junior ensign. Len was distracted by the ship's service accounts—he couldn't get November to balance. He spent every off moment at them, wisely waving off my weak offer to help—much too complicated to explain, as I am sure they were. Len hunched over the papers in his cabin, the Japanese far from his mind, as he muttered and ran his hands unhappily through his dark hair.

The day after sailing, on the twenty-seventh, we saw a ship coming our way. Although still a mirage floating above the surface of the sea ahead, she was evidently a merchantman. As we drew closer, we saw her boats being lowered from the davits, even while there was way on her. Her flag was Dutch. We drew up to hail her and assure her we weren't Japanese. Captain Pound told her she'd do well to go back where she came from. She was still sitting back there when we went on and lost her from sight, her boats still halfway down her sides as though those aboard were conferring about their next move.

As we ran south that day, we were heading for the Sulu Archipelago, the southernmost of the Philippine islands that stretch to the northeast tip of Borneo. The Japanese were known to be in force at Jolo, capital of the Sulu province—there'd been a report they'd occupied Jolo on Christmas Day. There was no way to get around the bottleneck of the Sibutu Passage at the other end of the Sulu chain from Jolo, heading as we were for the east coast of Borneo. The captain decided to slow the day's run so that we'd go through Sibutu Passage at night. It wasn't only Jolo itself we had to avoid, not only Japanese men-of-war, but Japanese air patrols as well. Once they sighted us, they could easily send ships or planes to intercept our course south. They might already have men-of-war patrolling the waters between the island of Tawi-Tawi and Borneo to interdict southbound ships trying to run the passage.

The word about the night's run soon flew around the ship. The sailors were ready, having long ago wrapped wallets, cigarettes and matches, snapshots, other keepsakes, in condoms, along with a supply of condoms, and secured them inside their kapok lifejackets. We were at general quarters by dusk, and things got quiet as dark came on, and we plowed the smooth roll of the Sulu Sea toward the Sibutu Passage on a dreadfully clear, quiet night, the shapes of islands visible, even miles away. Everything stood out, and surely, we thought, nothing more prominently for miles than the *Pillsbury* slicing her way though the quiet waters.

I don't know who first saw the shape bearing down on us, heading for us on a reciprocal course. On the bridge, the only voices were the exchanges between the captain and the exec. A voice from the gun director above us was reading off the yards of rapidly decreasing range. Where I was on the starboard wing of the bridge, I could make out a huge shape of thick black and white diagonals closing on us with great speed, a design taking no imagination at all to be translated into the camouflage of a Japanese cruiser.

In a flash, we were passing each other. The camouflage of the cruiser were diagonal stripes on the square sail of a

Moro vinta, one of those low, fast, narrow craft that sail between Borneo and the Muslim southern Philippines. Running before the wind, she raced by us to port, low in the water, the bellying square sail that had loomed so large in our alarmed eyes now shamefully small. Relieved laughter and a burst of talk ran around the ship.

We soon reverted to silence and tension. The next comic incident followed a quiet statement on the bridge that one of the four stacks, instead of exhausting a clear, hot vapor, was putting out white smoke, a result of an off-mixture of fuel oil in the fireroom. The captain spoke in low tones to the engine room, "Number two smoking white." The overcorrection was immediate, a huge shower of sparks roaring from the stack, lighting the sea red around us.

By the time we saw our fireworks display had not brought the enemy down on us, we had run the Sibutu Passage and were racing into the open waters of the Celebes Sea.

The coast of Borneo was off to starboard the next day. We could smell the oil of Balikpapan long before we reached the port and the low, green scrubby hills around it. We took on fuel, and that night went ashore to the Dutch officers club, drinking Heineken beer from large green bottles and eating small chow. The captain and the exec went back to the ship, leaving the younger element to order another round of Heineken, what would have been our third liter each. As we talked, we saw that one of our colleagues was paying less attention to the conversation than to a buxom Dutch lady seated some tables away. He called for a waiter, scribbled a note, pointing out the addressee to the waiter. The green-clad Dutch army officer sitting with the lady was the one who read the note, and he did not appear to be amused. We got up and helped our colleague back to the ship.

In late morning, the *Pillsbury* was lying at the fuel dock when the air raid siren sounded. On a hill above us, a 40-millimeter antiaircraft gun—the kind the British called "a Chicago piano," in memory of Al Capone—began popping at something out of sight. From behind a hill, a low-flying, mud-colored, Japanese scout bomber came on us, much too close, right down on the water, flying down our beam. Tracers, hastily fired from our Lewis guns, sailed toward the plane like a shower of arrows before curving hopelessly aft of his tail section. The gunner facing aft had his part of the greenhouse open—some said he was waving at us, and others said he was unlimbering his wobble gun to give us a good raking where we crouched in surprise on the deck.

Captain Pound gave the word to get underway before the plane was out of sight.

In a rain squall, two mornings after that, we bobbed about in the blue-gray waters off Surabaya, waiting to take the Dutch pilot aboard. Once in the harbor, we moved slowly down a narrow strip of water toward our berth in the Dutch navy yard, passing a few feet from *Pillsbury*'s sisters lying in column, bow to stern, alongside the dock. The sailors on the ships turned and those walking on the dock stopped to stare at the holes in *Pillsbury*'s skin and her stacks.

Chapter 10

The broad flat avenues of the port of Surabaya in east Java, like the thoughts of its citizens, were still uncluttered by war. An orange-haired girl, freckled, with a full figure and a complexion much the same color as her hair, part Dutch, part Javanese, pedaled past the Oranje Hotel on a bicycle four times during the day, as dependable as the sidereal dispensation. Against the heat, the shops were closed from noontime until late afternoon, the city then awakening for the hours remaining before nine at night.

Lunch in Surabaya might be elaborate. Rijsttafel was served in the Oranje Hotel dining room, a separate building in the hotel courtyard, the middle hours of certain days being set aside for the ceremony. A bald Dutchman with thick glasses, his frame bulging the lines of a white linen suit, sat long-torsoed at the white-linened table for the rijsttafel rite, napkin draped beneath his jowls. Beginning with a conical heap of rice on his plate, the next step was the consideration of one curried meat sauce versus another. Once he'd applied the suitable one, a waiting line of turbaned boys began shuffling past him. The first bore chutneys. The boys following, a tray in either hand, carried on each tray smaller dishes with condiments and garnishes from the spice islands of the Indies, half a world away from the peanuts, raisins, coconut, tomatoes, onions, of a pale, mild Stateside curry. Multiplying the number of boys (ten) times the trays (two) times the dishes on each tray (eight to twelve) gives an idea of the opportunities open to the devoted eater. The choices ran from fried plantain, bland and sugared, to Makassar fish, a dried minnow dyed bright red, pretending to be an anchovy, dropping its disguise when it was too late, burning hot on the unwary tongue.

"Jungen!"—"Boy!"—the Dutchman would shout, clapping his hands for another quart of Heineken. The Dutch were more comfortable as colonial masters than the Americans in the Philippines. "The Dutch, like the British, are respected," I remember a traveled American saying at the Army-Navy Club in Manila: "Not like us." Clapping his hands, frowning, he'd shouted, "Boy!" to make up for the national weakness.

The behavior of the Javanese was far more deferential than the Filipinos had been. The Javanese looked different, too, wearing sarongs, the men wearing velvety black Muslim caps or scarves tied around their brows. In the countryside on the edge of Surabaya, the women with baskets on their heads not rarely were bare-breasted above the sarong fastened about the waist. That was all right, but their teeth were black, gums and lips red with betel juice, an acquired taste, like Bols gin.

Smoke from the strong, highly perfumed tobacco of the local cigarettes was the endemic scent of Surabaya, drifting through the city day and night, not at all unpleasant unless you had to smoke them. I spent some free hours shopping for Camels in thin metal boxes, flat fifties, they were called, and for round, sealed canisters of a hundred Chesterfields or so, operating as a member of a consortium. By the end of January, we had ferreted out, cornered, and smoked all the American cigarettes. Some of us went then to British alternatives, such as Players Navy Cut. Others preferred the hot spiciness of the local cigarettes to the harsh weedy Virginia leaf of the British brands—either one soon brought on a gritty throat.

The archetype Dutch colonial who'd set aside an afternoon for rijsttafel was not a lonely centerpiece in the dining room of the Oranje. Three times a day, families made up of ruddy, blond mothers, towheaded children, and lean, longheaded fathers, sat at their tables. At the other tables were white-clad businessmen and government officials,

Royal Navy officers in whites—Dutch, the British came
later—and green-clad army officers. Finally, the Americans
walk into the dining room, look around, wondering where
to sit and, once sat, wondering what you can get to eat
around here.

The city seemed to shrink from us, not unfriendly, certainly not hostile, more politely curious, but not asking
what it was we wanted, why we were there. I don't remember being reproached for having abandoned the Philippines.
On the contrary, you might think no one realized what had
happened fifteen hundred miles to the north. Of course,
they did know and may have been too polite to say anything about it. Maybe they didn't want to have to think
about it. You couldn't blame them, what with having lost
their homeland to the Germans a year and a half before.

The Dutch had given us working space in the Surabaya
navy yard where we kept a wall map showing the waters
the Japanese sailed in their conquest of the lands of Southeast Asia. In December, it had been the South China Sea to
the Philippines, Malaya, and to Hong Kong, where the British were overwhelmed on Christmas Day. The Japanese
were ready to come south from the Sulu Sea after taking
Jolo the same day as Hong Kong. In the first weeks of January, Japanese transports, escorted by aircraft and men-of-
war, were in the Celebes Sea, landing troops in the cities of
the northern Celebes and eastern Borneo. By mid-January,
Japanese taskforces were enroute in Makassar Strait, in Mo-
lucca Passage, sailing into the Ceram Sea, by the Bismarck
Sea to New Ireland and New Britain. Pins went in the map
along the coast of Borneo at Tarakan, at Menado in the Celebes, at Amboina in Ceram. Pins were put in as the
messages came in, sighting reports from the PBYs of Patwing 10, messages from the Dutch Army and Navy, from
planters—Dutch, British, Australian—telephoning in from
outlying islands, telegrams from missionaries, hotel owners,
district residents, post offices.

While the members of Hart's CINCAF staff now reunited
in Surabaya were—like our comrades in the Asiatic Fleet—
the same people we'd been all along, Hart had become the
naval commander of ABDACOM, an American-British-

Dutch-Australian command. At the end of December, Roosevelt and Churchill had called that arrangement into being to give us a name before the Japanese rolled over us. ABDACOM was a British general with an American air force deputy, a British air marshal in command of the aircraft, a Dutch general commanding ground forces, plus Admiral Hart. These men had never worked together before—most had never met before—and had no agreed strategy for directing a motley assortment of ships, men, and aircraft. Our assignment was to stop the Japanese at the Malay barrier, stretching from Malaya across the Netherlands East Indies—where we were—to New Guinea east of us. The islands we called a barrier were stepping stones for the Japanese.

Hart was at the other end of Java along with the rest of ABDACOM. In Surabaya sometimes, we had tall, elegant Adm. William A. Glassford with us. At times he was elsewhere, whether as COMTASKFORCE 5, or later as COMSOWESPAC and also as CINCAF ADMIN. When he had his flag aboard the cruiser *Marblehead*, a gleeful friend told me, Glassford's costume on the bridge was black baseball cap, striped blazer, eyeglasses on a black ribbon that retracted into a button on his lapel, white shorts with high white socks, black patent leather evening pumps. With us consistently was Adm. William Purnell—heavily freckled, nicknamed Speck. He'd been Hart's chief of staff in the Philippines and was now, off and on, his chief of staff again, or Glassford's. It was Purnell, recently promoted from captain, whom we saw every day. He exercised firm authority in an easygoing, confident way and was liked and respected by his subordinates.

Many of the Japanese landings were lightly opposed if at all. One exception was the landing at Balikpapan, the oil port where the *Pillsbury* had gotten underway in a hurry three weeks before when the Japanese scout bomber had flown down our length. Admiral Glassford, as commander Task Force 5 aboard the *Marblehead*, with the cruiser *Boise* and four of our destroyers, left Timor for Balikpapan when the word came of the landing force there. *Marblehead* soon suffered an engine breakdown, and *Boise* tore her bottom on a rock. The *Boise*, by far the most modern American ship around, happened to have been in Philippine waters on an escort mission when war came. Not a part of the Asiatic Fleet, *Boise* had been drafted into Taskforce 5 but saw no action in these first months of the war. Something always happened to prevent her, thereby earning her the name in the Asiatic Fleet of "The Reluctant Dragon."

So the four destroyers, *Ford, Pope, Parrott, John Paul Jones*, alone attacked the Japanese landing force the night of 23–24 January, making two runs through the far stronger but confused Japanese force, firing torpedoes and their guns, sinking five Japanese ships and getting out with four men wounded, only one destroyer having been hit by enemy fire. The Japanese went ahead with the occupation of Balikpapan, but that did not diminish the lustre of this first engagement of United States surface forces against the Japanese.

The first few weeks, Hugh Lawrence and I shared a room at the Oranje Hotel. Around the middle of January, something rare, a PBM, a large patrol bomber, was in Surabaya, returning to the States that night. We got the word they'd mail a letter for you. We weren't supposed to say where we were, and I didn't, but I did write the note on Oranje Hotel stationery. Like a lot of devious behavior, it was unnecessary. I had sent a short commercial cable home about that time to say I was all right but not saying where I was. Postal Telegraph noted on the copy delivered to my parents the place of origin as Surabaya.

Our room was on the second floor, the louvered door giving onto an open walkway from which we looked down into the windows of the dining room, at the palms and flowers in the courtyard surrounding it. From the end of the walkway, just to our left, you could see out to the boulevard in front of the Oranje. Sitting outside the room were a table and chairs, where we'd have friends up for a gin and quinine water. (We were taking quinine pills, as well, when we had them.)

Above each bed, a mosquito net dangled from the ceiling, and inside that oriental tent was a bolster—the Dutch wife—around which you wrapped yourself those hot nights.

On February 3, I had been on watch at the navy yard all the night before and was fast asleep in the room. I bounced out of a heavy sleep—this time taking care with the mosquito net—to pad out to the walkway in my skivvy shorts. I came wide awake as a Brewster Buffalo screamed past at the level of our floor, the street reverberating with the straining of its engine. The pilot of a Japanese Zero had fallen in right behind the Buffalo, firing as he went by, the misses thudding into the street and the buildings on either side. They disappeared up the street as fast as they had come, leaving the boulevard quiet until the drone of a formation of high-level bombers moved into the silence, heading for the airfield and the navy yard.

The Dutch pilot had taken our street in his rush to get back home, where he landed, the Zero still on his tail. When he jumped out of the Buffalo, the Japanese pilot strafed him at the same time the Japanese bombs from on high began thudding along the airstrip. The Dutch pilot survived with three sets of superficial wounds from combat in the air, from the strafing, and from shrapnel in the bombing, whereas a room boy in the Oranje had been killed by the ricochet of one of the Japanese bullets.

The decorum of Surabaya was shaken by this raid, the first of what would be many, the navy yard being a favorite target of the Japanese. We worked in a barnlike open space, with the coding machines and the other cipher apparatus hidden behind partitions. The first week or so of the bombing, we'd close everything up and go outside and stand around an above-ground shelter nearby, sidling into it when the bombers were overhead. We spent a lot of time that way, waiting for something to happen, especially as the raids became more frequent and lasted longer, so you might be setting aside four to five hours either side of midday. Anyway, the shelter didn't strike us as being much safer than the building we were in. We kept on working, diving under our desks if the bombing seemed to be close.

Not that we were cool about it. The Surabaya zoo was outside the normal target area, and we took to going out there for a sandwich and a beer at midday when off duty. In one cage gibbons swooped, long-armed, on their trapezes, swinging down to hang backwards on the bars, cooing softly when you scratched their backs—a species commonly called wou-wou for their soft talk.

An old orangutan had invented a two-person game played with a stick, lazily tapping it against the bars to lure the innocent, tossing the stick on the ground outside the cage if he sized you up as a sport. He'd blink at you with his small bright eyes in the huge red head, looking from the stick to you and back to the stick. You'd pick it up and hand it back to him. He'd offer it back to you, and you'd take it. He'd hold on to it, giving it a small tug so you'd tug back. He'd hold on tighter, and so would you, beginning to pull the stick back and forth between you. When you had a good grip on it and didn't seem liable to let go, the orangutan would suddenly yank it to him banging you against the bars. He'd fall back on his haunches, one long arm curled around his red head, baring his teeth, in a moment flipping the stick on the ground with the other arm, betting you were simpleminded enough to play again. Those of us whom he'd thus instructed would sit at a table a short distance away, drinking beer, making sure he had a stick to clack against the bars. We looked up and down the walk, he peered out of his cage, all of us waiting for the next victim to wander by.

People who'd been en route to the Philippines were joining us in Java. One such officer, newly assigned to the staff, heard us speak of the zoo as a refuge during raids and asked how to get out there. After one raid was over, he reappeared at the navy yard. "All right, you sons a bitches!" he said, by way of introducing his subject. He'd been sitting by himself at a table during the noon raid, drinking beer and smiling at the apes. A Japanese Zero came in over the treetops purposely to strafe him—so he claimed, as though we'd tipped off the pilot. Bullets had clipped the tree under which he'd been sitting, the macerated leaves drifting down on the table below which he crouched. We wondered later how the apes had fared under the Japanese.

One afternoon at the Oranje, an American in civilian clothes came up to our table to introduce himself to Lawrence and me as Jess Reed. He was a captain in the Marine

Corps reserve who had been in Java on contract with the Dutch government to train Dutch pilots in Brewster Buffaloes. He told us of two naval reserve officers who'd had been training the Dutch in PBYs. They had also stayed on in Java, rather than going home when the war started, as had the other Americans on contract. All three wanted to go on active duty right there in Java. The next day we had fried prawns in a ginger and honey sauce at a Chinese restaurant named Kit Wan Kie, where Reed took us to meet Lieutenants (jg) John Robertson and Hardy, the two PBY pilots. We turned their request over to Lieutenant Commander McDill, the flag secretary. It seemed to take Washington forever to decide. Reed and the others were often waiting at the Oranje to see if I had any news. Reed kept after me, and I kept after Mr. McDill, and he kept after the Bureau of Navigation in Washington until the approval came through, and the three were recalled to active duty.

Within days, Reed was killed landing a P-40 in Surabaya. Robertson was shot down in his PBY over Makassar in a brave attempt to bomb the Japanese ships lying there. Hardy was able to get out of his flaming PBY when it was strafed on the water by Zeros, the way many of these planes were lost.

I learned later that my sister had known Reed at American Airlines where they both worked. Reed had been given leave by the airline for the job with the Dutch. He had gone to Harvard where his father taught, my sister told me, and she knew the wife Reed left behind him. I've always wished we'd worked that out before he died, although, like a lot of things you later wish you'd done, it made no real difference in the end. Those three have always seemed to me particularly admirable. They could have gone on home, but they insisted instead on coming in on the losing side.

After a few weeks in the Oranje, Hugh Lawrence and I moved out to a gray stucco house, cool with terrazzo floors and high ceilings, at 445 Darmo Boulevard where other staff people were billeted. "*Ampat ampat lima* Darmo Boulevard," you'd tell the taxi. I learned more of the Javanese dialect of Malay in one month than I'd learned Tagalog in the Philippines the previous eight. The house was in a tree-

lined suburb, and if you half closed your eyes against the
tropic ambience, you might almost be home.

One evening, Hugh and I and a lieutenant we worked
with put on our whites to go out on the town, the town having loosened up a great deal after the bombings started. I
was feeling good about being back in proper uniform, having replaced the hat I'd left Christmastime in the house
Topside on Corregidor. I'd outfitted myself at the same
place we were going that night, a club where a large black
man in the purple livery of a doorman stood in front. Americans assumed, without giving any thought to it, that a
black man must be a fellow American, and were surprised
when Dutch came out of him rather than English. I went
there one night to try on officers' hats and found one that
fit pretty well. While I like to think I would not do such a
thing now, I justified taking it because I was taking the hat
of one of those strange officers at the bar, just in from the
States. If not exactly in the category of the Japanese enemy,
whoever owned the hat was not one of us, either, not of the
Asiatic Fleet, that is. Ethically, I owed him nothing.

Hugh and I had arranged this night to meet Len Sulkis,
as we did when the *Pillsbury* was in Surabaya. The lieutenant with us was an academy man, a regular. When we had
our first drink, Len brought up an incident he'd been brooding about—some outrage, some atrocity of naval
discipline—a subject he couldn't talk about aboard ship.
The lieutenant with us calmly defended the system, explaining the necessity of the occasional injustice, justifying
it in this case. As they argued, Lawrence and I listened,
cheering points well taken, objecting as necessary. That
went on through drinks and dinner, arguing about the navy.
The discussion superseded whatever plans we'd had for the
night, and Len barely made it back to the ship. You'd have
thought we'd be talking about the war. Perhaps we did, and
I wonder now what we might have said about it. From then
on, when we went out, Len was always looking at his
watch, but nevertheless, we ended up every time in a rush
to get him back to the ship in time.

Admiral Hart was relieved in mid-February by Adm.
Conrad Helfrich to give the Dutch command of the last

days in their Indies. Changes in the occupants of the command slots made little difference to our work, but Hart's relief was discouraging, leaving us, as it were, in the hands of strangers. We continued to handle the messages between our command (whatever it was called) and Washington and Corregidor, painfully deciphering the traffic in the joint system we shared with the Australians, the British, and the Dutch. We gave the most care, naturally, to the messages to and from the ships of our own Asiatic Fleet where our friends were. (We still thought in terms of the Asiatic Fleet no matter what others called it.) What we communications watch officers did in Surabaya was what we'd been doing in Manila, watching the established order go to pieces, our work, no matter how conscientiously done, having no effect on the outcome. Unfortunately, that's how it was for everyone on the Allied side, no matter what role they played. People fought gallantly and lost their lives in making the Japanese pay for their victories, but we were hardly more than anguished observers. The Japanese had the initiative, and we were left to react.

On 15 February, the British garrison in Singapore surrendered to the Japanese. If anyone had any doubts about the outcome, the fall of Singapore wiped them out—except the Dutch. They seemed to be ready to fight to the last man and to take the rest of us along with them.

On the nineteenth, a number of ships were sunk in a heavy Japanese air attack on the port of Darwin in northern Australia, the *Peary* being one of them, taking many of her fine people with her. After limping south from Corregidor the day after Christmas, the same time we'd left on *Pillsbury*, she was attacked by both Australian planes (through a misunderstanding) and by the Japanese before reaching Darwin. There, many of her crew came down with malaria. We'd last seen Bill Hirst when he went aboard the *Peary* at Corregidor. When she got to Darwin, he'd signed on as ship's company. On the nineteenth he went down with her.

The port of Surabaya was untenable for ships without air cover—"lack of air cover" was a key phrase of those months—and the communications officer, Commander

Lineaweaver, told us to pack up again—transmitters and receivers, cipher machines, codebooks, and cipher folders. Hugh and I and our gang of radiomen joined the rest of the staff in a narrow gauge train one night and set off once again, this time to Tjilatjap on the south coast of Java. Sailors were calling it Slapjack before we got there.

Chapter 11

The channel into the steamy port of Tjilatjap on the south coast of Java was so narrow that a Japanese air attack on the ships lying in the port was not only predictable but repeatedly predicted. Tjilatjap harbor was full of ships, men-of-war coming and going, merchant ships that had come down from Surabaya or fled Singapore were moored out in the stream. "We'll be all bottled up in here." There are people who can't be satisfied with the immediate disaster. They insist that the worst is yet to come. The Japanese seized the oil fields at Palembang with parachute infantry in mid-February. So, the Japanese would not only bottle us up by sinking a ship athwart the channel but, at any moment, we'd have Japanese parachutists floating down on our heads.

One night, some of us took a boat across the dark water of the harbor to climb the ladder up the side of a Dutch passenger ship. We went down one deck to eat in the blacked-out dining saloon, saronged waiters padding around barefoot, in blue light, to bring us drinks, a curry, cake, cognac. A ship's officer came by the table to show off the life jacket he wore, fitted with light, bell, horn, and water bottle. He was proud of it, pointing out features he'd added after being torpedoed first in the North Atlantic and again off the coast of Africa. Here was the real danger, nothing fancied about it: these merchantmen waiting in the harbor, indecisive, heeding the claim of the Dutch authorities that they'd stop the Japanese here, hold on to Java. That was as empty as MacArthur's prewar boast that he'd cut the Japanese to pieces if they dared to land in the Philippines. Many of these merchant ships would be doomed by waiting too long to get safely south.

The dining room of the Grand Hotel was in a central courtyard, like the Oranje Hotel in Surabaya. There the resemblance ended. Rice, served with what looked like a resubmission of a former set of meatballs, was the standard menu of the Grand Hotel. In fairness, it should be added that sometimes there was fish. The hotel's breakfast roll was acceptable, but you couldn't help wondering if it, too, was coming around for the second or third time. The best place to eat ashore was the general mess of our radiomen. Its provenance was large navy cans. Coffee was always hot there, night and day, where the radiomen messed and worked in the rooms behind ours. At any hour, you could hear the bass thumping of a keyed transmitter making *V*s and the shrill stutter of the incoming messages on the receivers. General mess, but also private—the radiomen, having sampled the hotel menu, felt sorry enough for Hugh Lawrence and me to have us in for the occasional meal.

After trying what Tjilatjap had to offer, I was tending toward giving my exclusive custom to the Chinese up the street for his dependable roast chicken, agreeably accompanied by a large bottle of Heineken. Where water was concerned, we hurried to soap up under the dribble of the tepid shower when the unsavory stuff unpredictably did run, but we never thought of drinking it. At the end, I was having roast chicken and beer for breakfast. The accommodating Chinese would bicycle it over any time of day.

After all, we hadn't come to Tjilatjap for the food. Surabaya was untenable, and Japanese troops were coming ashore on the islands all around Java, landing at Bali on 18 February, brushing aside attacks on their landing force by our aircraft and ships. Everyone we knew had left or was leaving, the higher ranking by air, others by ship from Tjilatjap, the most valuable ones by submarine. Some of our ships were still in Tjilatjap, but most of our staff was going or had gone. The radio guard had been passed to our detachment in the Grand Hotel. That meant we were the

CINCAF/COMSOWESPAC/COMTASKFOR 5 radio station until properly relieved. We wouldn't be relieved until the command—actually it was Admiral Glassford in his role as COMSOWESPAC—settled down somewhere and was ready to take over naval communications from us.

A lot of our people came through Tjilatjap, but not to stay. Our office, cum living accommodation, was at the top of the right end òf the U-shaped, one-story, tin roofed hotel, our door giving directly into the street. Friends from our ships—before they all left—knew where Hugh and I were staying and found it amusing to announce themselves by hurling handfuls of gravel on our tin roof. After you'd reacted badly for two months to loud noises, a rain of gravel on a tin roof a few feet above your head could really get you up out of a chair with its suggestion of paratroopers at the door.

The end room was our reception area, and the room behind was set aside for sleeping and cipher work. We didn't have a pressing load now of ciphering and deciphering. The radiomen could decipher message headings on their own and put the message on the broadcast schedule for a ship or ships to pick up. They gave us a copy if we were an addressee. For the rest, Hugh and I would look over the dispatch file, breaking the occasional message just to keep up with the bad news. Some messages we couldn't break, lacking the appropriate cipher system. By the end of February, we'd pretty well cut back the secret material to what we needed to do our job.

If one of us was working alone in the back room on a dispatch, the other off somewhere on an errand, anyone at all could walk right in on us and often did—Dutch, British, Australian, Javanese, American—with the cipher machine humming, the day's key settings and the dispatch files open on the table next to the Colt .45 automatic pistol you'd taken off because the damned belt chafed so. You'd jump up and walk the visitor out the door backwards, pulling it shut behind you while asking what you could do for him.

One of our early visitors was a white-haired American diplomatist. The radiomen fed him supper one night, and we all sat there listening while he told about being on the

Japanese black list, your mind drifting off to wonder, not for the last time, if any of those black lists really exist. Anyway, we had to get him out of Java before the Japanese came. We treated his age and high office with respect and saw to it he got on a departing ship. We had fun the next few days going in to say good-bye to the radiomen: "I've got to be running along. I'm on the Japanese black list."

Among the circuits guarded by our radiomen were those of the submarines to whom they broadcast messages, some of which Hugh or I might have enciphered at someone's direction and put on the broadcast schedule. At night, the submarines would surface and call us to acknowledge they'd copied our messages and to send their own traffic, the radiomen hanging over the receivers to get those messages. In February, one of our submarines, the *Shark*, was out of touch and feared lost. She was on our minds. Either the radiomen on watch would come in to say, "Nothing from the *Shark*," or you'd go in to ask them, "Anything in?"

An American reporter called on us. He wore the natty khaki of a British Guards officer, hat, blouse, trousers, polished shoes, a careful mustache to go with it—no regimental insignia, just brass letters, "Press" or maybe it was "Correspondent" on his lapel. He sat down opposite me in the outer room and began to grill me about the *Shark*. He had picked up something about her being missing and wanted me to confirm it. He became testy when I, a junior officer still wet behind the ears, refused to tell him anything. He wanted me to know he was on a first-name basis with Bill Glassford. He may have thrown in Gen. Sir Archie Wavell and Air Chief Marshal Sir Dickie Peirse before stomping out, cross at himself for wasting time on me. However he got out of Java, it was not through our auspices. My response was the emotional one of a callow ensign: I thought the fate of one of our ships was none of his business, that he didn't care a whit about the *Shark* or the people on her. To him it was just a piece of news that could benefit no one, only puff him up for a day were he the first to report it. The announcement of her loss could lead to needless despair for families with husbands or sons aboard.

Shark might turn up safe, her transmitter broken down, something like that—what we were hoping for. In retrospect, looking back on it with the perspective given by the years, I still think it was none of his damned business, and I continue to hope he was among the last to find out what happened to the *Shark*. (She'd been depth-charged and sunk off Makassar in early February, we later learned.)

A B-17 pilot came in lugging a Norden bombsight, of all things, and asked if he could park it with me. He patiently explained to me what a Norden bombsight was—as though it were not about the most widely-publicized artifact of that epoch—what it was used for, that it was secret, and that I shouldn't let anyone fool around with it or let it out of my sight. He gave me the name of a colleague who would be along in the next few days to claim it, and I should give it only to him and to no one else who might come in on some phony pretense or other trying to get it away from me. He was a nice enough fellow, but like a lot of army people, he thought navy types belonged to a different subspecies, maybe not quite bright. I stuck the bombsight under the bed when he left and forgot all about it until his colleague showed up, as promised, and relieved us of the bombsight. Thank goodness. It was fitted in a canvas bag, about the size of a sousaphone, and was remarkably bulky, weighing more for its volume than anything else we had except a gasoline generator.

Among the few people who could not be allowed to fall into Japanese hands were the cryptanalysts—Japanese language officers, mathematicians, and radiomen—of the Fleet Radio Unit on Corregidor. These were the Station Cast people who had been kind enough to put me up and give me Christmas dinner on Corregidor. They came through Tjilatjap one day in late February, arriving by submarine on their way to Australia. They were standing around, blinking, in a patch of shade near our place, gulping in the fresh air, pale from their confinement, when I went over to say hello. I really wasn't thinking about the hat I'd left at their place, but I couldn't help noticing a redheaded ensign, about my age but smaller. What got my attention was the way the tops of his ears were recurved on themselves by the weight of the hat resting on them. I took the liberty of lifting it off his head—easily done, it was so large on him—and looking inside it. He hadn't bothered to put his own name in it, probably not expecting me to be hanging around Tjilatjap waiting for him. "That's okay," I said, putting it back on him, "Forget it."

Hugh did a nice thing about that time. There was a plane leaving for Australia with room on it, and he suggested I take it, and he would stay to clean up things. Both of us weren't needed. "Hell, no," I said. "You go," taken aback that I hadn't thought of making the suggestion first. Neither of us went.

Hearing a hubbub in the street one day, I looked out to see what the fuss was about. It was a bunch of soldiers who turned out to be Australians heading for our door. We knew that among the more than sixty thousand British troops at the fall of Malaya and Singapore were some fifteen thousand Australians. This group had piled on a coastal steamer as the place was coming down around their ears and made their way to Java. They all talked at once until a sergeant quieted them down to act as their spokesman. I didn't understand him at first, and that set them all to shouting again. He got them quiet and it turned out they wanted transport to Australia.

"Oh, what you want is the RAF office up the street there," I pointed. "They take care of you British."

That really set them off. From the welter of words, I could pick out some colorful terms for Britain and the British, from which I inferred they were bitter about Singapore and directing their bitterness at the British command. I don't remember how we took care of them—maybe through the RAF without the Australians knowing it. Australians from Singapore kept coming in small parties of escapees, announcing themselves by throwing the door open, stamping in, cursing horribly, calling us "Yank" and "cobber" and "mite." It's one thing for an American to listen while an Australian denounces the British, if he's so minded, but a great mistake to agree with him, expressing anti-British sentiments being an Australian not an American prerogative.

We'd seen something of war's cruelty to the innocent, the women and the children. Now we saw the anguish visited on men helpless to keep their families from fear, from viciousness, from pain and death itself. In the last days at Tjilatjap, the families came, Dutch mostly, British, a few Americans, officials, business people, missionaries. With our own homes and families safe thousands of miles away, nothing but our own skins to worry about, we could carry on without those distractions. I admitted to myself that I found these days exciting. I knew it was selfish of me, and I said nothing of it, any more than I volunteered my feelings when I was fearful, as indeed I sometimes was. "No strain in the Asiatic Fleet."

The families began pouring into Tjilatjap toward the end of February. Car keys began to pile up in the office. Ordinarily it was the man of the family who'd park the car in the street in front of the hotel—adding to the row lined up near the office—and ask you to look after the car. You'd take the key and nod and wish him good luck, a shared falsehood, he pretending he'd be back soon, and you that you'd stick around to look after his automobile. He'd pick up one of the children and his wife another, take a third by the hand, and the little group would walk slowly off to where they'd find their ship, strictly a matter of luck which one they were put on, the one that made it to Australia or the one the Japanese sunk.

Sometimes it was the wife, maybe young and alone, no children, her husband having joined his reserve unit. The worst of it was the family outside the office saying goodbye to each other, the man climbing into the car turning it around and heading back to his reserve unit in Batavia or Bandoeng or Surabaya. You couldn't look at their faces.

The Japanese sent a plane over Tjilatjap occasionally, but they didn't sink a ship in the channel, nor did they overwhelm us with parachutists. Instead, the Japanese put submarines outside the entrance to Tjilatjap, and naval task forces, aircraft carriers and cruisers, to roving the Indian Ocean south of Java, lying in wait for the ships to come out.

The *Pillsbury* was back in Tjilatjap after expending her

torpedoes in the attack on the Japanese landing force in Bali Straits. We were counting on her to take our party aboard as soon as the word came from Australia that we'd been relieved of the radio guard. But she was told to make for Australia, and *Isabel*, a yacht that used to carry the flag of CINCAF in the good old days back in Shanghai, was assigned to take us and our equipment. Lt. Jack Payne was her captain, amiable and unflappable, although capable of expressing himself vigorously at having to sit around Tjilatjap waiting for us.

Lawrence and I drove one of our cars down to the quay to see *Pillsbury* leave. We were feeling sorry for ourselves, our friends going on without us. The day was dark enough as it was, the sky overcast, a yellow streak low on the horizon, trying to rain, spitting, black clouds blowing across the sky, dirty gray scud moving fast just above us. The *Pillsbury* came fast from her anchorage past the quay where we stood, churning the water yellow, the wind ripping the tops off the waves. She had a foaming white bone in her teeth. We could see our friends on the bridge as she raced by, some of them bareheaded, foreheads white where their caps had kept off the sun, hair whipping in the wind.

We watched her go, and crept silently back to the hotel to find Lt. James Dempsey sitting at a table in the outer room. Dempsey was a short, compact officer with a bulldog jaw who had come ashore from command of an S-boat to take over a larger, fleet-class submarine, the *Spearfish*. She was lying somewhere under the water outside Tjilatjap, and Payne had been told to put Dempsey aboard her. You had to wonder what it was like for them, waiting out there for their new skipper, Japanese submarines sitting out there with them, also waiting for ships to come out of Tjilatjap. Dempsey did considerable sitting at that table before we could finish our business and go aboard *Isabel*.

The next and about the last person to turn up was an American P-40 pilot, a young, hatless fellow in a leather flight jacket, another determined jaw, who wanted to get to Surabaya. He'd been shot down at Bali, and he'd heard there were P-40s in Surabaya. We stood around and argued with him. "What do you want to go there for? Look, it's all over. We're about the last ones, and we're going as soon as we can."

He wouldn't listen. "Just tell me how to get there." We gave him directions, the pick of the cars, one with gas in it. He checked the oil, jumped in, and left. We watched him drive off, and I've always wondered what happened to him.

Jack Payne came ashore on 1 March to get briefed on the locations of the Japanese in the seas south of Java. Besides the submarines, we knew they were using aircraft and surface ships, and we knew they were sinking ships, too. Despite our intense personal interest in seeing the *Isabel* elude the Japanese, we had nothing useful to tell him. We did know the Japanese were beginning to land on Java itself and that we were keen to get going.

Finally, that afternoon, the message from Perth said they would take over guarding the circuit, relieving and freeing out detachment and *Isabel* to leave Java. We acknowledged the message immediately, went off the air, and began loading our gear yet again: transmitters, receivers, coding machine, gas generator, ciphers back in the canvas bag to be hurled over the side when the time came, piled on the truck ourselves, rattled down to the dock, and scrambled aboard *Isabel*.

Before we could get out to sea, Payne had to deliver Dempsey to *Spearfish*, then rendezvous with a U.S. merchant ship, the *Seawitch*, and escort her safely to Australia. Search for the *Spearfish* was carried out in bright moonlight, the *Isabel* cruising around the rendezvous for a couple of hours before the submarine came rearing up out of the sea. She must have been at periscope depth, watching for us as anxiously as Payne was looking for her. Dempsey quickly went aboard, and she submerged.

Then we had to wait for *Seawitch*, *Isabel* zigzagging about a silver sea. Around midnight, the lookout sighted the track of a torpedo heading right for us. There was no time to maneuver, only to watch. The torpedo passed right under *Isabel*, for some reason not exploding. I remember being pretty numb by then. We all were. We'd seemed ordained to sail foolishly about in the moonlight until the Japanese submarine got us lined up and torpedoed us. The surprising part was that it hadn't exploded.

Seawitch showed up before the submarine had another shot at us. Luckily, too, the weather went bad as we ran to sea away from the submarine, hoping to avoid Japanese air and surface task forces.

But the sky was blue the next day. Inevitably, a Japanese scout plane found us and circled some time, looking us over, quite low, before flying off. The *Seawitch* sent an indignant message by blinker searchlight to this effect: "Why didn't you shoot that plane down?" Payne, who had no guns aboard capable of hitting the Japanese plane, replied, "I wanted him to get low enough to hit him with one shot."

Beer had been stowed in a chest for some future beach party, and Jack Payne ordered it served out to all hands. Drinking aboard a U.S. man-of-war is strictly forbidden, but Payne generously broke that rule, thinking it might be one of the last decisions he'd ever make. We stood around on deck sipping the beer, not happily—for we expected Japanese planes or ships soon to be upon us—but more or less gratefully.

A Patwing 10 PBY left Tjilatjap after we did and passed overhead—it must have been around the time the Japanese plane circled above us. The pilot identified the familiar shape of the *Isabel* below one wing, and on the far horizon the ships of a Japanese cruiser/destroyer task force. On getting to Perth, he reported that he assumed the Japanese had found and sunk us both.

The *Seawitch* was worth attacking, but the Japanese had many richer targets than little *Isabel* among the ships in the Indian Ocean south of Java. That, and the weather getting terrible that night, probably saved us both.

About this time, I remember, the *Seawitch* signaled "I am leaving you." I think she left because she was more seaworthy than *Isabel* and didn't want to hang back waiting for us to struggle slowly through the seas. It may be, too, that her captain had found frivolous Payne's reply about the Japanese plane. That day or the next we were in the radio shack, bracing ourselves against the wild pitching of the ship, listening to the signals of ships under attack. (We had radio receivers but no transmitter.) I remember that the gunboat, *Asheville*, came on the air with a series of *R*s: "*R-R-R-R*", the signal for "raider," meaning an enemy surface ship. (For air attack a ship sent a series of *A*s.) The signal stopped abruptly.

In the next few days, we thought the *Isabel* would go to pieces with no help from the Japanese. We were taking blue water right over the ship. Interior compartments were flooded. Payne was worried because our fuel supply was low. We spent all the time we could above deck, living out of cans. I recall how we lowered each others' spirits by declaring that we'd escaped the Japanese only to come apart and sink off the friendly coast of Western Australia. By the time Jack Payne thought we could make port and were near enough to Fremantle to break radio silence, lacking a radio transmitter, he could say nothing about it.

We came into Fremantle on 7 March 1942. We found a truck and drove ourselves and our gear into Perth where COMSOWESPAC had settled. Headquarters was in an office building on High Street. We parked in front, and I took an elevator to where I'd been told to go. In a dark hall I ran into Commander Lineaweaver, who was hurrying somewhere, as usual.

I tried to be casual about it, suddenly proud that we'd brought the men and the equipment safely through. "The communications gear from Tjilatjap is out in front, sir. Where do you want it?"

He stared at me. "Horton! We thought you were lost."

But there was no word of our friends on the *Pillsbury*.

Chapter 12

In those first stunning weeks of war, danger and death were parceled out with blind equity. Whether flying, aboard ship, ashore on Bataan or in Java, officer or man, there was no privilege of sanctuary. Only the Japanese onslaught was sure and overrunning us. One unit would be lost and another slip, somehow, through a crevice to safety. How it ended for you had nothing to do with courage or cowardice, prayer or defiance. And there was no fairness in the chance that took some of us to safety in Australia, three months into the war.

We didn't know then the extent of our losses. Our friends on the *Pillsbury*, so far as anyone knew, might have been rescued by the Japanese or swum ashore. That's what you wanted, to pretend they might be all right, somewhere. Until Bataan and then Corregidor fell, you could pretend those people would be all right too. When Corregidor fell, you couldn't keep up the pretense.

For me, that message was like a curtain slamming down, cutting off the friends on the other side of it, ending that segment of life, setting as distinct a boundary as marriage, as the birth of the first child. I go for months without ever thinking back to that place where one time ended. Yet, if I live to be a hundred, 6 May 1942 and the final message from Corregidor will lie there and come into my mind whether or not I summon them.

No matter how hard you tried to be offhand about it, assure yourself you'd done nothing underhanded, committed no breach of conduct, you could only feel uneasy about being spared. Like a good many other parents, mine got a telegram in June 1942 saying that, "The Navy Department exceedingly regrets to advise you that according to the records of this department your son . . . was performing his duty in the service of his country in the Manila Bay area when that station capitulated." I'd sent a number of cables and letters home by then, but I reassured them. So did the navy. I didn't tell anyone of the strange comfort I found in being declared missing, a link, no matter how false, with the friends I'd left behind.

Then came a real opportunity to relieve my uneasiness, thanks to Adm. William Purnell, still chief of staff. By then we were operating under the name of Allied Naval Forces Basing Western Australia. He put around a memorandum asking for volunteers to return to the southern Philippines to destroy caches of aviation gasoline we'd left behind, keep them out of Japanese hands. I went right in to see the admiral to volunteer. Purnell seemed pleased, with my attitude anyway, and accepted me right away.

A relative newcomer to the staff was Lt. (jg) Merrill Stewart. Unwilling to be outdone in a bid for adventure, he also went in to volunteer to Purnell. A reserve officer, Stewart had been called to active duty as an intelligence specialist and had gotten as far as Surabaya enroute to assignment to the 16th Naval District. He'd joined us there and been put to work as a communications watch officer. Stewart was a few years older than I, having finished college, and had been coaching tennis and teaching history at a prep school in Pennsylvania. He was a stocky, athletic person with a penetrating, determined look in his eye, dark hair cut short on his head. Stewart had a quick sense of fun and a bold, easy way with others. He was determined, even stubborn, quick to take offense if treated offhandedly. And competitive. He didn't like not knowing something that another person knew or not knowing how to do something that another could accomplish. He'd do his best to learn it. For that reason, in Surabaya, he quickly became a useful communications officer.

I told Stew, when it became clear that the volunteer force

was made up of the two of us, that destroying gas dumps was a pretty shoddy objective. (I'd kept that criticism to myself when I'd volunteered myself to Admiral Purnell.) My idea in volunteering to go back to the Philippines was to locate our prisoners. My motive was strong—make it up to the comrades I'd abandoned—but the scheme itself was weak, falling apart as soon as you began to define it. Locate the prisoners and—well, then what? Seize the camps? Set prisoners free in the Japanese-occupied Philippines? Burning dumps of aviation gas in Mindanao might be humdrum, but it was practical. My idea was romantic and foolish.

Nothing changed in our lives. Stewart kept at what he was doing, now handling intelligence functions for the staff in Perth and Fremantle. And I kept on working as communications watch officer on the staff of commander, Allied Naval Forces Basing Western Australia. Allied meant ships flying the same ensigns as in Java: Dutch, British, Australian, and American, most of our American vessels being submarines on combat patrol in Japanese waters. The surface vessels did convoy work and occasionally went after blockade runners, merchant ships, some of them so heavily armed as suitably to be described as raiders, carrying strategic minerals from Japan to Germany.

Hugh Lawrence and I had been billeted at first in the Commercial Travelers Club in Perth. When it seemed we'd be staying in Perth for a while, we looked for other quarters. It was Lawrence, who knew how to do things right, who found them. Lawrence, Stewart, and I soon were living in a house on the edge of the Swan River on the road from Fremantle to Perth. As household staff, the three of us had one of Admiral Hart's former stewards and the Asiatic Fleet pastry cook, Chinese lured into the naval service from good Shanghai restaurants. We had far better dinners and fancier desserts than we appreciated.

The house was a convenient way station for friends on the way into Perth from Fremantle. They'd stop on the way, sometimes just stay with us, drinking, eating late. Or after an evening in Perth, they'd drop by in the early morning on their way back to Fremantle. In the some two months we lived there, on only one phenomenal night did the three of us eat dinner alone. It wasn't just company for dinner, either. I was awakened one dawn by a friend sitting on the end of my bed, an Australian girl giggling on either side of me. They'd helped themselves to an eye-opener at our bar. I must hear the girls sing the songs he'd taught them, and they sang tunelessly, "The Monkeys Have No Tails in Zamboanga" and "We'll All Go Up to China in the Springtime."

We had two fireplaces, usually a fire in them, often when it was far too warm for it, everyone crowded into the room, drinking and talking all at once. Everyone had his stories of narrow escapes and told them and repeated them, too. One night, some friends came by with a Royal Navy midshipman we had to meet. He'd been in the skytop of the *Repulse* or it may have been *Prince of Wales* when the two of them were sunk in December, the day Cavite was bombed. When the ship had listed sufficiently on its way over, he dived 130 feet—they said it was—into the water. A gangling, towheaded youngster with British teeth, he was not doing the talking. He sat on the couch with a drink, hat on the back of his head, laughing, while the others hung over him, gesturing, telling his story—not that they were there. They'd turn to him, "Isn't that right?" He'd laugh and shake his head. They'd ask, "Isn't that how it was?"

"It's your story now, old chap, no longer mine."

The same social germ in Lawrence that had gotten us the house and our steady stream of guests led to his inviting several senior officers of the staff, lieutenant commanders and commanders, to dinner. It was a wonderful evening of comradeship. We had drinks, followed by an excellent dinner. They seemed really to appreciate having been asked, and we agreed, when they'd left, that obviously they'd enjoyed themselves.

The next day we were moved out, the house had new occupants, and the chief steward and the pastry cook were happier serving a more senior and better behaved clientele. The two Chinese were past middle age and had gotten tired of unexpected place settings at dinner, the irregular hours, the loud guests.

We moved into a perfectly nice house at the top of Mount Street in Perth, with a large living-room window overlooking the Swan River far below. Our friends from the ships complained that it was not convenient, not on the way to anywhere. When we asked them up, they said it was hard to find. Anyway, the old hands—what was left of them—were all going home. Of the twenty-five of us who'd come out a year before from San Francisco, by mid-1942, only Hugh Lawrence and I remained together.

General MacArthur, his seat transferred to the east coast of Australia, was condescending to being idolized by the undiscriminating Australians. As the Philippine Islands belonged to him, our plan to return to the Philippines was sent to his headquarters for blessing. We had by then elaborated on the aviation gas bit, adding reconnaissance of prison camps, getting in touch with guerrillas, perfectly sound proposals.

MacArthur's reply was to this effect: "The navy, having been responsible for the loss of the Philippines, will have nothing to do with regaining them." While I put these words within quotation marks, they may not be the exact language of his typically graceless words. Close enough.

The reply infuriated Purnell and disappointed us. No one was really surprised by it, coming from MacArthur. Stewart and I began to think of other expeditions. Patwing 10 was flying patrols out of northwest Australia, their arcs occasionally intersecting the patrols that Japanese bombers flew out of Kupang airport in Timor. The planes would look each other over from a safe distance, like a pair of dogs that have met before, deciding not to challenge each other, the Japanese apparently as grateful for a quiet period as were our aviators.

Our scheme was to sneak ashore and destroy the aircraft at Kupang in a hit-and-run expedition. We spent a lot of time poking our fingers at charts, checking depths, landing spots, figuring where the mangrove swamps were. We argued in our written proposal that a raid on Kupang would annoy the Japanese psychologically as well as destroying aircraft. The psychological bit is often included to dress up a doubtful proposal. But we were striking few blows at the

Japanese. The attack on Tokyo on 18 April 1942 by Col. James Doolittle's B-25s was a stunt with a psychological objective. In its small way, our idea of a raid on Kupang was similar.

In case a strike on Kupang didn't appeal to our betters, we began collecting information on Denpasar airport in Bali, an alternate target for a seaborne expedition.

In a pleasing sign that Stewart and I were being taken seriously, Theodore Cathey, who had just made Marine Gunner (warrant officer), was detached from the cruiser he was serving on and assigned to work with us. Ted was an amiable, tough, accomplished career Marine. Adding a professional dimension we lacked, he was, if anything, keener about our plans than were we. The three of us took the train into the countryside, hiked through the desert, tested communications equipment, being careful to spot pubs for lunch, spend the nights in small-town hotels, hardly more comfortable than the desert itself.

Our first obstacle was personnel. We wanted to train the few men we needed ourselves—Marines, sailors, whatever we could get. Stewart's intelligence duties had put him in touch with the Australian army, and he got Purnell's permission to talk to them about coming in with us with a few men. To our credit, we always thought small rather than big, favoring a small team of compatible people for our first operation or two.

Naively, we hadn't thought that transportation would be an obstacle. On the one hand, we might infiltrate by PBY, take rubber boats ashore, and return to the plane or a rendezvous to be taken out. The advantage of using an aircraft was that we might be able to talk friends in Patwing 10 into supporting us. We really preferred going in and out by submarine, thinking the risk of warning the Japanese to be less and the chances greater for being retrieved. The trouble was getting a submarine, even though we had become essentially a submarine command, Commander Submarines Southwest Pacific. Combat patrol was the only mission the submariners could think about, despite continuing problems with torpedoes. (Defective torpedoes were banging harmlessly against the hulls of Japanese ships or running impotently beneath them during the early days of the Pacific War.)

When Admiral Purnell was ordered to Washington in mid-1942, we lost our sponsor, and our plan lost prestige. A bold plan in which an admiral is personally interested commands considerably more attention, we learned, than a harebrained scheme being pushed by a few junior officers.

Lawrence got married, and I was best man at the wedding. Stewart and I diverted ourselves by taking on a white British bull puppy. Skipper grew, but not much, a genetic puzzler. His father, a large brindle bull, had attracted notice in Perth by hamstringing a horse pulling a milk wagon. The horse had to be destroyed, and Skipper's father was given a retributive death sentence. He had been so mild an animal before the crime that his partisans suggested the horse had provoked him.

Then Stewart got married, and I was best man at his wedding. I remained in the mess with the bulldog and another two or three officers, new people, but all right. Stewart and Cathey and I feared that our anti-Japanese plans had been stored in the bottoms of the file cabinets of those who could approve them did they want to. Being canny about these things, Stewart drafted an earnest personal letter to Admiral Purnell in Washington. Without enthusiasm, I put my signature next to his at the bottom expecting nothing to come of it.

Convinced we were getting nowhere, I persuaded the flag secretary to forward my request for flight training. That got me into surgery for a deviated septum in my nose.

Then the flag lieutenant, personal aide to Adm. Charles Lockwood (COMSUBSOWESPAC), had orders to return home. The flag secretary called me in to astonish me with the announcement I was to be the new flag lieutenant. When I reminded him of my request for flight training, he ended the discussion by telling me, "You don't want to be a plane driver."

I did, too. Nevertheless, I called on Admiral Lockwood to state that I was honored to be chosen for assignment as flag lieutenant. Meanwhile, I was trying to reconcile my wishes—assignment to a destroyer, to go back to the Philippines, to raid Kupang, for flight training—with the navy's intentions.

At the same time I was calling on Lockwood, a dispatch was on its way from the Navy Department ordering Stewart and me to report to Chungking as assistant naval observers. That was Admiral Purnell's answer to Stewart's letter. He was sending us to a place where he thought our thwarted ambitions would find their outlet.

Stewart, the bulldog, and I got on a British merchant ship—there being no handier way of getting to China from Western Australia—and, eventually, in February 1943, reached Calcutta, the jumping off place for China.

Chapter 13

One winter night in February 1943, Stewart and I reached the bottom of the navy's valley outside of Chungking in Sichuan Province. Torchbearers led us, climbing, past rice paddies on stone paths, as though winding through dark gardens. I knew nothing then of the endless tracings of stone paths from field to field, from house to house, from one village to the next across this immense land. Even less could I know my feet would trace score after score of miles on flagstones, cobblestones, round stones, long flat stones, on black stone paths through mountain passes, on greasy stone walks in cities, on white stone paths along river banks, the nights of stumbling, tired, as we walked that night on stones set next to paddy dikes. The oily flames lighted the paddy right around us that night, spookily casting the rest of the world into darkness.

It was to be a familiar sight that year as more people arrived in the valley at the end of a long day's flight. From the veranda at the end of the valley, you'd see a torchlit party in its nimbus of orange light, climbing stone paths in the dark from the road below. Let that small circle of light stand for what we knew of China and the pitch darkness represent the infinity of our ignorance.

We arrived, most of us, with a myth set in our heads as firmly as anything else we believed. The myth was a fighting China, bravely resisting the Japanese invaders. Pervasive among Americans, the story typically was spread by Henry Luce's influential *Time* and *Life* magazines, simple and sentimental exaggerations undisputed by official American propaganda. The myth was based on a trace of truth that was true, to the extent it was true, of the recent past, but not of the weary China of 1943. The China of 1943 was a divided country, much of the coast, the major cities in eastern China and along the large rivers, being in Japanese hands. We knew that. What we had to learn was that the Chinese were a divided people.

The myth was the rationale for the Office of the Naval Observer, Chungking—soon to be Navy Group China. We were officially pledged to the assumption that all the Chinese needed was help, military equipment, the tools with which to finish the job—maybe some advice in how to use them. Left out of that picture were the motives of the leaders of the only two significant Chinese factions, the Nationalists and the Communists. The overt struggle—outright civil war at times—they'd been waging since 1927 had ostensibly been put aside in the pretense of a common front against Japan. Actually, the two factions were leaving the task of defeating Japan to the United States, themselves getting ready for the eventual and decisive struggle to decide which of them would rule China.

Mythology aside, we worked in a real political situation. The United States continued to recognize the Chinese government dominated by the Nationalist Party, the Guomingdang, led by Generalissimo Chiang Kai-shek. When the Japanese took the wartime capital of Nanjing on the Yangzi River in 1937, the Nationalist government moved to Chungking further to the west up the Yangzi. The Japanese set up a puppet government in Nanjing to rule China proper. The Chinese Communists had their headquarters in Yan'an in the north. Thus, three different political entities claimed to rule China, each having some degree of control over large parts of it. The Nanjing government's power came from the barrel of a Japanese gun. It had authority, not legitimacy. The Chinese Communists held what they called liberated areas, and during the 1940s, they steadily infiltrated the areas claimed by Nanking and Chungking. It was our opposition to Japan's attempts to turn China into a

Japanese protectorate, our refusal to accept Japan's hegemony in China, that led the Japanese to attack Pearl Harbor.

The valley near Chungking was a huge bowl, open as far as the hills around it, the land sloping lower in the direction of the Yangzi River, hiding the river from our sight. The intensively cultivated farmlands of Sichuan surrounded us and were the main theme for as far as we could see. The steepest pitches were terraced, green rice growing bright in the red soil, water trickling through intricate canals from upper terraces to flood the rice plants in the paddies below. Only at the very tops of the hills, where the terraces ended, were straight dark pines allowed to grow. The same countryside rose from the river on the other side until the hills closed the horizon to us. To our right, on that far horizon, were smudges of the outskirts of Chungking, some eight miles away. In one of the last Japanese bombings of the city that year, we could see plumes of gray dust shoot up as bombs fell at the edge of the city, hear the distant rumbling of explosions under the whine of aircraft engines.

Our myth was housed, as it were, in the American center of the Chinese valley, a building longer than wide, more like a private house than institutional, sitting on the slope that climbed to close off the far end of the valley. If you were to face it, standing on the terrace in front, the wing on your left held a long living room with a couple of desks at the far end, easy chairs, a sofa, work tables, taking up the rest of the room. The strip of bedrooms, fronting one deep on the stone-paved terrace, ran from there to the wing on the right. That wing held the small mess hall and kitchen for the headquarters contingent—strictly Chinese food, eaten from rice bowls with chopsticks. Our bulldog, Skipper, chose the kitchen as his headquarters, appearing mealtimes to beg from tables, napping much of the day in shade on the terrace, sitting in on evening conversations after dinner.

On this stone terrace in the morning, we drank our tea from lidded porcelain cups without handles, sat there at the end of the day, feet up on the wall, to look down the valley. The view was remarkable for a sense of openness, of airy space between us and the lines of hills in the distance. Below us were buildings the Chinese used, barracks, offices, the valley crisscrossed by flagstone paths. During the day, Chinese troops sang patriotic songs, the music drifting to us as echoes from the valley. Strange bugle calls sounded morning and night.

At our backs, a mountain rose abruptly some hundreds of feet, closing off our valley from the hills behind. Stone was chiseled from the mountain for building in the valley. A pair of quarry workers would suspend a cut stone between them on a pole and step jerkily down the paths, calling in unison, "*hai-yo-HAI, hai-yo-HAI*." With the sweat pouring down their hollow cheeks and thin flanks, the regular chant did as much to relieve their pain as to keep time.

The headquarters element was then small. The one-room office at one end of the headquarters house, furnished with armchairs, except for the desks, had a family air about it. Our commanding officer, Adm. Milton Miles, often sat at his desk in the far end of the room, the door behind him leading to a small bedroom. He didn't sit for long. Miles was impatient, not much of a sitter, more of a pacer, a runner-around, always going off to look at something. In the valley, he dressed simply, without insignia on his khakis; like the rest of us, wearing shorts in the hot Sichuan summer. He had graying curly hair, brown eyes in a pleasant face, somewhat sallow in complexion. Miles had that comfortable trait in a senior officer of being easy to talk to, putting you at your ease. In that, he was like Admiral Purnell, another officer confident enough to put stiffness aside without, either one of them, dropping all protocol. Certainly I never made the mistake of forgetting Miles's rank, despite the easiness about him, any more than I had Purnell's. Miles liked being called by his naval academy nickname, Mary, and many of his juniors did so. While I was not one of them, I never once felt I could not give Miles my honest opinion, and I fear I often gave it without being asked. I can't think now of an example of his taking my advice, although he may have done so. I do remember times when he did not like what I said. Yet, he was always kind to me, considerate, and later on when I disagreed with him and was close to insubordinate, he treated me with a tolerance I hardly deserved. His fault, I think, was being far too decent an officer for the job he'd been given.

Off and on during that year of 1943, I was included in the small family circle of headquarters, sharing, with one roommate or another, a bedroom off the terrace. There were few naval officers there, early on, and my tenuous grasp of how the navy works—how things ought to be done—was unusual enough to be useful.

Our valley belonged to Gen. Tai Li. He and Miles headed the Sino-American Cooperative Organization (SACO), the joint organization of the United States Navy and the Nationalist Government. General Tai was chosen by the Chinese Government to work with the navy, and thus our headquarters were near his in his valley. The navy did not go looking for Tai Li. It was the Chinese government that decided that Miles would be assigned to Tai—and vice versa—for the navy mission in China.

Major General Tai, a graduate of the Whampoa Military Academy in the brave days of the 1920s—the surge of reform, hot nationalism, and the crusading Northern March—was head of the Bureau of Investigation and Statistics (BIS). This government agency, combining political with security functions, worked in secrecy and semisecrecy, the semi part being what we in the Navy Group saw—to the extent that we saw it and understood what we were looking at. The secrecy and Tai Li's role in suppressing the Communist Chinese along with more democratically motivated dissenters, tasks delegated to him by Generalissimo Chiang Kai-shek, made him feared in China and earned him a questionable reputation with many foreigners. At the time a typically facile description of Tai by a foreign writer called him "China's combination of Himmler and J. Edgar Hoover." Miles saw a great deal of General Tai, in the course of working with him, and knew him far better than any foreigner. Miles's evaluations of Tai range from the apologetic, even defensive, all the way to laudatory, always erring toward generosity. I never heard Miles admit that Tai himself frustrated our mission as much as he helped it. Maybe Miles never saw it that way.

Our mission in China started with Admiral Ernest King's

telling Miles the Navy had "to send someone to China to find out what is going on out there. . . . You are to go to China and set up some bases as soon as you can. The main idea is to prepare the China coast in any way you can for U. S. Navy landings in three or four years. In the meantime, do whatever you can to help the Navy and to heckle the Japanese." Those orders could justify just about anything. Miles described his first activity as reporting the weather.

> Weather in the western Pacific . . . tends to come out of China and, as a result of the Japanese invasion, very little weather information from the mainland was reaching our naval forces in the western Pacific. If we could send observers to China, however, we could surely do something in that field, and, in addition, we could no doubt help ourselves in other ways while also being of some help to the hard-pressed Chinese.

King's order gave Miles license to define his mission as broadly as he liked. At the other end of the scale was the narrow task of reporting the weather coming out of China. Miles's words above show that he saw right away that other tasks could grow from that restricted objective.

I'd been a week or so in Chungking when Miles's executive officer told me to sit down by his desk while he talked about the constant problem for the Navy Group of getting air freight from India to Kunming in Yunnan Province. When Burma fell to the Japanese in 1942, the Burma Road closed. Now the only way to get supplies to China, since the Japanese held the coast, was by air over the Hump—the Himalayas and the mountains of Burma—the way we all got to China at that time. Our freight was entirely for use in our war: TNT, plastic explosive, ammunition, carbines and Thompson submachine guns, radios, batteries, and so on. It was especially galling to Miles that our stuff sat around India while the "army brought in canteen supplies—even brought in their peanut butter by air, though peanuts were an export crop in China." Miles could have gone on to point out that we in the Navy Group lived almost completely off the land, buying food locally wherever we were.

The United States Army and the army air forces controlled what came over the Hump, the executive officer went on to say. Gen. Joseph Stilwell, the China-Burma-India theater commander, had assured Miles more than once he'd see to it that navy gear was brought in. Miles didn't doubt Stilwell's good faith, but Stilwell didn't push his own people—our unit didn't rank high with him, even on a good day—and what orders he gave were ignored. Army people down the line decided what would go aboard a plane, and usually they decided it would not be navy gear. Materiel coming by sea from the States reached Calcutta and went by rail to Assam in northeast India, whence it was flown—or, if it belonged to the navy, was not flown—to Kunming.

At the end of these revelations, I was told to go off to India, find the navy gear in Assam, and get it moving over the Hump. The invoices I was stuffing into my suitcase did not reveal where the materiel was. It might be sitting on a siding of the Indian railways. It might have been off-loaded somewhere between Calcutta and Assam. It might be in someone else's godown rather than ours. I couldn't chase all over India after it. I was to go to the airfields in Assam, find what gear I could, and get it over the Hump to Kunming by persuading the army to carry it.

When I'd sent enough stuff over the Hump, I was to fly to Kunming and make up truck convoys for shipment to Chungking or to Camp One, a unit just being established in southern Anhui Province on the edge of Japanese-occupied east China. The materiel for shipment to future such units I'd arrange to store safely in Kunming. Here, again, was an assignment quite different from what I'd expected, more fitting to a navy storekeeper.

I didn't complain—I didn't know anyone in Chungking well enough to complain to him—but I remember seeking advice on carrying out my diplomatic assignment of representing the navy to the United States Army. In Miles's household was a fair-spoken naval officer who, I soon saw,

Figure 1. Self-portrait of the author on letterhead stationary of the USS *Wyoming*, August 1940.

Figure 2. The author with sister, now Jane Horton de Cabanyes of Madrid, Spain, in Glencoe, Illinois, on her birthday, February 2, 1941.

Figure 3. The author with the bulldog, Skipper, in Perth, Western Australia, 1942.

Figure 4. A view of the village of Xiongcun from the Buddhist monastery across the river. The grounds and buildings of Camp One, hardly visible beneath trees in leaf, lie along the riverbank, beginning at the leftmost of the trees and extending to the seventh or eighth of them. *Photo by Lt. Earl Colgrove, Navy Combat Photo Unit One, 1943 or 1944.*

Figure 5. Officers of Camp One at the June 1944 departure of Lt. Col. John H. Masters, USMC (kneeling, second from right). Standing, from left: Lt. A. Close, USMC; Lt. Spurgeon Benjamin, Supply Corps, USN; Lts. F. McGaha, J. Siegrist, Milton Hull, USMC. Kneeling, from the left: the author; Lt. E. Dane, USMC; Dr. A. Tucker, USN; Masters; Lt. W. Pickerell, USMC. Of those shown, surviving half a century later were Al Close, Jake Siegrist, Earle Dane, Walt Pickerell, and the author.

Figure 6. The Chinese training staff of Camp One with officers of the Loyal Patriotic Army. Seated at the top of the stairs are the author, Gen. Ma (commanding, LPA), Gen. Guo (camp commander), Mrs. Guo.

Figure 7. The author training a demolitions class, interpreter at his left and, looking skeptically from his right, three Marines (Sgt. Theron Herrin, Cpl. Robert Boger, and Sgt. Richard Young). The man at attention must have been asked to identify the type of fuse being displayed. Such a lecture would have been supplemented by practical field work. Spring 1944.

Figure 8. The Chinese wanted a weapon issued to every person submitted for training. They tried too hard at times to fill a quota. These *guazi* ("little devils") stand with GM1 Lawrence Conrad. Probably 1943 or early 1944. *Photo courtesy of Robert Boger.*

Figure 9. Admiral Miles was glad to have Maj. Charles Parkin, AUS, seconded to the Navy Group from the OSS. Parkin commanded Camp One from June 1944 until November 1944.

Figure 10. This is the musician whose bugle called forth Lt. Hull's scathing evaluation of the conduct of the night engagement at Ximoushi. September 1944.

Figure 11. Some who took part at Ximoushi stopped at Pact Doc for medical checkups on the way back to Camp One. Seated on the ground: Sgt. T. Herrin; PM2 H. J. Sauer. Seated on the wall above: AMM1 B. Van Dalsem, Jr.; the author; GM1 L. P. Conrad; AMM1 B. Colella; TSgt W. J. Tawater; PM2 T. P. Greco. September 1944.

Figure 12. Unaware that Japanese counterinsurgency force was just minutes away, a group from Camp One has joined Hull and his party. Kneeling, from left: McCoy, Tawater, Primos, GM1 J. D. Reid. Standing: MM3 R. J. Kosanovich, ?SM1? A. J. Wogan, the author, Hull. *Photo by Fireman First Class E. Arias.*

Figure 13. Marine Lt. Jacob Siegrist in the cowled parka assembling a war party in Camp One to leave for the operations area in Zhejiang Province. The soldier in the flight jacket carries a bazooka; the goggles are to protect his eyes from the propellant when the weapon is fired.

Figure 14. On the left is Lt. Wu, the former Shanghai assassin who embarrassed us Americans by hovering over us like a mother when we were in the field against the Japanese. With him is Alfred Liang of Hong Kong, interpreter, a fount of good advice to the Americans, a key member of Camp One's operational units, and always good company. Winter 1944–45.

Figure 15. Two of the finest officers at Camp One. Captain Chen Yuhua is on the left, and Maj. Ho, also known as Charley for some reason, is on the right. The Americans and they worked closely together in training and in operations. 1944 or 1945.

Figure 16. Zhejiang river crossing with capacity load on raft of lashed trunks of bamboo. The boatman is at far left. With too heavy a load, the party would make it across with water over the ankles. Hull is identifiable at far right with carbine slung across his back. 1944–45.

was a plausible authority on any subject that came up. His advice was this:

"Get yourself a few cases of Carew's gin from Calcutta. You see a pilot and you go up to him: 'Here, buddy, have a bottle of gin. While you're at it, take this gear along to Kunming, okay?' Nothing to it, Johnny. Trouble with our people—they don't know how to handle those guys."

I flew back to Calcutta to compare my shipping invoices with those of the Navy Liaison Office, and to see what hypotheses they'd offer about the whereabouts of missing freight—nothing new there. Then back to Assam, to Chabua, Dinjan, Jorhat—from those fields in 1943 our planes flew the Hump. Assam is in the valley of the Brahmaputra, the great river formed by its tributaries, the chief of these the Zangbo that flows from Tibet through the Himalayas into the valley of Assam. The flat lowlands here were filled with tea gardens run by British managers, the tea growing as rows of green shrubs beneath regularly spaced shade trees. Not a bad place at all for a tea-garden manager. The amenities were lacking for the rest of us. I settled at the Polo Grounds in Chabua where the air force had set up barracks on a muddy field that, indeed, had once been a polo field. The Polo Grounds became a swamp in the pouring, hot rain. Officers and men slogged through the mud, boots unlaced, wearing underwear shorts under a poncho, toilet gear in one hand. First to the latrine, sloshing from there to the washbasins in another leaky basha hut.

In godowns around the airfield at Chabua, I found navy gear. I started making my calls on army supply officers, explaining my business. I wore the same khakis as the others, but my navy cap drew puzzled stares. I was a lieutenant by then and wore on my collar the same two silver bars as an army captain, so everyone called me captain, and I gave up setting them right.

Some nights, I went to a screened hut where the pilots spread khaki blankets on tables to play poker—hundreds in dollar bills loose on the board. Some of them were fearfully young, reckless, noisy, frightened. Other pilots sat around and talked, others sat by themselves and read. I met a few of the pilots and this way got a few hundred pounds, I suppose, on this or that airplane. The pilots were on the move, and rarely did I see one of them a second time. I did cadge or trade the occasional book—I'd read anything I could get my hands on to pass the long wet days, even comic books.

During the day, I worked on supply officers, wheedling a planeload or a half or quarter planeload of navy gear over the Hump. I didn't know enough about China yet to be disillusioned at how poorly the Chinese worked together. I was only too well aware of how our own services got along—my mission was proof of that. It was vile and humiliating to have to go about begging favors. Nevertheless I accepted it. That's the way we are, I knew, and I found it easier to forgive our national weaknesses than I did, later on, to accept the Chinese as they are.

Finally there was enough gear in Kunming for a truck convoy. China would be paradise after India. I went back to Assam a time or two to remind the people I'd seen before of the continued navy interest in moving our gear. Or I'd start from the beginning again with their replacements. There was a lot of turnover. My Indian exile ended for good when an able navy warrant officer came to Assam with a couple of navy storekeepers. Between their professional approach and constant pressure on the army, the gear moved faster, sometimes slowing, sometimes stopping altogether, and negotiations—in Washington, Chungking, Chabua—would begin all over again.

I may have brought a case of Carew's up from Calcutta to Assam. I think I gave a few bottles to some of the pilots. I hope so. Maybe I drank the rest of it myself.

Chapter 14

Years later, my wife asked some of us who'd served in the Navy Group, "How did China get such a grip on you?" By no means did everyone who served in China during the Second World War feel as we did. Yet, for a small number, it's true that China has never let go. I can't answer her question in a few words. I know that China took hold of me from the first days in Kunming, and in the next two years, tightened its grip forever.

It's not enough to say that Kunming is a far more pleasing place than the Polo Grounds at Chabua, although it is. Of course, I was glad just to get away from the Polo Grounds, the heat, the mud, and the army supply officers who thought they were doing you a favor by flying a few boxes of navy freight over the Hump. Kunming is the capital of Yunnan Province: a good name, Yunnan, "south of the clouds." Kunming is some six thousand feet high, on a plateau with elegant blue and tawny mountains set about the horizon—actually, almost any view in China includes mountains—with clean, crisp air, and populated by blue-clad or black-gowned cheerful-looking Chinese. I couldn't see at first what it was in their spare lives that led them to be so cheerful. Later on, I learned that Chinese smiles and laughter don't always imply happiness. But, compared to a nation of sulkers like the glum Bengalis of Calcutta, even a false cheer serves to raise a visitor's morale.

For Americans in Kunming, the airfield on the outskirts of the city was the center of life rather than the city itself.

The American base was vigorous in early 1943 but not as big, as formal, as bureaucratic, as it would later become, not as cluttered with Americans, still a small town. Gen. Claire Chennault's American Volunteer Group, the Flying Tigers, was now part of the 14th Air Force of the United States Army Air Forces. As time went on, this force of khaki-colored, shark-mouthed P-40 fighter planes was augmented by silver, twin-boomed P-38s and P-51 Mustangs. In 1943, there were four-engined B-24 and green, twin-engined B-25 bombers that, along with fighter bombers, and always depending on the supply of aviation gasoline, were beginning to carry the war to the Japanese forces in China.

In the crispness of Kunming's air, even on a cold day, the sun was warm on your face, the sky a clear blue, and then there was the dust, gritty and dry in your teeth and hair and on your clothing. Wind took dust up from the runway, where it boiled behind trucks and jeeps running along the edge of the field and kicked up in the wash of idling propellers. (Rain turned Kunming's dust into instant soup, a clinging yellow mud.) Hundreds of Chinese laborers spent the days surfacing the airstrip and extending it. Ponies drew two-wheeled carts filled with stone onto the field, and workers trotted with baskets of earth swinging on poles across their shoulders. Squatting, hammers in hand, other workers pounded white rock into gravel. There were the Americans who thought that hilarious, and they took newcomers to enjoy the sight of people shattering rocks in their hands, snapping pictures of them to send home.

Most of the day, aircraft engines set up a backdrop of noise you'd hear without thinking about it, unconscious of raising your voice to speak over it. The C-47 transports, the ones the British called Dakotas, were the most common: a troop carrier with whirling propellers jouncing along the edge of the field, the noise dropping in pitch as the tail section swung about and the plane turned into the wind to take off, maybe bound east for the field at Liuzhou. The other cargo carrier was the C-46 Curtis Commando. You'd see them rushing into takeoff runs, their two engines roaring, heading back over the Hump to Jorhat. All aircraft in China burned aviation gas that was hauled by air over the Hump, ordinarily in drums. Bombers often had to fly in enough gas for themselves to mount a mission. Bombing raids on Japanese shipping along the east coast, on Japanese targets in Indochina, on men-of-war in Hong Kong harbor or on planes at the White Cloud airfield in Canton, fighter strikes at Japanese fields at Anjing or Wuhu on the Yangzi, air transport of people and freight around China—all depended on the import of gas. None of us in the navy minded competing for Hump tonnage with aviation gas—it was that darned peanut butter we resented!

In the spring of 1943, the Japanese were attacking the field from the air regularly. *Jingbao*—warning—was the term we all used for an air-raid alarm. Ordinarily the Japanese formations would be tracked across China by ground spotters with radios, giving time to disperse aircraft and get the fighters up. There was the occasional surprise and, at least once that I remember, a threat of disaster. Because of bad weather over the Hump, we nearly ran out of gas when the Japanese attacked the field several days in a row. The Japanese paused for some reason. Maybe they were out of gas, too. Then the clouds cleared, and plane after plane droned into Kunming with supplies of gasoline.

The raids brought Kunming some excitement—nothing that I couldn't have done without. We shaded our eyes from the sun to find the enemy formations high in the blue sky, Zeros sunfishing around them. Sometimes our fighters would drive off the Japanese aircraft before they could bomb, harass them so they'd jettison their bomb loads without damage. When they did get through to drop their sticks of bombs, they'd hit a plane or two on the edge of the runway, knock over an occasional building, kill or wound people on the ground with daisy cutters, the small antipersonnel bombs that burst to scatter shrapnel knee-high.

Sometimes good came of it. Toward Christmas that year, a C-47 flying Christmas cheer to Stilwell's headquarters was hit on the ground in Kunming. Friends who were there said it burned with a blue alcohol flame.

I had another personal reason to be glad about Kunming. I wasn't working alone. An interpreter named Peter Pan joined me to help get the truck convoys on their way. That's his foreign name, the surname properly pronounced to rhyme with the second part of "upon." Like other interpreters assigned to the Navy Group, he was more than interpreter, more a liaison officer between me and the various Chinese we worked with. Translating our words was only a part of it. Peter would represent us to each other—often misrepresent us to soften American brusqueness or to put a smooth patina on a rude Chinese refusal.

Somewhat like us Americans in China for the first time, and like most of the other interpreters, Peter had to deal with people he'd have had little or nothing to do with in other times. While welded strongly together by the culture that makes them unalterably Chinese, educated Chinese ordinarily didn't mix with workers, with Chinese soldiers, with the peasant class from which the Chinese Army drew its men. As intellectuals, they'd love in the abstract the people glorified in a propaganda poster, but they'd go out of their way to avoid talking with one of them in person. It was the Japanese invasion of China that forced Chinese of different classes to get to know each other.

Working with me, Peter would find himself for days at a time thrown with an earthy gang of ragged, smelly illiterates as we sorted through piles of crates and loaded them on trucks. "Bearers," Peter called them, avoiding the incorrect word, "coolie," with its imperialist taint, although their work was no less bitter for the euphemism. The Chinese laborers found Peter, a member of the educated class, nearly as strange a creature as the foreign devil standing next to him.

Our Navy Group interpreters had a standard disclaimer for the foreign-devil question. (The other common term for Westerner was "big nose.") Here's Peter, starting off with an embarrassed giggle: "Chinese people don't say 'foreign devil' any more. We say American friend, *meiguode pengyo*." Yeah, right, Peter. I'd hear him lecturing the laborers, trying vainly to stop the talking about the foreign devil. They meant nothing by it—it was just a term to them. I'd smile at them, and they'd give me big grins back, eyes crinkled, showing a lot of gums with teeth missing.

"*Ding hao!*" they'd call out, the universal phrase in Kunming those days. Thumbs-up all around, and I'd say, "*Ding hao!*" back to them.

Later on, in the farmyards, in the village streets, parents picked up their children to point us out among the Chinese soldiers. "Quick, quick. Look at the *yangguizi*"—the foreign devils.

On the back of their leather jackets, Chennault's pilots bore a message in Chinese asking people to help the wearer were he shot down or otherwise in trouble. The writing introduced him as a foreign friend who'd come to help fight the Japanese. I asked Peter why he was sniggering as a pilot walked past us one day. All he would say was that the term used to describe the pilot was "not very nice, not very good taste." He did say it wasn't as bad as "foreign devil."

Peter was of Cantonese stock, and he'd learned English in school before he learned the national language, *guoyu*, Mandarin. He was good about helping me learn to speak Mandarin, and he wanted to teach me to read and write Chinese characters. I told him I'd as soon remain illiterate if only I could learn to talk. Sometimes Cantonese friends of his would join us at a Cantonese restaurant in the city, the variety of provincial cooking being another charm of Kunming, a consequence of the overlay of refugees who'd fled their Japanese-occupied home provinces to Yunnan. "Don't listen to them," Peter would insist, causing much laughter, as his friends named things for me. He didn't want me learning Cantonese dialect or imitating their bad accents in Mandarin.

I remember Peter as darker than the sometimes lighter-skinned central and northern Chinese, but that might have come from his working outdoors so much with me rather than his natural skin tone. He looked the intellectual with his thick glasses, always neatly and simply dressed in military-style clothing. He had two *zhongshan* suits, one faded blue and one a more dressy black, what we called Sun Yat-sen suits after the founder of the Chinese Revolution of 1911, a high collar clasped at the neck—much the same style as our navy white service dress. I was sloppier than Peter in my khakis, my white uniforms packed away in a Calcutta warehouse.

Peter and I were friendly enough but always respectful of the other's position: face, that is. Peter addressed me as Lieutenant Horton in English, Hodong *Shangwei* in Chinese—Upper-lieutenant (equaling army captain) Horton. I called him Peter, but he was never comfortable calling me Johnny. I always referred to him in front of others as Pan *xiansheng*, meaning literally elder-born, an honorific for a learned person. As with the Chinese Communists, the term *tongzhi*, meaning comrade, was used by Chinese Nationalist officials with each other, by Chinese Army people— occasionally with me. I took that as a flattering, if fractional, degree of inclusion. I was careful about using *tongzhi*, treating it like the familiar form in European languages, not quite sure when to claim someone as my comrade. Reluctant to be the first to address a Chinese officer with a "*tongzhi*," the term came easily from my mouth after the first few cups of white lightning at a banquet.

Once I found the freight that had come over the Hump—I'm getting ahead of the order of events—Peter and I trucked it to a heavily guarded compound, a Tai-Li sanctuary controlled by one General Li, Tai Li's man in Yunnan. On the western outskirts of Kunming, the place was called Heilinpu, that Peter translated as Black Pine Grove. Down a drive among the dark pines, a hundred or so yards off the narrow, paved highway, was the godown where we made up the convoys of trucks to go up to Chungking or east across China to Camp One.

Across the highway from the drive into the compound was a narrow road, maybe three or four feet wide, paved with large flagstones, rubbed smooth. Near the edge of the highway, I found a slender ceremonial stone arch, shaped like a long-legged letter Π, traces of polychrome on its carved members, a soft rose, mostly, the arch delicately astride the road. I could stand under it and touch either side of it without having fully to extend my arms, just wide enough to let a small horse drawing a cart or a sedan chair pass through. The stylized curlicued top of it was no more than two or three feet above my head. I'd walk up from the compound to look at it, pass through it a short way on the flagstones that wound off into the dry countryside. No one, and I asked both Peter and General Li, could tell me anything about it. I was limited by my ignorance to ethnocentric speculations—seven centuries earlier Marco Polo might have ridden this road while in the service of Kublai Khan.

In the compound one day, I shamed Peter by catching him up on a remark he made about loyalty. It had to do with the safety of our weapons and ammunition in the godown. Peter assured me that General Li was trustworthy, responsive to General Tai, loyal to the government in Chunking—not to worry.

"What do you mean, 'loyal to Chungking'? Isn't everyone?"

Peter looked sick and changed the subject. I brought him back.

"Well," Peter began, giggling uncomfortably, "You see, sometimes the governor of Yunnan maybe have different point of view than Generalissimo Chiang Kai-shek."

Different point of view! In two years' time the warlords, Governor Long Yun—"Dragon Cloud," another nice name, would rise against the Nationalist Government in full-scale military rebellion.

Too bad poor Peter had to be the one to give me the first hint of China's disunity, of official and private corruption in the face of the Japanese invasion, of Chiang Kai-shek's balancing act, presiding over a China on the edge of flying apart into warlordism and feudal satrapies, even on the edge of giving in to the Japanese without formally surrendering. Peter didn't say any of that. It hurt his pride to talk about it, and I didn't push him. It's the sort of thing I had to pick up from others.

Near low buildings on the edges of the airfield twin-engined transports parked, cargo doors open to trucks loading beside them. At one side of the field, near General Chennault's headquarters, sat an airfreight godown where much of our navy gear was deposited, along with in-transit army shipments. In the course of discussing the endemic problem with our allotment of Hump tonnage—as he frequently does in his book—Miles remarks that, "Colonel

Fabius H. Kohloss of Stilwell's (Services of Supply) S.O.S. in Kunming once told us, with a twinkle in his eye, that he had no authority to ship anything to Kunming for us but that he certainly did not have time to sort out the things he found in his go-downs." In charge of the godown was young Sergeant Fallon who was, I suppose, doing no more than Kohloss generously had decreed. But Sergeant Fallon did it in such a friendly, reasonable, helpful, practical, and sensible way that he more than made up for every poky interrogation I'd suffered from a self-important officer of the SOS in Assam.

Not only did I find our gear neatly segregated in a corner of Sergeant Fallon's godown—he'd taken over a small aircraft hangar—but we could take our time, no hurry about moving it. And anything else coming in—"Sure, we'll just keep bringing it in here for you." It was there that Peter, the bearers, and I began to load our trucks to take the gear out to the compound at Heilinpu.

Sergeant Fallon's was a West Virginia outfit, and his men were the same Scots-Irish and border English, the same mountain people I knew from southern Indiana. Because some of them were illiterate and others not easy with their letters, Sergeant Fallon had to handle most of the paperwork. The men learned to know markings on the boxes as hieroglyphics rather than letters of an alphabet. Sergeant Fallon set the tone for the men, too. Every day they'd be waiting to tell me if any navy gear had come in. Often I'd stand with them in the early sun, watching the morning planes arrive, showing up as dots above the mountains. They'd say, "That's a GI," meaning an army C-47 or a C-46. "That's CNAC." (China National Airways Corporation, owned by the Chinese Government with Pan American Airways as the minority stockholder.) Or, "The B-25s have come back." The hospitable godown of the West Virginians was the closest thing I had to an office in Kunming, as friendly as any office I ever worked in.

In front of Fallon's godown, the CNAC plane taxied in from Chungking or from Assam and Calcutta. People I got to know in Kunming often met there, assembling to watch the DC-3, civilian equivalent of the C-47, bump to a stop and cut off its engines. Like meeting the morning train: Friends Ambulance people, British Quakers; a Red Cross worker, also British and also a Quaker; an older American with the Office of Economic Warfare, old China hand and a preclusive buyer of wolfram to keep it from the Japanese; an American assistant military attaché who spoke Chinese, as well informed as anyone I met, often passing through Kunming on his way to other parts of China. Also to meet the CNAC plane would be the Russian officer, in khaki with a red stripe around his hat, and some standoffish French officials. Neither they, nor the Russian, were members of the set, as it were, that gathered for coffee or made up our informal luncheon club. The French had long been an influential, even colonial, presence in Yunnan, Indochina being next door. They gave the impression, intentionally I think, that the rest of us had no business there.

I met an amiable civilian pilot operating a Link trainer, an early flight simulator, on contract with the Chinese Air Force. We quickly discovered a bond between us: In New York he'd been a friend of Jess Reed, the Marine aviator killed in Surabaya a year before. It was on coming to China that I began running into friends of friends. Even if it doesn't work out that the two of you become friends, the knitting of relations across time and continents lends a new texture to existence. I remember this aviator still with warmth, as I do some other members of our eating club, even as briefly we knew each other in Yunnan.

Because of similar connections, Miles accepted Stewart and me. Admiral Purnell had recommended us for our spunk. My service in the Asiatic Fleet—Miles had two tours there—meant that I knew, if slightly, many officers well known to him. I mentioned the *Pillsbury* and Captain Pound. "Froggy Pound," said Miles. I think he was inclined to trust me because I'd known friends and classmates of his.

The everchanging membership of the eating club sampled the provincial cooking of the refugee restaurants of Kunming, not rating a place by its looks. Someone said that the more rats running over your feet under the table, the better the chef. Someone else said you could spot the finer restaurant because the rest room was a bucket by the stove in the kitchen. The best places concentrated on good cooking rather than fussing about appearances or being obsessed about sanitation.

I became obligated to these passing friends for their good company as well as for their insights, the fruits of their experience, for intelligent answers to my naive questions. There was something unusual about each of us. The Quakers, for instance, were pacifists, conscientious objectors, as acceptable as the next man to the rest of us, even admired. I was distinguished only by being younger than the rest of the CNAC-meeting-and-eating club and by being a naval officer, a rare bird in that part of China. (The eating-club crowd may have found it funny to find a naval officer in the middle of China, but they spared me the dumb remarks I had to endure from others in Kunming.)

I lived at Hostel One, on the far side of town from the airfield, closer to Heilinpu. I shared a room with a signal corps major who wore a dented campaign hat, had a jeep assigned to him, and who was nice about giving me rides to the airfield in the morning. Sometimes I walked part way into the city, before a ride turned up, along a macadam road bordered by rows of trees, green paddy fields beyond them. (In my head, I see the trees as poplars, now as willows, as eucalyptus, as casuarinas. They may have been other varieties than those I seem to remember.) A canal, maybe twenty feet across, as wide as the roadway, ran next to the road, boatmen poling their loads between the high banks. At intervals, the canal edge dropped to water level, and women knelt there to wash clothes.

Flat, two-wheeled carts, drawn by small horses, were the same kind that hauled stone to the airfield, their wheels covered with old rubber tires stuffed with straw. Aside from our army jeeps and trucks, other wheeled vehicles were battered Chinese trucks or buses, bent out of line, off-center, drifting sideways down the road like hound dogs. Many of them burned alcohol as fuel, and others had charcoal generators smoking on their sides.

Where there were houses, a gaggle of urchins danced around to give you a thumbs-up—*"Ding hao, ding hao,"* the bolder of them thrusting out dirty palms for coins. They'd escort you to the end of their territory, where you'd be picked up and stared at by a new squadron of street arabs with runny noses.

The press gangs of Governor Long Yun's army marched canalside, doing nothing to conceal their mission. French influence was shown by the elegant French casques they wore for helmets. The conscripts were bareheaded, roped together, a line running around from one neck noose to the next, hands bound behind them. Their escorts had rifles slung on their backs, long, limber whips in their hands.

Set back in from the road at the edge of the city was a colony of stucco houses in the Western style, the brass plate of consulates—Britain or France or the United States—on the fronts of several of them. The houses were painted in earth tones, what I think of now as Mexican colors. Tomato, squash, melon, they're Chinese colors, too.

A pair of American officers with stylish mustaches lived in one such house where I went more than once for drinks. They had a still on the stove, thus rendering Chinese hard liquor into something tasting less pungent, a real chemical breakthrough. The end of the coil dripped into a vessel on the stove. When an inch or two of colorless liquid had built up in it, they'd take your glass—whoever's turn it was— quickly pour the new warm batch into it, deftly returning the vessel to the stovetop. They said they worked in airways communications. Maybe they did. They were a dashing pair, and I suspected them of doing something more exciting than that, what with the house. You'd have a hard time getting to your feet when it came time to go.

The main road passing through Kunming proper was wide enough for cars to pass on either side. Offices, shops, restaurants, were at street level in the weathered two-storied wooden buildings lining the way. Cats sat in front tethered by strings around their necks. On the sides of the road, you might see baskets of dead rats, lime sprinkled on their bodies, awaiting collection, the government paying a bounty for them as a health measure. When I was there, some entrepreneurs were arrested when found to be raising rats for profit. We'd walk up side streets, too narrow for a jeep to pass, looking for the Hunan or the Muslim restaurant, for Peking duck or mushu pork, some place where one of us had eaten once or a place someone had heard about.

There was a magnificent great wooden gate in the center of the city where cars had to stop to let one another through. (A friend, who was back not long ago, told me Kunming is all high buildings now, and the gate long since torn down.) Not far from the gate, General Li gave me a fine banquet at a Yunnan restaurant, Yunnan being famous for its ham and ways of fixing it. For one course there was a large fish. I'd been warned that, as guest of honor, I'd be offered its huge eye. It wasn't as bad as it sounds—maybe a little muscular.

After another trip or two back to Chabua, in early summer, I went up to Chungking, and the Navy Group set up a proper office in Kunming, staffed with supply officers. The navy photointerpreter shop supporting the 14th Air Force grew large. I passed through Kunming again in the next two years but found it greatly changed. Friends from the eating club had moved on, too.

Chapter 15

When I got to Chungking, I learned, to my envy, that Merrill Stewart had left in June for Hunan Province to found and command Camp Two, the second field unit of the Navy Group. (Marine major John Masters had left Chungking in February for Anhui Province to start Camp One, the unit I'd been sending truckloads of arms and ammunition from Kunming.) Stewart's unit was at Nanyo, a village near the city of Hengyang, south of Changsha. Hunan means "south of the lake," the lake being Dongting Lake, the largest body of water in central China, lying between Changsha and the Yangzi River. Stewart's first task was to train a class of Chinese soldiers, but he had his eye cocked north of Camp Two, where Japanese troops were strung out through the lake country and along the river. From Nanyo, Stewart wrote me about the opportunities for offensive action he saw there. As it worked out, months later, Stewart, another navy lieutenant, Joseph Champe, and I would be looking at intelligence of Japanese dispositions in the area, seeing them vulnerable to far more damage than the hit-and-run expeditions Stew and I had been planning for Indonesia the year before.

Instead of going immediately to join Stewart, as I hoped and as Miles agreed I eventually could, I first had another spell of trouble shooting, this time as communications officer in Chungking headquarters. I was experienced at ciphering and trafficking messages and could handle that easily enough. I knew nothing about building a radio station, the urgent task I had to pick up and complete. (Actually, Miles himself knew more about radio and electronics than anyone else in headquarters, certainly far more than I.) So, always the generalist, I depended on the radiomen who were, like me, in their twenties, but good technicians. I settled in one of the bedrooms off the stone terrace, dividing my working hours between the radio shack down the hill from headquarters, listening with little comprehension to plans for a transmitting antenna, and handling messages in headquarters house, keeping my ears open in the living room presided over by Miles.

I learned of the three major problems the Navy Group was having to deal with, one being the usual trouble getting equipment over the Hump. Another problem was caused by American empire building. The Office of Strategic Services (OSS) had used SACO as a device for getting itself established in China, specifically by naming Miles as OSS chief in China and assigning OSS people to work alongside the rest of us in SACO. Now OSS was preparing to weasel out of its alliance with the Navy Group, as shown by its sending OSS people into China without informing Miles.

The senior staff of the OSS operated more like corporation lawyers—as many of them were, starting at the top with William Donovan himself—than military men. The tactic they counted on was a takeover bid in Washington. A career of dealing in a straightforward way with officers and gentlemen had prepared Miles poorly for the OSS maneuvers taking place behind his back. But the Navy Department in Washington put a stop to the OSS scheme to seize the mission and prerogatives of the Navy Group in China for OSS and put the Navy Group out of business. As a result the OSS left the Navy Group and SACO, in turn sacking Miles as head of OSS in China.

The graver problem was the difference in what Chinese and Americans wanted to come out of our joint endeavors. The Navy Group, like General Stilwell, was single-mindedly dedicated to carrying the war to the Japanese. Like Stilwell, we were running into opposition from the Chinese. Significantly, Tai Li had put a peculiar emphasis on the kinds of Americans he wanted Miles to bring into SACO, defining "old China hands" as anathema to him. You could under-stand how Tai Li, a member of the revolutionary generation, wanted no foreigners with the old treaty-port mentality sit-ting across the table from him. But Miles went overboard in deferring to Tai's presumed sensibilities, not merely barring persons of that stripe but anyone who knew anything at all about China and the Chinese. "Our recruits should not be 'old China hands,'" he wrote the Navy Department. "The less they know about China, the less they will have to un-learn. We can indoctrinate them all here, so that they will meet with Chinese approval." Whatever the benefits in good relations with the Chinese, our innocence of China and Chi-nese ways meant that we bogged down badly in the slough of Chinese manners. We wasted expensive time learning that Chinese objectives were not the same as ours. What's more, when our doubts showed themselves, the Chinese were learning—the more suave among them, anyway—what we Americans wanted to hear, and they saw to it that we were mollified, for the moment at least, by hearing it.

Quite aside from these larger considerations, I look back on that miserable summer without sentiment. Sichuan Prov-ince is famously hot and humid in the summer months. Ev-eryone of us in the valley shared that and the prickly heat, sweat popping out all over us as we drank nothing but hot tea, our main defense against polluted water. Despite that, I had constant diarrhea. With that, and the moderate diet, al-though we had enough to eat, I was fast losing weight. Stewart had packed a pair of my khakis by mistake and wrote that he'd lost enough weight at Camp Two to get into my thirty-inch waist. I wrote back that I could wrap my trousers around my waist twice now, a slight exaggeration. I was running up and down hill, always soaking wet, knowing I was in way over my head with the hateful transmitting an-tenna, and forever anxious about delays in getting material for installing it. I felt insulted, as I raced about meeting deadlines, mostly self-imposed, by having to stumble over lounging officers, push by knots of them talking, waiting noisily to be given something to do. Sorry for myself, I be-came self-important and testy. I remember hurrying through the living room late one Saturday on some vital task with a headache so strong I could hardly see. A Marine colonel for whom I had immense respect and liking, seeing that I was taking life so seriously, said: "Don't forget, Horton, you are to lead us at sunrise service in the singing of 'Jesus Wants Me for a Sunbeam.' "

I went to lie down on my bed for a minute, and that's the last I remember. Delirious with fever diagnosed as cerebral malaria, I may have had dengue fever, also known as break-bone fever for the severe pain in head and limbs. A week or ten days of August were lost to me except when I came to, once or twice, being sick into a bucket next to my bed. My roommate at the time had a lot to put up with.

When I went back to work, creeping feebly about, my ears buzzing with quinine, I was all hunched over. The strain of chills and fever had popped my intestine through its inguinal exit, so that along with other debilities, I now had an active hernia to favor. Stewart came on a visit to Chungking, and we vied with each other for gauntness. He had been in a mission hospital in Hengyang with acute bronchitis. We sat at a table in the mess hall to plot operations on Dongting Lake, the bulldog with us. He slept most of the time under the table, awaking occasionally to snuffle at us, reassured by familiar smells and voices, to drop off to sleep again.

Stewart and I briefed Miles on our plans, reminding him we'd worked well together in Australia and would make a good team for amphibious operations in Hunan. Stewart had gotten Miles to ask for Ted Cathey, our Marine comrade from Australia, to be sent to the Navy Group. Joe Champe was planning mining operations in the Yangzi River on his own, and we persuaded Miles—or so I thought at the time—that amphibious operations could best succeed with the four of us working together. Miles refused to let me go until my hernia was repaired. I didn't argue and neither did the army, accepting me as a patient in the Calcutta army hospital sight unseen. When I left in October, Miles told me to take some leave once I got that fixed. I must have looked as bad as I felt.

I took the CNAC flight to Kunming and got off the plane at the familiar parking place to pay my respects to my old West Virginia friends at the airfreight office. They shook their heads gravely when they heard where I was going. Planes had been radioing distress calls all that morning about being attacked by Japanese fighters over the Hump. Flying the Hump you had, on the one hand, the prospect of getting lost in bad weather and, on the other, of being shot down in good weather. I walked over to our CNAC pilot to be absolutely sure he had given this development his full consideration. "Never mind," he said. "There's bad weather to the east over Burma, and we'll duck into that." (It was good policy to fly CNAC because their pilots had more time over the Hump than the army's young transport pilots.) We weaved around high thunderheads, ducked into others, creaking, bouncing heavily, scud and murk blowing past outside. All you could see were the wings waving up and down until landing at Dinjan in Assam. By the time we got to Calcutta, my intestine had crept back in where it belonged. As that was the only evidence to show I was a bona fide rupture case, I worried the doctor might think me malingering. He didn't. I entered the army hospital, and my rupture was repaired.

Once out of hospital, I got together with Joe Champe who was in Calcutta making up a supply list for the Dongting Lake operation. We collaborated on a personnel list, asking for some men we knew by name. Joe was a naval academy graduate who had left the navy early and worked as an engineer. Older than Stewart and I, short of stature, he was full of energy and ideas, interested particularly in mining operations and technically gifted enough to know how to carry them out, which certainly I did not.

It was a good team. None of the three of us cared about status in a hierarchy. I knew Ted Cathey didn't. Stewart commanded Camp Two and would be responsible with Ted Cathey for training and leading the troops. Joe would handle mining and demolition operations, and I'd be in charge of the water craft. Joe and I agreed to meet in Changsha after the first of the year so I could go along on the first mining expedition in the Dongting Lake area.

I wrote Miles two letters from Calcutta about these plans, asking in one of them that Stewart come to Chungking for a final discussion to be sure we all agreed. While I didn't say so in the letters, I knew staff work was loose in Chungking, discussions ending with oral understandings, good only for the moment. Another weakness in Chungking was that schemes quickly became grandiose, once the Chinese got their hands on them. They had a keen eye for the equipment involved— "the more the better" would have made a good slogan for Tai Li and company. Champe, Stewart, and I were dedicated to starting with a simple project that we could justify, understand, and manage. I wanted to get all that nailed down tight so that we wouldn't be driven off course later on. Feeling confident about the future and happier than I'd been for months, I followed Miles's order to take some leave and went off to Darjeeling, hill station of the British raj in the Himalayan foothills.

I got back to a cold and misty Chungking valley in mid-December 1943. I was in good health and of good morale. The latter was soon to be shaken.

Stewart and Champe briefed me on a meeting I'd missed concerning our plans for Dongting Lake. Tai Li had not been present, but his leading staff members were there, and they were reshaping our plan to fit their objectives. The meeting had started off well enough, naming a Chinese commander of the operation and naming Stewart as his chief of staff. There would be ground forces for amphibious operations, a squadron of armed sampans for raiding Japanese installations and attacking their river craft, junks for transporting troops on operations, craft for minelaying, all as we had proposed. Then Tai Li was quoted, ex cathedra, no-discussion-if-you-please, as being in favor of our plan but as having decreed that one such unit was insufficient. There must be another in Anhui Province at Poyang Lake, similar country to Dongting and some two hundred and fifty miles due east of Changsha. The meeting ended by stating that the previous plan submitted, ours, that is, was "eliminated . . . because two units ought to be started simultaneously."

We were uneasy about the decision, the idea of starting a unit in Anhui being completely new to us. Joe Champe and I decided there was nothing wrong with another unit, if that's what they wanted. It needn't concern us. Because of his experience at Camp Two, Stewart was suspicious. In these meetings, he said, even if the Chinese agree with everything you say, and they never do, still nothing happens. Then you meet and go over everything again, and they agree, and again nothing happens. Stewart put this more vigorously than I do here. As a matter of fact, he got quite worked up.

There was to be another meeting with Tai Li in the chair. I was skittish about any meeting with Tai Li present. I'd been a working guest at several of the banquets Tai had given for visitors from Washington in the past year. I'd been impressed by the first one. The later ones, identically staged, the same toasts, the same speeches, identical remarks by the Chinese and, almost as predictably, the same by visiting American officers, no matter who they were, had led me to ask questions, largely of myself. Others seemed to regard those dinners as heartwarming examples of Sino-American chumminess. First thing in the evening, some remarkably handsome young women in form-fitting silken cheongsam dresses greeted you, Tai Li introducing them as former undercover agents in occupied China. Oohs and aahs from the visitors. Just as you were having fun trying your Chinese on a couple of them, gazing short-breathed into their laughing eyes—poof! They're gone. The speeches begin.

Miles had hauled me to several meetings with Tai Li on various subjects. Each one was an inoculation, raising the level of skepticism in my bloodstream. I confess I was beginning to dislike Tai, not for his reputation but from watching him at our meetings. His prominent facial feature was a lack of nose bridge between his eyes, not uncommon, but a trait exaggerated in Tai Li, giving him the look of a predatory insect, his eyes particularly protruberant. His words came in bursts of a Zhejiang provincial accent, in sibilants, hissing and clicking noises. He'd gesture with one hand in front of him, grabbing at the air, clawlike, then sum up quickly, slicing the air with one or both hands, sitting back in his chair as though the last word had been spoken on that subject. And, what's more, it usually had.

I saw him make decisions without listening to other sides of an issue, showing an arrogant narrowness of mind that could conceal from him his own limitations. I didn't like the way he dominated our meetings. Furthermore, at no meeting I'd attended had our own objectives been talked over beforehand, our tactics rehearsed, nor a distinction made between what was vital to us and what was merely convenient. If Miles had an insight into what the Chinese intended to gain from a meeting, he didn't share it with me.

As a generalization, I'd say that Americans generally don't prepare for meetings with foreigners as carefully as they should, and as the other side often does. In my own Chungking experience, we did not, and the Chinese did. And Tai Li always seemed to get his way. Of course, Miles was not required to take me, a junior officer, into his confidence before a meeting. Miles didn't like postmortems, either, and was impatient with me when I complained, as I was soon to do again, after a meeting with Tai Li.

On 19 December, eight Americans, among them Miles, Stewart, Champe, and I, trooped down a stone path to the Chinese hall: tea, hot towels, and greetings all around, eyes stinging with charcoal fumes from feebly burning braziers, Tai Li in the chair.

Expanding on our modest plan to begin at Dongting Lake, Tai Li repeated that we'd expand operations to Poyang Lake and declared that we'd start training also at Nanning in Guangxi Province and in Guangdong for operations in Canton.

Miles defended our plan of starting in at Camp Two and said we should try it for three or four months to learn from it before trying to set up training in other areas. Tai Li insisted on setting up a parallel unit under Camp One in Anhui, and just here my career took a sudden turn, although the record of the meeting does not show it. Tai Li pointed at me and said that I should be put in charge of the work in Anhui. I objected, and Miles told me to keep quiet. From there on, our plan and the meeting was transformed into a China-wide spotting of locations for amphibious operations: Dongting, three places in Poyang Lake, two places in Guangdong, two or three places on the east coast,

Fuzhou or Wenzhou and Changzhou near Amoy were mentioned—just a start, it was said at the meeting, more to be added later.

After the meeting, I protested to Miles that Tai Li had broken up a functioning team, that getting one tidy operation started was worth far more to us than great plans on paper, that Miles had been right in wanting to wait to see what we'd accomplish at Camp Two before starting other units. I thought then, as I would feel more strongly as time went on, that Tai Li preferred to mollify us with grand plans but postpone the actual operation we'd proposed. The first implied requisitions for more equipment from us without disturbing the Japanese, while one real operation meant far less equipment from us along with the threat of stirring up the Japanese. I don't remember that I had the temerity to say all this to Miles—talk like that made him angry precisely because the same points could never be far from his mind. While Miles probably was interested in the grander plan that was described at the meeting, he must tacitly have assumed concessions from Tai Li could be bought only by promises of sizable material help.

I did object that day to Tai Li's reassigning our people—me that is. But the subject was closed, and Miles told me to get ready to go to Camp One.

As it turned out, Stewart was right about the Chinese dragging their feet. By the time the Japanese launched the *Ichigo* campaign against the American airfields in the spring of 1944—five months later—no operations were underway at Camp Two. Champe had made one reconnaissance along the Yangzi, and a class of Chinese troops had started training. Stewart was having trouble getting small boats built. Camp Two itself would be abandoned when the Japanese drove south through Changsha and Hengyang in the summer of 1944.

In May, Miles sent Stewart to the the east coast to organize coast watchers near Fuzhou, putting another officer in command of Camp Two. Miles always speaks highly of Stewart and said that he relieved Stewart because of his poor health. It was true that Stewart hadn't been well. I would visit Stewart and Champe at Camp Two before going on to Camp One. Stewart was pushing his Chinese opposite number hard to get the Dongting Lake operation started. The Chinese were complaining, and I think that's why Miles felt he had to move Stewart. He wasn't getting along with the Chinese.

Miles says, "As things turned out, this sampan navy was never to be launched, for the Japanese beat us to the punch." Even though by the end of April 1944 nothing had happened, a dispatch went from Chungking to the Navy Department on the first of May repeating the decisions of the December meetings and elaborating on them. There would be "large units" at Dongting and Poyang, each with three river steamers and thirty sampans each. Smaller units at five other sites would be about half that size. The dispatch asked for 38 officers and 258 men to staff this force. The steamers and sampans were to be armed with Oerlikons and .50-caliber machine guns. So far the Navy Group had not launched one river raid. Nor any other kind for that matter.

So much for our careful planning.

Chapter 16

When Ted Cathey—now first lieutenant, USMC—arrived from Australia, we started off, four of us in two jeeps, to drive from Kunming to Camp Two near Hengyang in the province of Hunan. Ted, Lt. (jg) Guy Lloyd, a bomb disposal officer, and John Cahill, aviation machinist's mate, first class, were assigned to Camp Two. I was to take the second jeep to Camp One near Huizhou in southern Anhui Province. I'd like to have driven to Hangzhou, the closest city to Camp One, to be able to say I'd driven the first jeep all the way across China. But the Japanese garrisoned Hangzhou as, indeed, they did much of the country around Camp One. You had to watch where you were going.

I looked forward to this adventure, more expedition than mere motor trip and a lot more fun than flying. We jammed the jeeps full of freight for Camp Two, our own gear, plus gasoline. We couldn't count on finding fuel between Kunming and the railhead south of the city of Guiyang in Guizhou, the province adjoining Yunnan to the east. The railhead had reached Dushan on its way north to Guiyang, I'd learned in the course of collecting traveler's lore. I told Ted we'd been warned to look out for bandits skulking on slopes above the road, preying on travelers, deserters, mostly from provincial armies, it was said. We should keep the jeeps close together, let it be seen that we were armed, watch for ambushes at bends in the road and at blind hilltops. Deserters! Ted was indignant.

He sat with me in the lead jeep and, beginning with what

would cause a Chinese soldier to desert in wartime, asked questions about China and the Navy Group. It was easy to tell him how poorly the ordinary Chinese soldier was treated, often beginning his service conscripted by a press gang. I was careful talking about the Navy Group, concealing my bitterness at being reassigned by the imperious Tai Li, although not hiding my disappointment that we wouldn't be serving together. Ted would be hearing enough gripes about the Chinese and about Chungking headquarters without my starting in on that. Ted had the virtues of the ideal Marine. He'd put up with a lot of bitching in his time, and I didn't want him thinking less of me because of my carping about the outfit he'd just joined.

Unless it rained or was unusually cold—these were brisk winter days—we drove with the top down for visibility, visibility both ways. We wanted a good view of the terrain around and above us, and we wanted bandits to be awed by the sight of us. Sitting next to me Ted held a Thompson submachine gun across his lap, ready to advertise it. I could take a hand off the steering wheel and reach behind me and grab a carbine to wave in the air, the following jeep mounting a similar demonstration. Neither Ted nor I were fond of the Thompson, but it did make a fearful racket, and were he close by and not fidgeting about unduly, the weapon could discourage the fainthearted ambusher.

That first day, we bowled along smooth, level, dry roads through the scrubby, red-earthed, nearly deserted countryside east of Kunming. Except for the occasional truck or someone on foot, we had the road to ourselves. There were few rice paddies, mostly stunted pines on low eroded hills. We passed the desiccated body of a soldier along the road, not far out of Kunming, the rags on him so tattered that no one had passed poor enough to take them from him. Bodies of soldiers were not infrequent on roadsides, stragglers dead of sickness or malnutrition, left to crows and vultures by companions hardly in better condition than the corpse. This led Ted to consider the other side of the desertion question.

At Chanyi the road branches, one road going north to Chungking, ours east to Guiyang. Until Guiyang where another fork went north to Chungking, we'd be on the upper

leg of the old Burma Road. On this trip we were introduced
to Chinese hotels, finding little to recommend them over
the outdoors. A Chinese hotel featured creaky movement
around the building all night, shouting up and down stair-
wells, slippers scuffing along passages, hawking and spitting on the other side of a flimsy wall, an engine roaring
outside where, beneath a light powered by a noisy gasoline
generator, a truck crew assembled, tested, and disassembled
a carburetor. The hotel staff was often busy bumping furni-
ture from one floor to another, setting up dining room tables, cooking, going about seeming daytime duties during
what otherwise would have been the dead of night. Long
distance phone calls, too: every call in China was long distance, the voice of the caller rising in proportion to the distance the electric talk had to travel down the wire.

On otherwise deserted stretches, we'd glimpse soldiers in
the mist of the hillsides above our road, idle bunches of two
or three, sometimes a dozen of them. Some wore washed-
out summer uniforms of mustard yellow, blankets around
their shoulders, others in quilted jackets and trousers of
blue, faded to lavender. All wore the typical tight, round,
cloth caps with a small visor. A few slung rifles on their
backs. The first to see us would point us out to the others,
those sitting on the ground getting up to see us better,
speaking rapidly, eyes hard on us. Their very aimlessness
seemed vicious because of what we'd heard of them. But
they looked lonely, abandoned. Only one of the groups we
passed showed active hostile interest in us, waving rifles
and running down the hillside as if to intercept us. There
was a straight downgrade ahead, through boulders lining
the road, and we speeded up to whiz through before they
could reach us.

We went through or around towns and villages, mostly
around, as the old way passed by narrow cobblestoned
streets through the centers of the towns. Driving was slow,
even on the straight stretches of level road on the edge of
the villages. The children, the dogs, the hogs, the carts, all
seemed to know the threat from trucks careening down the
road. They were unused to jeeps, even less to our honking.
Once the way was parted for one jeep through the gawking

villagers they'd close up in back of us, children running behind, blocking the way of the other jeep.

We reached a walled town one night, crenellated along the top of the walls, towers on the corners. The high, roofed gate in the middle of the wall had been closed at twilight against bandits and wandering soldiers like us. Standing outside in cold and drizzle, we presented ourselves to muffled figures faintly silhouetted on the battlements against the wet sky. The great doors were pulled back barely enough to let us in, the jeep engines roaring as we passed through the narrow opening. We parked in the yard in front of the two-storied hotel whose courtyard was surrounded by galleries, a typical old Chinese inn. Hanging by their stretched necks, pressed ducks and chickens dangled like deflated footballs along the upper gallery.

On this trip as well as later on, I tried to compare what I saw in China with what I'd known before. Inevitably, finding few metaphors for China in experience, I turned to an imagined Europe of the middle ages or to my own country a century and a half before. These trite analogies were stimulated largely by surface appearances of material backwardness. Still, often I felt that I'd been transplanted in time as well as place.

Beyond Chanyi, the road began to climb. The higher we climbed, the colder it got, the road slicker, the cloud thicker around us. We could see barely a hundred feet ahead. At each climbing hairpin turn, we had to be ready for the truck, clutch out, freewheeling at us down the middle of the road. Less terrifying, but maddening, was the truck grinding uphill, refusing to move over to let the faster jeeps pass. In one prevoyage briefing, we'd been told to fire a .45 into the air. Unseemly, overbearing behavior, it was also persuasive.

The road to Guiyang was all the same, mountains, clouds, and freezing cold. We ground in low gear and four-wheel drive through the greasy muck of a climb on the Burma Road that was famous for the seventy-two hairpin turns winding up the face of one mountainside. All the others on the way to Guiyang were Chinese. We seemed to be the only foreigners traveling. Traffic was piling up, the going slow in the thick, slippery mud. Getting out to stretch our legs where our way was blocked by a stalled truck, we were soon smeared with mud to our knees. Foundered trucks were canted along the roadside, some deserted, some with crews picking over engine parts on a tarpaulin. Many trucks were loaded with heavy aircraft bombs for our air bases in Hengyang, Guilin and Liuzhou. Where trucks had collapsed on earlier days, bombs were thrown helter-skelter about on the roadside.

Clouds froze on the shrubs along the road and brown grasses were flattened by the burden of ice. We'd been complaining of the cold, sitting still in our jeeps, clad in wood ODs over long underwear, dry boots, sheepskin jackets. Then we caught up with the first soldiers—we must have passed a thousand soldiers on the road that one day—moving in formation toward Guiyang, slogging head down through slush and freezing mud, barely turning their lowered heads to see us creep by. None of the men had more than straw sandals on their feet, and many went barefooted. The cold causes the skin to crack and to gape in deep slits along the sides of the feet and ankles, flesh showing red in the crevices. At the rear of each column, as we came up on it, were the stragglers, the lame, the sick, last the litters with the dead on them, covered with straw. That they were carried we took to be a sign of a disciplined unit. You could understand the temptation to leave a dead comrade by the road rather than haul him further on that dreadful trail.

On the high plateau of Guizhou before reaching Guiyang, we ran on flat roads through the land of the people the Chinese call Miao and who call themselves Hmong. We didn't know who they were, these different-looking people. The women wore white caps, rather like the traditional Dutch woman's cap with its high crown and turned-up corners, their blue blouses cut lower than the Chinese, half exposing their breasts, below that wearing full blue skirts.

We had fuel enough to reach the U.S. Army supply post in Guiyang, but no further. The grinding climb had burned up the ration we had calculated to last us all the way to Camp Two in Hengyang. The headquarters of the Services of Supply (SOS) in Kunming had ruled that gas could be issued only by specific authorization from that headquarters. They surely would not approve of issuing it to navy travelers, I was informed flatly, and there was no point arguing about it or bothering to ask Kunming. As I turned to leave, I was greeted by an old friend, young Sergeant Fallon, late of the airfreight godown in Kunming. He completely agreed that SOS headquarters in Kunming should not be bothered. He typed up a piece of paper that I signed, obligating the navy to repay SOS for the gas he'd issued me. Thanks to Sergeant Fallon, we were able to drive south through Duyun to the railhead at Dushan, then the end of the rail line being extended from Liuzhou in Guangxi, northwest to Guiyang.

Dushan was an old city, overrun by temporary guests, a boomtown ankle-deep in mud, full of railroad workers, rain staining the new raw-pine buildings along the rutted road. As we drove into town, a half dozen young women in blue cotton gowns with slit skirts, lipstick and rouge on their broad coarse faces, were picking their way through churned-up mud on the road's edge, frowning at the remarks tossed at them by passing soldiers and laborers. When the railhead moved north to Duyun, the whole temporary population of Dushan, whores and all, would pick up and move with it.

We stayed in a new, jerry-built, leaky hotel in Dushan. The smell of pine pitch from green lumber failed to subdue the haze boiling from the ripe buckets in the latrine below the stairs. The plump hotel manager from Shanghai, in a long black gown, talked on the phone much of the night, otherwise clearing his throat to sing selections from Chinese opera in a falsetto piercing enough to vibrate right through the shrunken panels of our door.

At the railhead, we watched the jeeps being strapped on a flatcar behind the steam engine. It was a relief to get our seven hundred pounds of gear into the compartment of our train instead of having to unload it, reload it, watch it, sleep with or on it every stop along the way. The pullman car was in a state of decayed elegance, lacking everything that had made it first class except the frayed antimacassars on the tops of the seats and the courtliness of the old steward. He brought us tea and asked if we knew the foreigners who'd ridden with him when the car was new, missionaries and tobacco buyers they must have been. He remembered them all. Along the road, we'd lived off the land to save our rations for a likely emergency. Profligate now, we opened cans, supplementing the usual eggs, greens, steamed bread, endless pots of tea, with hash and stew.

Pairs of military police in good khaki wool uniforms came into the compartment to demand our papers—nothing like the soldiers on the road, these tall, well-fed fellows with their high leather boots, abrupt manners, harsh faces. Red tassels hung from the butts of semiautomatic Mauser pistols in the wooden holsters they wore at their sides. When they moved on, I got up to watch them, haughty and barking rudely at Chinese passengers.

At Liuzhou, the Guizhou-Guangxi line petered out and the Hunan-Guangxi line began, a bottleneck on the supply route caused by differently configured railway cars. The train from Liuzhou took us north along the Xiang River. Having known nothing of them, we exclaimed on seeing the karst hills of Guilin from the windows of the train. Like many Westerners, we'd thought the conical, hanging mountains of Chinese classical painting to be traditionally stylized versions of entirely imaginary landscapes. The hills around Guilin, although different from the equally surprising sacred mountains of Huang Shan (Yellow Mountain) in Anhui Province, are, like them, models for these representations.

When we got to Camp Two, I learned that Stewart had finished training one class of soldiers. He was waiting for a second draft of students. He'd wait five months before they appeared. When I loaded a jeep at Hengyang for the first lap on the road to Camp One, Stewart and Joe Champe were determinedly heading north to Changsha to try again to prod the Chinese into action.

Three of us, Sgt. E. P. Jensen, USMC, a Chinese cook named Tai, and I, took a jeep to Camp One. The direct route goes northeast from Hengyang straight to Huizhou in the far south of Anhui, but the Japanese sat athwart the northern half of Jiangxi Province around Poyang Lake. So we'd drive south first, then dogleg northeast through

Jiangxi to Anhui, Japanese to the west of us, Japanese to the east holding parts of Fujian and Zhejiang provinces. Maps of that time show a thumb-shaped salient of free China pointing toward Hangzhou. Right at the top of the thumbnail was Huizhou and our destination, Camp One. From Hengyang, another flatcar took the jeep south to Shaoguan, and there we put the jeep on the road, heading north-northeast into the thumb.

Tai, slight in build, pale and shy, spoke English, Cantonese, and Mandarin. He wore a light blue *zhongshan* suit and cap with the blue and white Guomindang sun as a cap device. Assigned to the kitchen staff at Camp One, he would serve as our guide and interpreter on the way there. Tai was sensible but nervous, an apprehensive expression showing often in his large brown eyes. Seeing no apparent cause, I speculated Tai might have been pressed into Tai Li's culinary service with the additional duty of informing on the Americans. A gentility about him seemed inconsistent with the role of either kitchen help or informant. He never gave me reason to think my idle suspicion was true.

He and Sergeant Jensen were good traveling companions, despite silences that might last for an hour, Jensen so taciturn that I had to pull comments out of him. I laid this to a Scandinavian reserve, but he was a free enough spirit, I observed later, in the company of other Marines. During our drive, when I tried to get a conversation going, I might elicit no more than a syllable from each of them.

There were German Christian missions along the way, we knew, with a reputation for correct hospitality, if not warmth, for American travelers. I thought staying with them would put a needless strain on both sides. We did stay at a Belgian mission, set among green fields and orange groves—somehow anomalous—at Nanfeng. Our hosts, the priests, served an elegant liqueur they made of the oranges. The mission doctor was a refugee from Germany who'd served as an infantry officer in the German army in the 1914–18 war. He was courteous enough to an American officer, but still a patriotic German, unhappy that the Russians were then pushing the German armies back in the Ukraine. He was another anomaly, slumped in his chair, insisting that he was as good a German as any Nazi—they had no right to consider him anything less for being a Jew.

On the walls of every mission we visited were faded sepia portraits, enlarged photographs of priests or of ministers and their wives and children. The portraits had been hung to honor these martyrs, murdered by Chinese Nationalist troops during the Northern March of 1927 or in the early 1930s by the Chinese Communists when Mao Zedong had his stronghold in Jiangxi Province.

One day, we passed through sterile stretches of fields, rough and grown over, deserted villages without life, not a pig or a chicken, the roof joists fallen in, the walls crumbling, the doors stove in. I know now that we'd passed through the area of the Jiangxi Soviet, one of several enclaves the Communists held in south China ten years before our passage. The Jiangxi Soviet became the best known of these bases after the apotheosis of Mao Zedong who had been in charge there. Under siege by the Nationalists, the Communists broke out to the west from these fastnesses, thus beginning the Long March that ended a year later in Yan'an. The Nationalist troops had scorched that earth after the Communists left.

At the time, I asked Tai to explain the desolation. If he knew the answer, and he may well have, he told me nothing. We'd get used to our Chinese colleagues treating the Communist question like a shameful family secret, looking shocked if you brought it up.

The lack of bridges over rivers slowed us down. A dozen times, we waited in a line of trucks to squeeze our jeep aboard a ferry. Some might hold no more than a jeep and one truck. The ferry might be a set of planked-over oil drums hooked to a cable spanning a river, the ferry being set at an angle to the current so that the flow of the river pushed it across. Much of the road followed broad valleys, and sometimes the old route ran straight from us to Japanese-held towns, the fork running north from Nanfeng being an example. At various points, the Chinese had ditched across the width of the road to keep Japanese vehicles from driving right into our salient. I knew that. Yet, more than once at a fork in the road, I questioned Tai closely to be sure we were taking the proper one—we had no reliable map. I didn't question Tai's good faith, but I could think of nothing more humiliating than motoring carelessly into the arms of the Japanese.

Days of rain had wet us and our gear until we had nothing dry to put on when we arrived at Huizhou, soaking wet. While the jeep was welcome, my coming could have been awkward. Masters hadn't asked for me. I'd been assigned by Miles, by Tai Li actually, to run Camp One's own amphibious project in Poyang Lake. (I never did, by the way.) Masters was happy with his competent executive officer, then 1st. Lt. Earle Dane, USMC. Outranking Dane, I became Masters's executive officer. Neither Masters nor Dane, who could have resented my bumping him from the exec's job, was ever anything but generous to me.

Chapter 17

Maj. John H. Masters, USMC, had left Chungking for Anhui Province with five other Americans in February 1943 to establish Camp One. He chose a site at the edge of a village near the city of Huizhou, often known as Shexian nowadays, the capital of Shexian County. The Americans took over the grounds of a temple on the riverbank, setting up housekeeping in temple buildings and a pagoda, eventually putting up other small buildings for quarters. Masters's opposite number, Gen. Guo Lizhou, and his staff occupied quarters in the village, next to the temple grounds, and space was set aside as barracks for the troops that were to come for training.

An incidental feature of the site was the natural beauty of its setting, although it had not been chosen for that reason. The green river curves around the site, running fast over the dark sand and shingle of the beach in front of the camp. The presence of the Americans didn't keep the village women from washing their clothes as they had forever, more or less, before the foreigners came, nor did it prevent the village children from playing on the parade ground that overlooked the river when it was free of classes or formations. The opposite bank of the river was steep, suitable for the butts of a rifle range, the students firing across the river from the camp side. The range was dug below and well to one side of the whitewashed buildings of the Buddhist monastery that looked down on the camp from the heights of the far side.

The village, Xiongcun, "Heroes' Village," is some seven hundred air miles east of Chungking and a five-mile walk over stone paths from Huizhou. The city of Hangzhou is a hundred miles east and slightly north of Xiongcun, great Shanghai twice that distance to the northeast. Both cities were occupied, of course, by the Japanese in those days. The enemy also occupied the nearby country to Masters's east in the province of Zhejiang, as well as the areas to his north and to his west.

A romantic description of the situation of Camp One is "behind the Japanese lines," useful to impress the folks at home or to puff up a unit history. There were no lines, actually, but rather areas that the Japanese dominated. We could survive in this piece of occupied China because it was mountainous and thus ideal for guerrilla warfare. Japanese garrisons held the towns, set up strong points at bridges, patrolled the railway line. We had the mountains and the help of local people. But the camp was not defensible against the Japanese. Sudden Japanese troop movements to the north of Camp One in early October 1943 led to Masters's sending extra personnel and supplies downriver to Chun'an. After the Japanese movement was judged to be the usual rice drive to seize the autumn harvest, the camp settled back to normal. We were never directly threatened in that way again.

Rather than a matter of lines, it was a matter of where you felt comfortable. We were confident those days on the Anhui side of the Qiantang River. The river, running north to empty into the sea at Hangzhou, is not the boundary between Anhui and Zhejiang provinces, but it became our practical, neighborhood boundary between free and occupied China. In Huizhou and the nearby towns of Tunxi and Chun'an, we Americans went about freely, and except some Korean assassins the Japanese sent at us, we were ordinarily as safe in our salient as if we'd been in Kunming or Chungking. Actually, we were comparatively safe in the Japanese-occupied areas of Zhejiang if we stayed in the mountains. Zhejiang Province was one of the three Chungking had assigned Camp One as our operational area, Anhui and Jiangsu being the two others. We were shy about moving into the flat delta country along the Yangzi River in central Anhui and Jiangsu. No place to hide.

Masters had as difficult a time getting settled as did Stewart at Camp Two. The first class of Chinese students did not appear for training until August, a good five months after the arrival of the Americans at Camp One, and he never did find out the real reason for the delay. In September 1943, he wrote:

> In plans and operations . . . we have no real authority. Our services are utilized mainly in giving technical assistance and in an advisory capacity. All of the troops come under the control of the Chinese authorities, and there is a hesitancy on their part to allow us to plan an operation for them or to let us participate in the operation. This, of course, applies to any operations in the field—training here at the school is almost wholly in our hands.

Those last sentences summarize the division of labor as the Chinese side preferred it: the Americans did the training, stayed away from operations and—this last point is important—handed out arms to the students who had completed the training. The apportioning of arms was an occasion for dispute between Chinese and Americans. The Chinese took the stand that every student brought in for training should be armed by the Americans. The Americans said that the student should have shown himself apt before being equipped. As the etiquette for this worked out over time, the Chinese brought in x number of candidates for a training class. The Americans then weeded out the seriously unfit and the children—no exaggeration, that—and trained the rest. At the end, weapons were handed out to the students who were judged to be qualified in their use.

"In training," said the same September report, "we have given each man instructions in each of the different weapons, viz.: Springfield Rifle, .30 cal. Carbine, Thompson Submachine gun, and Colt Automatic pistol. This was done with the original class at the request of

the Chinese authorities because it was not known with
what weapons these men would be supplied."

And, when that class had been trained, Masters discovered that

> Future requirements in weapons and demolitions depends
> (sic) on how many students are trained at this school and
> what type of military operations they are assigned to
> carry out. As yet, I have absolutely no information as to
> when I will receive more students, or what they will do
> when they complete their training. Training can be facil-
> itated if we can be given definite information as to when
> a group will arrive here, what that group is being trained
> for, how much time will be allotted for training, and
> where the group will be assigned to operate when it com-
> pletes its training.

Here was the running disagreement. The Chinese command wanted our arms and equipment. We expected the
students, once trained and given arms, to operate against
the Japanese. We wanted to take part in the operations,
eager to go after the Japanese as well as to confirm that the
weapons and training were being used as the Chinese
claimed. The intense interest of the Chinese command in
the distribution of arms at the end of training, compared
with their faint interest in the training itself, showed where
their hearts were.

The September 1943 report also included this:

> One factor which governs the training and operations of
> guerrilla forces is the attitude regarding the Japanese re-
> prisal system which prevails in China. The Japanese as-
> sign villages, towns, cities, and sections of cities certain
> zones of responsibility, and if aggressive action is taken
> by the Chinese in or near an assigned zone, the civilian
> population is ruthlessly punished. This reacts in two
> ways. In the first place, the guerrillas themselves hesitate
> to do anything which will subject innocent civilians to
> punishment. The second reaction is that the villagers for

well grounded reason are forced under the system to report any activities which might indicate guerrilla work in their areas. Both of these factors militate against any large scale accomplishment by guerrilla forces. Any work undertaken must necessarily be on an extremely small scale and only under the most favorable circumstances.

The only telling argument the Chinese command could bring against our zeal for operations was the Japanese readiness to punish the innocent for guerrilla actions. That went to our consciences, irritated as we might be when the argument was used hypocritically to keep us out of mischief.

We kept on pushing for operations, but it was their country, so we kept on training. By the end of 1944, more than 4,500 Chinese soldiers had been trained at Camp One. The training in guerrilla warfare was good: small arms and hand grenades, musketry, scouting and patrolling, ambushes and raids, night operations, unarmed combat. I taught demolitions classes in the spring and early summer of 1944. (The soldiers enjoyed seeing things blown up and especially liked making booby traps, becoming carried away with joy at seeing an innocent spring one.)

With Jensen's and my arrival in March 1944, there were eight officers at Camp One, five Marines, three navy—the doctor, the paymaster, and me—and thirty-two men, navy and Marines. Despite the statement in the Camp One monthly report in March 1944 saying: "No additional Americans are needed in this camp," in July, eight more navy men came. (Two of them were aerographers, accompanied by three other weather specialists from the 10th Weather Squadron of the army air forces. They did valuable work, separate from other camp activity.) In October 1944, two ensigns and ten more navy men arrived. From then on, we had some fifty Americans at Camp One.

In July 1944, a medical unit of three doctors, a dentist, and a dozen navy corpsmen, was sent to support the Loyal Patriotic Army (LPA), the Chinese unit that furnished most of the trainees to Camp One. We were responsible for Pact Doc's security and communications. The medical unit was two-days' walk to the north of us. Another day beyond that was the headquarters of the LPA at Wangjiaqiao—the Wang family bridge.

Fifteen or so more people than needed at Camp One, plus Pact Doc, added administrative headaches that a leaner outfit would not have suffered. Had we had been content to sit back and do nothing but train Chinese and keep house, it would not have been a bad life for the American officers and men.

The so-called wardroom for the officers was simply the central hall of the officers' quarters. Rooms off to the side—cells, really—were where we slept. There was hardly room for the two double bunks in the room I shared for a time in 1944 with Lt. Milton A. Hull, USMC, and Lt. Walter D. Pickerell, USMC. The bedsprings were a netting of rough, reddish rope, eventually sagging into a hammocklike pouch that called for restringing. Doctor Tucker came by to grumble if we didn't rig our mosquito nets at night.

The table in the central room, the wardroom, was used for eating, for typing, for enciphering and deciphering dispatches on a small hand-powered cipher machine, for letter writing, for drinking tea and arguing, for cribbage, checkers, backgammon, poker, and bridge. For privacy, you went walking along the river bank.

Peanut Hull, built like the star football player he had been in college, showed the natural attributes of leadership that some big men have—easygoing, friendly, always greeting everyone cheerfully by name. I learned that year that Peanut was also valiant, energetic, spirited, a top-notch young officer, and fun to be around. Peanut—the nickname he'd brought with him hardly fitted, but that's how we knew him—had a Florida accent and a surprisingly high voice for his size.

Until we tired of it, Peanut and Abie Pickerell and I set booby traps around each others' beds, firecrackers of instantaneous fuse or a blasting cap, nothing lethal. We'd often forget what we'd done and spring it ourselves—perhaps why we gave it up. Pickerell had a bad knee and took to going about with a cane. Doctor Tucker certified him unfit, and he was ordered home in the autumn of 1944. After he left, it was said, quite unfairly, that once out of sight of camp on the way into Huizhou, he threw the cane into the rice paddy and ran for it. He had talked so much of his previous service in the London embassy that he was accused of finding service in China inferior.

Outside our door was a walled yard, a compound formed by a storeroom at the other end that served also as the camp bar or club. In good weather, we'd sun outside in the compound and have a drink of one homemade liquor or another at sundown. Often the farmer would pick that time to trot by with honey pots on a shoulder pole. He'd dip the liquid fertilizer into furrows of the vegetable garden outside our walls. A miasma strong enough to make the landscape shimmer would creep over the walls and spread around us, sending us coughing into the wardroom. The smell of human fertilizer in the fields was so constant that we were hardly aware of it; when freshly put down, it caused the eyes to tear up no matter how hardened you'd become.

Our river raced green and clear in front of the camp, a refreshing bath on a hot day. You'd tiptoe barefooted, in skivvy shorts, upriver from one end of camp, to leap in, fending yourself off rocks, bouncing through the rocky shallows, as the camp raced past on the shore. You had to claw your way out over the rocks at the end of the run or be carried, we said, inaccurately, right down to Hangzhou. Tucker remarked at lunch one day that the snails in the shallows were hosts for schistosomiasis, a filariasis that causes, among other things, elephantiasis. We had a few exemplary cases in the surrounding villages, one symptom being an extraordinary enlargement of the testicles. It was enough for Peanut to hear the affliction might bring on impotence and he gave up swimming. I continued to ride the rapids on Tucker's assurance that, by keeping out of the still waters along the river's edge, one could avoid the fluke.

During the rains of the spring and fall equinoxes, the river would lap up along the beach and surge past the camp in brown waves, tossing up logs, the odd dead chicken or swollen dog rolling by. Persistent heavy rains forced us to suspend training, leading to bouts of poker or bridge in the wardroom, interrupted only for meals. We began to play a version of poker called red dog by rules that led to the pot in the middle of the table to go from nothing to a large amount in stunning geometrical bounds. More than once, when he was losing heavily, Bud Masters would get up from the table and Spurgeon Benjamin, the paymaster, would groan, "Sir! Colonel Masters, please? Oh, no."

Masters would come back from his room with a squat, black-leather bag he kept under his bed. Of a kind you don't see any more, with its brass lock and black-leather handle, the flexible top opened a wide mouth to reveal the commanding officer's confidential funds. Benjamin had to count and certify the funds were there at the end of the month. He needn't have taken on so. Masters always put the money back. It was conniving at gambling with public funds that frightened Benjamin.

Masters took me with him when he called on General Guo, the Chinese camp commander, so that I would get to know Guo and his staff, be able to represent Camp One in Masters's absence. We'd walk across the temple grounds to the high blank wall of a somber gray building, a door and some widely spaced windows the only openings in its bleakness.

Along that gray wall, to the left, at an open window was the telephone, manned by the sergeant operator, a former hostler—*mafu*—retreaded to care of the telephone, there being no horses. You'd tell him to ring up LPA headquarters and ask one of the American friends up there to the phone. You'd wait, standing on one foot and then another, walk around outside, come inside to sit down, the hostler grinning and nodding, his free hand wiping the gray stubble on his shaved head as he shouted into the phone. *"Wei!"* he'd shout—"Hello!"—over and over.

The hostler was usually good for a ghost story. All the soldiers and the villagers believed in ghosts. That's not the way to put a matter of fact. You might as well ask one of them if he believed in pigs, if there really were such things as ducks. We ran a patrol of our own at night to check on the camp sentries. One night, a sentry box was turned over, door down, to teach the old soldier asleep inside a lesson.

The work of a ghost, the hostler reported the next day. The wispy figure crossing the paddies at dusk, the light floating along a path across the river—all ghosts and devils: *guizi*, the same word as the devil in foreign devil, Japanese devil, and no less real than the others.

After greeting the hostler, you'd pass through a door and turn right, go through an inner door, and that was General Guo's office. A call on Guo began with ceremony, bowing—Americans bobbing their heads awkwardly—and asking after each other's health. We'd sit in Guo's cold office and wait for the tea to be brought, wrapping hands gratefully around the hot cup. He might have a charcoal brazier burning on the floor. His office was no colder than the wardroom. Not until the end of 1944 did we have a fifty-five-gallon drum for a stove in the wardroom, whereupon we all immediately caught colds.

Ordinarily, unless anger broke out into rudeness, Guo followed the etiquette of circling around the subject for a while before getting to the point. He was always in uniform, a Sam Browne belt distinguishing him from inferior officers, the blouse and trousers quilted in winter. He had high cheek bones, a wide, thin-lipped mouth, the kind of nostrils you could see straight into if you wanted, and he wore black-rimmed eyeglasses. He smiled a good deal, toothily, out of politeness, occasionally with amusement. He had an unenviable job, fending off our requests—sometimes demands.

Often, when we were in General Guo's office, the hostler would be bawling into the phone, arguing with an operator somewhere on the line. You and Guo and the interpreter would have to move your chairs closer, put your heads together, repeat what you'd said. We haggled more or less politely about some point or other: the training schedule, the charcoal supply, gasoline for the generator that powered our radio transmitter. We paid for supplies, but they were hard to get. And there was always the question of Guo and his people squeezing an exorbitant commission out of the price we paid. Some of the other Americans fretted about squeeze more than I ever did. A general in the Chinese army, thanks to inflation, got a salary of maybe ten American dollars a month—less than that as inflation worsened.

The budget to run the camp—and to feed the students, who we were always insisting be better fed—was low to begin with and gravely trimmed by inflation. I assumed that Guo and his supply people chiseled us and I didn't see how he could have managed otherwise. I doubted he was getting rich from it.

We'd see Guo socially at banquets, at ceremonies, such as graduation of a class, or when invited to hear a visiting Chinese opera company. The opera came courtesy of the Chinese equivalent of our USO. A session lasted for hours, and a troupe stayed for days. After the first one, most Americans had to be ordered to attend their second. Sometimes we'd see Mrs. Guo, attractive enough to get our avid paymaster sidling up to her closer than social distance of either culture allowed.

We constantly insisted with Guo that we start operations against the Japanese. We knew this was out of his hands. Gen. Ma Qiqiao, commanding the LPA, had to agree. So did the Third War Zone commander, directly under Chungking. So did Tai Li. We pestered Guo so he'd pass the word on to General Ma and to Tai Li. We cultivated our obsession and Guo got thoroughly sick of it.

Chapter 18

Admiral Miles was surely as eager as we were to get the Americans at Camp One into action. He had definite ideas for missions in our area of operations, shown as early as August 1943 in a memorandum he wrote Tai Li on the occasion of the graduation of the first training class at Camp One. There, he suggested the huge railway and highway bridge over the Qiantang River at Hangzhou as a target for sabotage. He pointed out that Japanese troops occupied the area of the railway line running from Hangzhou to the city of Jinhua in Zhejiang Province east of Camp One. (Jinhua was one hundred miles southeast of us.) He suggested that railway bridges and sections of track be destroyed.

Miles would remind Tai Li of these missions when the two of them came to Camp One on an inspection of east China in June 1944. At the same time, Bud Masters had been promoted to lieutenant colonel and ordered home to a new assignment in the Marine Corps. Maj. Charles Parkin, AUS, had served as Masters's executive officer in 1943 until recalled to OSS. OSS had released him when he asked to be reassigned to Camp One, and he was to take over from Masters.

Miles reached Camp One on 4 June 1944 and talked with us until Tai Li arrived on the sixth. Miles was a good listener. He was impressed by the morale of the Americans at Camp One, and by the zeal of our young Marine officers in particular. When Tai Li arrived, Miles raised our morale a notch by backing our drive to get into operations. He

went further than we ever had by trying to get Tai to agree
to Marine officers leading Chinese troops in combat. Miles
reported to the Navy Department in Washington that he had

> two purposes: (1) to give the Chinese some ideas on
> leadership, and (2) to give our people a little pep. Gen-
> eral Tai, like the rest of the Chinese, will not permit this.
> He is perfectly willing to take command of Americans,
> but will not reverse the process. Why this exists I cannot
> say. It is perhaps because they feel that we would be
> treading on their sovereign rights by taking command of
> their troops. I wonder if the English feel the same way
> when we take command of their troops.

It was just after D day and that's what put the compar-
ison in Miles's mind. I would have been surprised had Tai
agreed. Miles went on to say that

> (Tai Li) has agreed that the Americans going into the
> field should have supervisory powers and he has stated
> that if the Troop Commander does not carry out his ad-
> vice he should be executed.

This, it may not need saying, was poppycock. Refusing
to let Americans command Chinese, as was Tai Li's prerogative, he tried to cover over his refusal by volunteering this
dramatic and unabashedly false offer to sacrifice a Chinese
officer over a difference of opinion. Miles continued:

> (Tai) has stated that he will issue the necessary orders to
> the Commanding Officers of the troops which are ac-
> companied by the Americans. In such cases the Ameri-
> cans will be responsible for planning an operation and
> for supervising its carrying out. I asked him to define
> (sic) the limits of this authority. He said that when the
> American says that a job must be done, he will tell the
> Troop Commander his plan for accomplishing this job
> and will lay before him all the details for doing it, in-
> cluding the time and methods (the time portion of this is
> of considerable importance). Once the plan has been de-

cided upon the troop will carry it out as planned and the American will supervise it. The supervision will take the form of constant inspection and if the American sees something is being done wrong, he will inform the Troop Commander that is not the way to do it, but to do it this way.

Without challenging the ambiguities here proposed by Tai Li, Miles followed up with a memorandum of understanding in which Tai Li agreed—for the moment—to five groups of American officers and men going off "to supervise" graduates of the current training class in sabotage operations. Targets were those Miles had specified previously. (He named me, a Marine sergeant, and a pharmacist's mate, to "river raider supervision," a shred of the tattered plan that Stewart and Champe had been struggling to put across in Hunan.)

We'd given Miles a full briefing on the treatment of the Chinese troops, starting with their being roused before dawn by bugles—as were we, but that wasn't the reason for our complaint. Mustered on the parade ground, they'd sing the doleful hymn, *"San Min Zhu Yi"*—the Three Peoples' Principles—or the rousing patriotic song *"Qi Lai,"* then be harangued by General Guo or his political officers for an hour or more on the thoughts of Sun Yat-sen and the Confucian homilies of the generalissimo. We couldn't object to this boring and sacred regimen—it was probably worse on the Communist side—but we told Miles the students were always worn out. We had complained to Guo about the hiring out of the students as corvée labor, taking time from class to repair roads, sometimes working all night, showing up in time for morning indoctrination. We told Miles about the poor health of the students and the little we could do to make up for their lack of medical care. Dr. Tucker and his pharmacist's mates ran a clinic to treat the common complaints, scabies, trachoma, leg ulcers, but Chinese pride prevented our supplementing the troops' poor diet in their two meals a day.

In the letter to Washington, Miles went on to speak of what we found most objectionable in the treatment of the

Chinese troops by their superiors, going beyond callousness to brutality.

> I had a rather heated session with (Tai Li) yesterday about the mistreatment of Chinese troops by the Chinese officers ... on the firing range the trooper will miss the bull's eye or fail to squeeze the trigger and he will get batted one from behind or kicked in the ribs. ... one officer batted a soldier over the head with a small stool. ... The day I arrived here the Company Commander of one company batted a student across the face with a belt and the belt buckle hit the student in the eye. ... and it appears he may possibly lose the eye. ... Dr. Tucker was ordered by Colonel Masters to supervise the treatment of the student. ... I told General Tai if that particular thing was done in the presence of an American Officer it might create a serious rift between us. ... (one of our people) would most certainly lose his temper and slap the officer down and perhaps kill him. General Tai agreed that perhaps that would be a good thing. I told him that under no circumstances would I want that to happen, but he had to issue orders that no student would be physically punished by anyone while in our training classes. ... He said that was a good idea and immediately went out to find out all about the student who had been hit in the eye.

We admired Miles for putting these cases directly to Tai Li. We didn't expect bad officers to reform any more than we expected Tai Li easily to give us our head in operations against the Japanese. But Miles had put Tai Li on notice and elicited lip service to Miles's vigorous if courteous testimony. We told Miles, too, of the obvious difference between the way many—not all—of the Chinese officers and the Americans treated the students. We saw signs that the best of the Chinese officers and noncommissioned officers were paying attention to the way our people respected the Chinese in the ranks. Good Chinese officers didn't need our example in leadership. It was rather that they appreciated it.

At this time, a landing on the China coast was much on

Miles's mind. "When I had been in Washington a couple of months earlier, Admiral King had given me important new instructions. 'Be ready on the China coast,' he had told me, 'for Fleet landings possibly by December.' That had been in March 1944 and now it was May."

"Six months," Miles wrote later. "'That was all the time we had to make our preparations for the Fleet landings. . . .'" As late as November 1944, a landing—or a variation of it— was still on the agenda in Washington.

> In view of Japanese successes inside China, the increasing difficulty of supplying China from India and the increasing importance of preventing the Japanese from withdrawing forces from China in order to increase their strength elsewhere, what support can now be given from the Pacific? Before undertaking an amphibious assault and subsequent major land fighting on the China coast, to what extent can we conduct "Philippine Express" and "Marianas Express" operations to unoccupied or lightly defended points (on the China coast)?

We knew in June, as we'd assumed right along, that a landing was being considered. (In a small notebook I kept, I find a nearly illegible list of intelligence requirements I passed on later that summer to a Chinese general in Zhejiang Province. Among others, "defense fortifications such as forts or guns which the Japanese have or intend to install along the coast and in defense in depth back from the coast," and questions on enemy order of battle, ship-repair facilities, communications in coastal areas and behind the coast. I wonder now whether I was an unwitting participant in a program to deceive the Japanese.)

A landing on our China coast would have suddenly taken us from the end of the line into the vanguard of the fight. It wasn't the first thing on our minds, though. We were pressing for local objectives, and Miles's agreements with Tai Li on 8 June were consistent with our ambitions. The landings on the China coast never did take place. With the capture of Iwo Jima in February 1945, according to Miles, "all these potential mainland efforts were left completely astern. . . ."

Shortly after Miles left, and consistent with the understanding he'd reached with Tai Li, Peanut Hull and I and our party of a pharmacist's mate, a gunner's mate, and three Marine sergeants, left for the Wang family bridge, seat of Gen. Ma Qiqiao, commander of the LPA. I was to spend the summer either at General Ma's or hiking about Anhui and Zhejiang Provinces before getting back to Camp One.

It was a hot, three-day, June walk north to Wangjiaqiao. The last day, we were honored by General Ma's sending an officer with hostlers and horses to meet us. All but one were scrawny little things, maybe a hand or so taller than a Cavite calesa pony. Peanut, being the heaviest of us, got an exceptional animal, a thickset Mongolian gelding of a light chestnut red with a graceful swinging trot. Peanut knew how it hurt to see him instead of me astride this Tang horse brought-to-life. He turned in the saddle to cackle at me over one shoulder.

We had to try to ride apart from each other. Except Peanut's placid Mongolian, the little beasts went after each other with their teeth or ran sideways to kick, carrying on their feuds without regard for their riders. We might as well have had no reins or the horses no bits in their tough mouths. The hostlers carried long, limber whips—the kind the sergeants in Kunming used on the conscripts—and ran alongside to lash the horses for misbehaving. My horse, when not attacking his own kind, rolled the whites of his eyes at me, gnawing at my knee with yellow teeth.

Ma received us with a banquet, where we exchanged endless toasts to each others' governments and people, to victory, in good Shaoxing wine. The Chinese officers put their minds to getting you drunk at these banquets, singling out a victim—often me as senior American officer present—and ganging up for one toast after another. And the finger game where you were required to shout your guess at the total number of fingers displayed by your fist and your opponent's.

The site of headquarters proper was a farmstead, set in a bamboo grove at the foot of a hill, a flatness of rice paddies beyond the thickets. Ma put us up in a grand house, now used as a rice granary. The American and Chinese members of our party—there was always at least one interpreter with us at Ma's—sat on stools at a round table set near the door in the great central hall. We ate better than a Chinese soldier but, over the summer, all of us lost weight. The summer of 1944 was a time of drought, and the farm people wisely kept their animals back in case they needed to eat them come winter. Thus, we took our rice with eggs and greens. For breakfast we ate *xifan*, a hot gruel of wet rice, accompanied by pickled vegetables. With little taste for the pickles, we tried to get *youtiao*, crullers, twists of deep-fried dough, enough like doughnuts to make you homesick. Walking for days on that diet or on less, as we did that summer, did trim a body. I was down to a hundred and ten pounds by October.

Peanut and I shared a room and slept in ancient, roofed Chinese beds, carefully tucking the mosquito net all around the bedroll, less against mosquitoes than the rats that scuttled about all night on the rice sacks. Even if you exercised due care, a rat would sometimes get in with you. The rat was not keen on staying, once he found you there, and the game from there on was to see who could get out of the net first.

General Ma, a Mongol from the northwest—they're all named Ma, meaning horse—was short, with a frog face, large prominent eyes, words croaking from a wide-lipped mouth; really froggy. He was always courteous to my face when I pressed him to get some operations going but, as time went on, became less and less available. I'd have to wait, days sometimes, to see him. He was traveling or in conferences or not well. Actually, he was in poor health, and our being there did not improve it. The whole game with Ma was one of waiting. We spent the summer waiting to sally forth with his troops. Ma waited for us to give up and go home. We wouldn't let him forget the commitments Tai Li had given Miles in early June. Tai Li had come up to Wangjiaqiao to visit Ma after the visit to Camp One—no way of knowing what he'd really said to Ma of the agreement with Miles. I doubt that he ordered Ma to comply.

"Unit One spent a long and unprofitable time trying to cajole and at length to force General Ma (Commander LPA) to allow operations in his area," Charlie Parkin, now commanding Camp One, wrote to Miles in the autumn of 1944:

In my opinion Gen. Ma, for understandable reasons and also for reasons not too clear, does not want to be bothered with Americans in his operational area. Some of these reasons I would say are the following:

The fear that some Americans will be killed or hurt since he has been told by General Tai that he is *personally* responsible for the safety of Americans.

I believe this order of Tai's has done much to hamper Americans getting out and seeing anything.

His dislike of advice (especially from American junior officers).

The political situation in the Yangzi area. The fact that there are Communists there (although well-known to us now was not known for certain last summer). Also the various Central Govt. and Puppet setups that Ma has might become compromised by a threat of operations in the area.

Ma's unwillingness for Americans to check on just how much operation is going on in the LPA area.

Ma is obviously saving much of the material given him, whether for assistance in the landings or for other reasons I don't know.

Ma does not want the Japanese to get hot and bothered by the Americans in the area and start pushing about with punitive expeditions.

In an earlier letter Parkin had cited another reason why he thought "the Chinese do not at present wish to leave or have Americans deep in the Yangzi Basin. (General Ma seems to be especially anxious to keep Americans out because of political pressure from head city leaders in occupied areas.)"

Parkin is right about Ma and his reasons. That's a good analysis of senior Chinese officers in general. I doubt, though, that Ma was husbanding any gear against the day of a landing on the coast. Ma and the others, both Nationalist and Communist commands, were playing a bigger waiting game—waiting for the Americans to defeat the Japanese and saving their own strength for the coming civil war.

Chapter 19

One of the targets assigned us by Miles was the bridge over the Qiantang River at Hangzhou. Curiosity led me recently to look up the entry for Hangzhou in the *Encyclopaedia Britannica*. "A railroad bridge over the Qiantang River was completed in 1937," says the entry, "but it was destroyed in December of that year when the city fell into Japanese hands." ("Damaged" would be a more appropriate word than "destroyed," apparently.) As I remember, Chungking sent us either bridge plans or dimensions from which we knew it was a formidable target in size alone. That gave us nowhere near enough information to plan an attack. In late 1943, Charlie Parkin, through General Guo, had sent at least two agents to report on the bridge. While the record is not clear, Parkin himself may have briefed and debriefed one or both of the agents. The description of the bridge and its defenses submitted by the second agent gave us a better idea what we'd be up against.

The Qiantang river bridge has 13 archways. At each end of the bridge there is a sentry platoon comprising a strength of 40 men. In the center of the bridge there is a sentry squad of 12 men. Beside the sentries there are about 10-15 gunners in the middle of the bridge.

The agent also reported that "The enemy division stationed in the city of Hangzhou (has) about 10,000 men." The difference between his figure and our higher estimate of Japanese troops in the Hangzhou area had no effect whatsoever on our estimate of risk. The Japanese troops stationed on the bridge were enough by themselves to strongly suggest our approaching the bridge by water.

I'd listened to Joe Champe on this. The Champe method employed a pair of sampans, linked by a line of the proper length to hold them on either side of a single bridge pier. The sampans would be loaded to the gunwales with TNT or plastic explosive and drifted downstream on either side of the pier. The current might clasp them tightly to the pier. If not, they'd need to be tightly fixed to concentrate the explosive blast on the pier, rather than have it dissipate into the air. The sampan crews would activate firing devices with a short time-delay and slip discreetly away in a third craft before the Japanese sentries became aware of their presence. The idea's simple enough. You might want to try it at night.

The agent also said that "In evening there are lights on the bridge, and at times a searchlight is used." So far as cover was concerned, "No foliage or houses can be found within about two *li*s of this bridge," he reported, and added that

No train traffic can go over the Qiantang river bridge. The damaged part is a length of three archways. Boards and planks are employed to cover the wrecked section. Only empty trucks are able to run over the repairing. The goods dispatched from Hangzhou to Zhuji or Jinhua are mostly military equipment, while from Jinhua to Hangzhou are mostly foodstuffs.

Trains, that is to say, had to stop at either end of the bridge. The damage to the bridge led me to question the point of mounting a complex and dangerous operation against a bridge, no matter how impressive as a work of man, useful only for empty trucks and foot traffic. In June we learned, "General Guo informed the Camp Commander that on 17 May 1944, six men previously trained in this school, attacked and damaged pier number 8 of the Qiantang River Bridge near Hangzhou." I don't think we ever got a fuller statement than that.

We decided that we'd never be able to depend on the information we needed unless we got it ourselves. Carrying a camera, Sgt. Charles Shero, USMC, and I left General Ma's in August for the headquarters of General Pao, commander of the 3d Column of the LPA. Jimmie, one of the interpreters from Camp One, a short, stocky man, round-faced, wearing eyeglasses, was with us. We must have been met by guides along the way to lead us. The scheme called for me to drop off at Pao's and, from there, Pao would get Shero within sight of the bridge.

The Chinese—it may have been General Ma—agreed to his going only on the condition that Shero wear civilian clothes. Whatever benefit there was in the disguise was vitiated by the suit of shiny blue pajamas the tailor made him. They may not have been irridescent, as I seem to remember, but they did give off a ghastly light in the sun. We walked due east from Ma's headquarters at Wangjiaqiao, toward Hangzhou, Shero slouching along in his garish pajamas, much too thickset with his rolling gait to pass as a Chinese, even from a distance. Only his thick curly black hair looked at all Chinese, and that not much. Shero and I both knew this was, for him, a dangerous expedition and, I thought, a quixotic one as well.

If not in country occupied at that moment by the Japanese—a gray zone rather than a transition from white to black—at the end of the first day of walking, we were close enough to be careful. From there on, we slept by day and moved by night, as was our way in Japanese areas. We were less likely to be recognized as foreigners, reported by informants of the Japanese if we passed through villages by night. Actually, although we didn't do so on this walk, we could pass through the streets of Japanese-held towns at night because the Japanese buttoned themselves up in pillboxes come dusk.

Moving by night, we avoided the heat of summer sun as well as hostile eyes. On a moonless night, treading the narrow paths alongside a rice paddy was perilous. Step a few inches in the wrong direction, and you plunged into the mire, sometimes a six- or eight-foot fall. Our leading phobia was the fear of stumbling into one of the great vats set in the fields at ground level, full of night soil, human manure, that is. As with horrors generally, our preoccupation was out of proportion with the odds favoring such an immersion. The prospect was dreadful.

On other expeditions, tramping through dark village streets with a detachment of Chinese troops—this time Shero and I were traveling light—with nothing shining but the moon, the villagers could hardly see a foreign face, even if they noticed figures larger and heavier than normal. If a window swung open or a curious villager came out a door with a lantern, without a word a soldier would break ranks to bang the shutter shut or push a man back inside.

Sleeping by day was restless. Not just the daylight. You'd often be in a dusty farm outbuilding with the meal sacks, chickens walking on you, clucking and pecking, hogs grunting outside. If you were lucky, a Chinese soldier, pledged to the death to protect you, would be awake to shoo the chickens outside from time to time. Another day, it would be ducks quacking. The soldiers tore strips of cloth and tied the ducks' bills shut. A soldier might tuck a chicken into a knapsack on leaving at dusk, looking to a good meal in the morning. Sometimes a soldier would snatch up a duck from a dark farm pond. This was frowned on, the rule being we paid for food, but I shared more than one illicit duck or chicken dinner.

One morning before dawn, after an all-night walk, Shero, Jimmie, and I were met by a guide in the streets of a deserted village. He took us to the top story of a large building, looming over the street in the moonlight and told us to sleep there as immediately we did.

That morning, we woke to sun streaming into the loft of a rice mill and to shrill voices welling up from the street below, Chinese schoolchildren shouting their lessons in unison. We went quickly downstairs to find the rest of our party eating breakfast in a ground-floor room. The noise came from the schoolroom across the street. The people of this village had suffered so many depredations from Japanese troops, they'd set up a fastness in the hills and the whole village retired there for the night. By day they came down mountain paths into town to carry on the business of life as normally as this life allowed.

Waiting for us in another room, courtesy of General Pao, was a newly made, shallow wooden tub, a vat of hot water, soap and towels—a luxury best appreciated by those who've spent some gritty days on foot, not washing with anything more than a damp hot towel along the way.

We had a breakfast of *xifan* and pickles, were stared at by the schoolchildren, and went to market where goods were displayed on counters crowding the narrow main street. The people were polite enough but standoffish. Jimmie said they appreciated the "American friends" but were concerned about reprisals from the Japanese, once word got about that we'd been there.

A soldier led Shero and me up the side of a grassy slope on the edge of the village and left us there, pointing to the shade of a cluster of trees. Awaiting us was a watermelon, the green skin glistening with moisture from the cool inside, a knife stuck in its belly. We stretched out and ate it all. The wind tossed the branches of the trees above us, fleecy clouds passed by, and we napped.

We had lunch with General Pao, Shero, Jimmie, and I. Pao was tall, lean, bald as a Buddhist monk, which he resembled more than he did a soldier. Pao was a handsome man, courtly, not only an officer but a gentleman. He'd cooked lunch himself—a hobby, he explained—and had prepared the acorn squashes as his mother did. The squash at noon had sugared vegetables in the center. The evening squash at the same table had ham, an artistic way of dealing with short rations. For dessert that night, we had tapioca, "pearl rice," Jimmie called it, asking if I'd ever tasted it before. I didn't say I'd come to loathe tapioca in childhood, but then my mother hadn't fixed it the way General Pao's mother did.

Pao gave Shero an escort from there, and I went back to Ma's to wait. The records don't show how far he walked. The 1 September 1944 monthly report says Shero returned to camp from a reconnaissance mission on 21 August. I can't find a report on the trip. I do know the Chinese did not let him get as far as the bridge. Good thing, too—he could easily have fallen into Japanese hands. This anticlimax, typical of guerrilla warfare, did not put an end to dreaming about a Qiantang River bridge expedition. Chungking kept up a persistent, uninspired interest in the bridge, and a couple of our people were kept working on it. I scratched it from my own list.

We kept in touch with Camp One by messages enciphered in a simple double-transposition system based on a key word changed periodically, probably not often enough. We sent the messages by an agent radio set when we could. Often Camp One couldn't hear us. I cursed them, grinding a hand generator while Sgt. William Tawater tapped out *V*s over and over on his key. So then we'd read them over the phone. If we couldn't raise the Camp One hostler/operator, we'd use the courier that ran between the LPA and General Guo. We stopped using him the first time he was stopped and shaken down by "bandits"—meaning Communists—on the road from Wangjiaqiao to Huizhou.

Peanut and I went off together on an expedition from Ma's, where or why I can't remember. I find no record of it. The drought-stricken countryside under a brassy sky is still before my eyes. Peanut walked with a quick, hip-twisting shuffle, always ahead of me. More than once the rage fed by exhaustion rose in me, angered at his agility. In one wide valley, everything green parched dull and tawny by the sun blazing at midday, I saw Peanut stop at a teahouse canted on a slope of caked mud far ahead. I dragged up, minutes later, to where Peanut sat in the shade of a leafed awning, grinning at me, his shirt soaking wet.

As soon as I eased myself down across from him, I forgave him and sipped from my own bowl of burning hot tea. We talked about cold beer and cherry Cokes with ice in them. Jimmie was along, again, and asked what a cherry Coke was. So we talked about soda fountains in drug stores. One of the soldiers asked what we were talking about and Jimmie turned about on his stool to explain. We listened to him trying to put an American small town that he didn't understand himself into terms the soldier could. I kept on talking to keep us there, to postpone getting up. If

you rested even a few minutes on those hot days, you paid
for it, your leg muscles seizing up. You rose painfully, hob-
bled off stiff-legged, like a woman with bound feet, until
things loosened up and you could swing your legs freely
again.

These small, farm-country teahouses, flimsy tables, three-
legged stools and crude benches, bamboo poles propping up
a roof of branches or banana leaves, sat in valley bottoms
where the paths crossed. They sat in the V of mountain
passes where weary climbers from either side met. Astrin-
gent green tea made your mouth pucker, flakes of leaf and
stems floating in it, leftover scrapings from the bottom of a
sack—the first sip started the sweat into your eyes, the second, sweat running down your back, finally from every
pore on your body. Even if you'd been crisped like a leaf
by a hot wind as you walked you'd sweat and shiver with
the sudden cold.

The woman running that teahouse in the valley was a little ageless thing, scrawny and dried up in black blouse and
trousers, tottering on bound feet, with the kitten face of a
girl I'd known in high school. She was noisy, joking
coarsely with the soldiers in a cracked voice, but delicate
and girlish with all that, not at all impressed by the foreigners, treating us like the others, insulting us with words we
didn't understand, making everyone laugh, soldiers, the
farmers with their wide straw hats—even sober Jimmie
couldn't help giggling, one hand over his mouth.

We went on from there, closing on a rounded mountain
with great green flanks, its top so far above us, as we
neared the bottom, that it was blue with haze. There were
fields, terraces, houses, until halfway up, above them barren
pasture, cliffs, waterfalls gone dry, trees at the very top. We
had to cross it that day. Steady walking, only a standing
pause to look back and get a breath, sweating from the
climb, now, took us to the top by late afternoon. On the
down trail, we met a party of blue-clad, brown-faced farmers, all bone and tendon, staggering up the trail with loads
on their poles. They paused to talk, not putting their loads
down, propping a stick to rest them on. They stared at us,
their mouths open, laughing at Peanut and me with the

shock of hearing us speak Chinese. Jimmie scolded them. *"Laobaixing!* How many *li* of road to the next village?" We were heading for a village in the valley that stretched for miles into the distance below. They saw we looked tired and lied so as not to discourage us.

"Oh, fifteen *li*"—five miles.

"That's not so bad," we said, knowing they'd tempered the distance and hoped they hadn't overdone it. They had. Three hours later, ten or twelve miles farther on, we reached our village and tried to get lodging and something to eat.

Rarely did I think of the simplicity and the austerity of our life as hardship. One of our group, years later, spoke of the effect of China on him: ". . . respect for the people, for the suffering they endured. I had seen much deprivation and suffering in the USA during the depression years of the 1930s but nothing to compare (with this). . . ." That's right. Hardship for us was walking through a drizzle, for the Chinese an unending hard rain. As desperately tired as I'd get and cross, wobbling the last miles, I came to enjoy the walking, moving through country at a man's pace, walking to green tea and new faces in the next village, standing on a high ridge in a breeze coming all the way from the China Sea. I was letting go the idea of ever getting to sea, of being a real naval officer. This was a great adventure, I knew, and knowing that, I was in no hurry to go home.

When I returned from the walk with Shero, I started waiting again at General Ma's. Hardship for me was sitting around, waiting for Ma to decide. Not always sitting. Part of the time, I had a painful boil on my rear end. I could not walk far or barely straighten up to move about.

But, on 27 July, I sent a dispatch to Camp One from Ma's headquarters. "General Ma states men will be gathered in two weeks. Training to be finished one month from now with immediate operations. Suggests 'rehearsal' on Jap garrison near here . . . ." Luckily, my boil burst, in its loathsome way, in time for the "rehearsal." In September, we set off to attack a Japanese fortified town.

Chapter 20

I could only imagine the grumbling negotiations carried on among General Ma, Tai Li, and the Third War Zone Commander, before Ma called me in to say he'd acceded to our wish for an operation. What we were granted resembled nothing we'd proposed to him. Ma announced that a place called Ximoushi was to be the objective of a raid. He invited Peanut Hull and me to go along. Of course, I agreed right away. Ma did insist that we wear Chinese uniforms, so that we'd not be spotted as foreigners. I compromised, despite my distaste for disguising ourselves. Ever after that, we wore our own motley all-American outfits on operations.

North of Camp One and LPA headquarters three cities—Ningguo in Anhui Province, Guangde and Anji in Zhejiang—formed a crescent of Japanese garrisons in 1944. In the upper northwest corner of Zhejiang, right at the Anhui border, are clustered four villages some five to fifteen miles from Anji. Each village is a communications nexus at a junction of stone paths, three of the villages being also on unpaved motor road. The most remote village was Ximoushi—Westfield Market, in English—some eight or nine miles on foot from Anji and some forty miles from Ma's headquarters. We'd walk farther than that on soldiers' routes through the mountains. Anji was headquarters of the 103d Battalion of the 70th Division, with three hundred or so Japanese and one hundred renegade Chinese puppet troops. From Anji, Ximoushi could not be reinforced by road, as could other outlying garrisons. Japanese troops would have to come along stone paths. As in the other three villages, the Japanese had expelled the villagers and fortified the site as a strong point.

When we assembled on 15 September to leave for the headquarters of the 2d Column of the LPA, we saw that none of the Chinese with us wore uniforms of the same livid green as our American contingent. Peanut Hull and Gunner's Mate First Class Conrad, both extra large, loomed as though dressed for a costume party. The rest of us, of slighter build, might pass for Chinese soldiers, at a distance in dim light. Feeling foolish, we walked thirty or forty miles north to Yaozun, headquarters of General Wang, commanding the 2d Column of the LPA.

Wang was a thin, white-haired man with thick glasses, dressed in a good wool khaki uniform, amiable and, if anything, too deferential to Peanut and me. He had the word from Ma and Tai Li, no doubt, to please us. He and his staff briefed us on Ximoushi and presented an operational plan for the raid. Their intelligence showed 140 Japanese as garrison in Ximoushi and no puppet troops with them. The Japanese had infantry arms, eight machine guns, rifle-grenade launchers, and a small artillery piece, probably 37 millimeter. There were five pillboxes on the perimeter of the village, protected by barbed wire, the whole town surrounded by a bamboo palisade described as ten feet high. Inside the fence were communicating trenches, dry moats, mines around the pillboxes, booby traps in the wire. The pillboxes, twenty feet high and twenty to thirty feet in diameter, walls of unfired brick six feet thick, had good fields of fire over the rice paddies for their machine guns. The only terrain allowing a close approach was high ground west of the village.

General Wang pressed us for comment on the plan for the raid, clearly inviting us "to supervise" the operation. The plan looked fine to me, but I didn't say so until Peanut, on whom I was completely dependent for intelligent opinions on tactical subjects, had spoken. Not only was the plan good in itself, said Peanut, but he admired the logic of its presentation, the way it considered contingencies, and approved it right down to the headings, the paragraphs, and the subparagraphs. He said it might have been prepared by a Marine, the highest possible compliment. I then announced that we endorsed the plan. And we did. It was a good plan.

Essentially it was this: Wang would attack with one of his battalions, a third of it in reserve, with the purpose of making such a ruckus that the Japanese in Ximoushi would ask for reinforcements. Our troops would not try to get through the Ximoushi defenses unless a good opportunity arose. That seemed wise. With the light arms we and the Chinese had, the place looked impregnable to me.

Another of Wang's battalions would take positions along the paths leading from Anji and another garrisoned village nearby to ambush the Japanese reinforcements that would be moving at night along the paths. Peanut and I would get as close as we could to fire our six 4.5-inch rockets into Ximoushi, adding to Japanese apprehension. Conrad would command three Marines and our two Lewis guns at one ambush site. Pharmacist's mates were distributed about to handle casualties. All units were to be in position at 2300 on the twentieth, to begin the attack an hour later at midnight.

Late the night of the nineteenth, I walked with General Wang to a small village four miles north of Ximoushi. In the candlelight of a farmhouse, his battalion commander told us that Ximoushi had been reinforced by the Japanese, as usual, to be ready in case the Chinese attacked to celebrate the anniversary of the Mukden incident of 18 September 1931, another tradition, apparently. The reinforcements had returned to Anji on the nineteenth leaving about 150 Japanese on station, and General Wang decided to go ahead with the attack on the twentieth. That morning, we met the regimental commander who would lead the attack, and he said he'd take our rocket party as close as he could get us, putting us on the forward slope of the hill west of the village, some six hundred yards from the nearest pillbox.

We ate lunch in midafternoon and set off for the village near Ximoushi I'd visited the night before, some seven or eight miles away. I noted in my report that "the movement of the men was superb." We were forever impressed by the way the Chinese took to night operations. I added, "Most of the soldiers were trained at Camp One . . . there was no talking above a whisper nor was there any confusion."

It was here that a teenaged peddler of *mantou*, steamed bread, exclaimed in delight at the sight of us halted in the dark of a village street, our weapons hanging off us, puffing on cigarettes. He came over to greet us and the soldiers tried to shoo him away. He offered bread all round—no charge, he insisted. He wore a conical straw hat, a light-colored blouse with wide sleeves, short blue trousers and, like the soldiers, straw sandals on his bare feet. He carried his wares on a tray in front of him, held level by the strap around his neck. When we formed up to leave the village, he came right along with us, the soldiers near us constantly turning to hiss at him to go home.

We'd walk a way in the darkness, stop, whisper, start in again, stop again, whisper, finally reaching a cluster of houses close to Ximoushi. Peering into the darkness, we couldn't see the village because of a strip of trees running across the valley floor. The regimental commander came to guide our rocket party into position and was immediately lost on a hillside. After more whispering, one of our soldiers broke into a farmhouse and came back, towing by the arm a terrified girl about eight years old. It took more whispering to calm and cajole her into putting us on the right path. When we'd stumbled and slipped our way to the slope facing the village, it was so dark, we could barely make it out, nothing like individual targets. We decided to fire the rockets toward the large black blob below us. I didn't mind the darkness at all, figuring that the same dark would keep the Japanese from seeing us.

Peanut destroyed my slight confidence by pointing out that we were standing thigh deep in brush, no cover at all, really. The Japanese would fire on us once we rained our rockets down on them, so we'd better be ready to move our two launchers away from each other after each firing until we'd expended all six rockets.

About those rockets: I was still at Camp One when they arrived unannounced and unexplained in a crate. We unpacked them and stood about like a bunch of aborigines, staring at them. Of course, we knew they were rockets and, between Marines and gunner's mates, we figured out how they must work: how to pull out a pin so that the spinner in the nose would arm the rocket in flight, and so on. We built a trough and Peanut himself aimed and fired one. We picked the wrong target, the hill by the rifle range, because the rocket whooshed off in a pleasing manner, unfortunately exploding with a loud crump across the river—unfortunate because we were confident of them, so confident we had half a dozen sent up for the raid and went about telling the Chinese how marvelous the rockets were.

At 2400, in a burst of blinding light, Peanut opened the engagement by firing his first rocket. It blew up in another flash of light on the near perimeter of the village. We cheered. I knelt by my launcher and fired my rocket. It shot off in flame into mysterious silence. I stood with my mouth open, listening for the explosion that never came. One after the other, the rest of the rockets ripped into the night and disappeared, as though we'd fired them at the moon.

As our party milled about, dejected, the *mantou* peddler showed up in the blackness of the slope above Ximoushi, grinning and handing out cold buns. He thought we were wonderful. He didn't care whether our rockets went off or not. I thought he'd follow us forever. He didn't, though. Like most rural Chinese, his village was the center of the known world.

I was standing, shivering, from the cold no doubt, waiting for something else that had not happened as expected. The Japanese had not opened fire on us. They remained quiet in the dark. So did the Chinese. The plan called for a show of force here to persuade the Japanese to call Anji for reinforcements. The first shot was not fired until 0035, and after that firing was sporadic and infrequent. General Wang explained that later, telling us Tai Li had decreed that each round of ammunition must account for a Japanese. A soldier should not fire until sure of hitting his target. I'm sure General Wang quoted Tai Li correctly. It was just the sort of political balderdash that Tai Li came up with, what with no one ever talking back to him. Wang, a real soldier, knew better.

From then until 0315, we heard Thompson submachine guns and carbines being fired, weapons we'd issued the Chinese. There were short bursts of machine-gun fire. Several grenades were used by the Chinese, and some Japanese land mines were exploded. We were told to withdraw from our hill about 0200, on the grounds the Japanese were coming toward us. We withdrew to the nearby cluster of buildings, where one of Wang's staff showed up to invite us to the command post, a mile or so away. Peanut and I sent the other Americans off with him and told the regimental commander we'd go back to our position on the hill. Wait until it was light enough to see the Chinese troops entering the village, insisted the colonel. Peanut and I huddled in a house to try to warm ourselves. It was bitterly cold. At first light, around 0330, we discovered the colonel had departed after ordering a general withdrawal. Peanut and I started back for the hill to see the Japanese positions in daylight. Meeting the troops coming down, we had to go back with them.

As Peanut and I walked tiredly back, just after dawn, drained of the exhilaration we'd felt hours before, a bugle blew behind us. "That's the garrison," I said. "They see we're withdrawing."

"The hell it is. It's the damned Chinese field music."

Peanut snatched off his green Chinese cap, he was so angry at the way the raid had gone, balling it up in his fist. He felt cheated, deeply affronted by the weakness of the attack. The plan had been good, but its execution dreadful. The Japanese could have thought they had nothing more to cope with than neighborhood vandalism.

My own emotion was embarrassment at the failure of the rockets. We'd lost face. The problem was that we'd fired them at too low a trajectory, as we worked it out later. Unless a rocket hit something at a wide angle—like the hill Peanut had hit on the test firing—the rod that projected in front was merely bent rather than being driven back to detonate an explosion. The first rocket Peanut fired at Ximoushi must have hit something squarely. The others skidded off into impotence.

A crate of bazookas showed up at Camp One later on,

like the rockets, as a nice surprise, no instructions to be found in the box. I was given the honor, as senior officer present, of firing the first projectile. In an unusual display of bravado, I disdained the goggles that came in the box and assumed a firing stance, tube on my shoulder, on the edge of the river. A gunner's mate touched two wires together and the rocket whizzed out of the tube, blowing back particles of propellant into my face on its way to a satisfactory detonation across the river. My face was covered with black pockmarks that eventually wore away. Luckily, my eyes were not affected. One of the gunner's mates impertinently suggested I had closed them on firing.

The rockets were fireworks—if they went off—and useful only in numbers for a barrage. Anyone we aimed one at was quite safe. The bazooka was a real weapon, rockets for display, the bazooka for business. We'd have had fun with the Japanese in those pillboxes had we a bazooka at Ximoushi.

When we got back to Wang's command post, we found a party in progress. One of the pharmacist's mates said Wang had been eating and drinking, toasting victory throughout the raid. This was the last touch for Peanut. I suppose poor Wang was scared out of his wits that something would happen to one of the Americans and Tai Li would put him up against a wall. I said nothing about the party, later on, when Ma felt he had to ask us to critique the raid. I liked Wang. He was a real officer, well read, telling us of the history of the region we were in. I wondered how a gentleman like him had gotten tied up with Tai Li. On the night we'd spent at his headquarters in a mountain village, made homesick by the smell of wood smoke, he'd served an unforgettable duck cooked with chestnuts.

Wang reported that eighteen of his men entered Ximoushi and engaged in the streets a group of twelve Japanese that came after them. The Chinese opened fire with Thompsons, killing eight Japanese and wounding four. The Chinese had one man killed by a mine in the Japanese wire. He looked it. We'd seen him carried by on a litter before dawn. Our pharmacist's mates treated the three men wounded trying to enter the village, one shot from behind by a carbine.

Before the raid, I'd noticed some thirty men dressed in tight, dark civilian clothes instead of the usual yellow uniforms. These darkly dressed men were those who'd penetrated the village. Most of the others just sat around. General Wang probably never intended to commit his entire force. That any men at all entered the village was incidental to the plan, but bold. We found later that Wang's 2d Regiment for some reason made a feint at the nearby garrison village to tie them down, contrary to trying to lure them out to an ambush. The Japanese at Anji fired an artillery piece toward Ximoushi at about three in the morning, we were later told, to demonstrate they were on the qui vive.

I was never sure about the raid on Ximoushi. Was it just a show, at the cost of a few casualties, cynically laid on to please us and end our everlasting nagging? Or was it a demonstration of lack of resolve and weak leadership? We went back to see General Ma to pay our respects and to vex him with a critique of the operation. We expressed particular annoyance at being protected, kept back from combat, knowing it was Tai Li's policy, but objecting to it at every opportunity. I quoted Charlie Parkin earlier about us juniors speaking so frankly to Chinese senior officers. It seems now as arrogant as it did then, a navy lieutenant and a Marine first lieutenant, neither yet twenty-five, telling General Ma how to do his business. I tried to be tactful, deferential about it, but differences in age, rank, and experience were obvious. Whenever I was tempted to lapse into the polite alternative, one zealous Marine or another would prod me from behind.

In early October, Lawrence Conrad, gunner's mate first class, Ben Van Dalsem, aviation machinist's mate first class, and I left the medical unit, Pact Doc, for Camp One. We'd dropped in for medical checkups after the rehearsal raid and were returning to Camp One, skinny, scruffy, clothes patched, unshaven.

My boots were nearly worn out from the summer's tramp but still capable daily of lacerating my feet. The morning the three of us walked into Xiongcun from Huizhou it was raining. I stopped, sat on a wet rock, took off the boots, threw them into a rice paddy, took off my socks, examined the oozing sores on the bottoms, sides, and tops of my feet, and put the socks back on. We splashed along the flagstones the rest of the way, through cool autumn rain, in stocking feet. My feet had not felt that good all summer.

At camp, we learned about the attack Charlie Parkin had led against a Japanese-defended bridge at Zhuji, on the railway between Hangzhou and Jinhua, a week before our raid at Ximoushi. The party included a Marine officer, six Marine sergeants, two corporals and a party of LPA troops. Negotiations with a commander of puppet troops under Japanese command led to his coming over to our side to join in the attack. The plan called for the assault to be made at dark, essential to allow the demolitions party to approach the bridge without being detected. As it turned out, the demolitions party was lost and did not arrive until daylight, and there was a council to decide whether or not to attack in this situation.

Sgt. James Rainey says that

Our aim had been to reach the bridge while it was still dark. We were late in starting, and the trail was rough and often uphill so that, what with stumbling around in the dark ... there wasn't a whole lot of dark left when we reached the point from which we would split up to go to our appointed tasks. Everyone was speaking in stage whispers so as not to annoy the Japanese. ... Someone, probably one of the interpreters, came to Jake (Siegrist) and me with two scrawny old men, obviously locals. We were told that they knew where we wanted to go and one of them was to guide Jake and the other was assigned to me. Jake and I both were a bit leery of these two oldsters, but we had little choice. I followed my local tour guide. ... Sure enough our guide took us right where we were supposed to go. ... There was a pillbox quite close but no one fired on us. We had twenty clams which we quickly placed on the rails with short fuses rigged with fuse lighters.

* * *

The action began when then Corporal Robert Boger, along with Sgt. Nelson Hillman, fired four 4.5 rockets from wooden troughs, as we had at Ximoushi. (I couldn't help feeling secretly pleased when I heard their results were only slightly better than ours.) "Two were duds," says Boger. "The other two went over the target and exploded in the middle of the town." The Chinese began blowing bugles. "The Americans were dumbfounded. We thought they were blowing reveille for the Japanese." From where Boger was lying in a railway cut, he fired a tracer from his Springfield rifle at a slit in the nearest pillbox. Immediately, machine-gun fire was hitting a rock next to him.

The commander of the Chinese puppet troops leapt to his feet and ran at a pillbox, a gun blazing in either hand. He fell with a bullet through his thigh. Many of the men who followed him were cut down by Japanese machine-gun fire. In their white shirts, purple suspenders and purple trousers, the puppet troops made good targets.

"On the day we left Camp One," Boger recalls,

for Zhuji Major Parkin issued to each of us a piece of chocolate about one inch thick and two inches square. He said it was for emergency use only and we would have to turn it in if we did not get captured, or *else*. After Hillman and I fired our rockets and things were going at a pretty good clip, I thought maybe I should eat my chocolate before it was too late. Hillman turned and saw what I was doing and got all excited saying that Parkin was going to be mad. I told him it looked like an emergency to me, and never did know who ate the chocolate and who turned it in.

The chocolate was an American issue called D ration, and we had very little of it, and the rule was that it was to be turned in unless we were faced with starvation or the sort of emergency that Bob Boger declared that morning.

The brief indecision about attacking appears to have caused some confusion. Jim Rainey says that

Just before the firing began, we were ready to set (the clams) off when two or three Chinese soldiers came running up and said that everything had been called off and that we shouldn't blow the rails. We were to sneak off and the Japanese wouldn't even know we had been there. Then we could come back later and blow the bridge. So we pulled off all of the clams and took off.

But when we had gone about a quarter of a mile we heard weapons being fired. I said, in effect, "The Japanese sure must know that we're here now. Let's go back and blow the tracks." So we did. Unfortunately, the fuses with detonators and fuse lighters attached had been jammed hastily into our pockets, so some of the fuse lighters didn't work properly and only about fifteen clams went off.

The demolitions party could not get near the bridge because of the fire from the Japanese pillboxes. After about thirty minutes of firing, the raiding party withdrew, Boger remembers, about ten miles before stopping to give blood plasma to the more seriously wounded.

In a report to Chungking, Parkin said two Japanese pillboxes were burned, ten Japanese and two puppet troops killed, and rails on the right-of-way blown in fifteen places. The LPA lost seven dead and six wounded, and the puppets who had come to our side had ten dead and seven wounded.

In a letter to Miles, Parkin wrote about the puppet commander and another officer operating in the Zhuji area. He described the former, Col. Xu Changshui, as still bedridden from the wound in his thigh:

However his men have continued to operate against the Japanese. Blowing rails, skirmishing and doing sabotage work. . . . He has proved most cooperative and willing to take Americans anywhere he is able. He has a tremendous personal following among the civilians in all this territory and is able to work against the Japanese almost with impunity due to this. He has a very loyal and able group of men working for him. Some 500 under his direct command. I have no idea what sort of American landings will be carried on here or on the Zhejiang coast and so have hesitated to take any action as far as organizing his men into a reconnaissance outfit. He told me ... he could take us or anyone else anywhere in the province or on the coast that we wanted to go. If there were any sort of a landing it can be imagined that such aid as he could give would be invaluable.

The LPA commander in the attack was Col. Shu Yiguang. Parkin said that, "he had been operating against the railway for some time.... He is a little more careful with Americans in that he does not give them the freedom of movement that (Xu, the other colonel) does."

Although the raid on the bridge at Zhuji failed, we'd established working relations with Colonels Xu and Shu. The difference in pronunciation of the two surnames was too fine for us. We pronounced both names as "Colonel Shoe." So we began to distinguish them by referring to Xu as Bad Leg—he who was wounded in the engagement at the bridge—and Shu as Good Leg. Our new relationship with them meant that we'd resume, as early as October, operations against the Hangzhou-Jinhua railway. We continued attempts to mount operations in the Yangzi valley to our north, but we'd been unable to establish a presence there. General Ma was no help.

Chapter 21

I took up my duties again as executive officer to Charlie Parkin, the most onerous among them having been absorbed by a newcomer, Lt. George Parker, USNR, a lawyer from Virginia who'd arrived during the summer. He'd taken over my ciphering duties and the compilation of data for the monthly reports. He could type, and he didn't try to conceal it. Unscrupulous persons deny an ability to type, just as they lie about knowing close-order drill or how to open raw oysters.

There was talk later on about unification of the armed services. With Charlie Parkin, a major of army engineers in command, a naval officer as exec and George Parker acting as exec in my absence, the Marines were already in a unified command. Being Marines, they were not entirely happy with this dispensation. Being Marines, they took it like men.

Parkin built a reputation for a scientific eccentricity by setting up a laboratory in the shower room where, in the usual course of events, water heated in a suspended fifty-five-gallon drum was released by a pull chain. There Parkin molded charges of TNT in bamboo containers, cooking granular TNT over a fire to melt it. He combined our surplus of TNT with native bamboo in ingenious weapons, useful in booby traps, as substitutes for the clams we used to blow up rails, for grenades, railroad or road mines, mortar shells, and other practical devices. No one doubted his ingenuity, but there was a general drift to the far end of the camp during his cooking sessions. Stung by our ignorance, Parkin pointed out in a memorandum that the process is quite safe. "T.N.T. melts at 176°F. and since water boils at 212°F., the T.N.T. can be melted in a container that rests in boiling water." He insisted, "T.N.T. *will not explode* after it has been melted and then allowed to harden."

When cold weather came that autumn of 1944, Parkin announced that one could keep warm, like a Tibetan, by not changing one's long underwear nor bathing during the winter months, benefiting from the insulation of body grease thus manufactured.

One cold morning, Art Tucker darted through the wardroom and out the door, completely naked, while the rest of us were at breakfast. We looked at each other and, as one man, got up to go outside, where we found him in the courtyard rolling on the ground in the first snowfall of the season. Later, he listed for us the healthful benefits of a snow bath.

Parkin showed more zeal at gathering intelligence than the rest of us. taking part in the briefing and debriefing of agents sent off to case targets such as the Qiantang River bridge and the railway bridge at Zhuji. In a letter he wrote Miles in 1946, Parkin spoke of the "many hundreds of hours . . . spent by my officers and myself in collecting intelligence. This necessitated many hours of conferences and many, many hours of walking." Many of these conferences and hours of walking—days, I would have said—had to do with planning future missions, operational discussions, establishing new liaisons with Chinese officials, as well as intelligence collection in the strict sense.

Chungking assigned Lt. Hilton Jayne, USNR, a specialist in Japanese order of battle, to General Ma's headquarters to exploit the LPA for intelligence. I didn't envy him the task of judging the authenticity of it. The Ximoushi experience led me to assume the LPA was good at local combat intelligence. Up at Ma's headquarters the past summer, Ma's intelligence officer had turned over to us intelligence reports that we then had translated. Some reported the finest local detail about the Nakajima battalion, let's say, based nearby at Ningguo: the names of his company officers and leading noncoms, the number of artillery pieces he had, where the men were quartered, the location of brothels, laundries, movie houses, and how the Chinese populace felt about him being there. Useful stuff if you were planning an operation against Nakajima in Ningguo—as we'd liked to have done. Didn't the term "rehearsal" imply raids against other garrisons?

If not used in an operation, such reports were merely annoying virtuosi performances, like an unpleasant violin concerto.

Another category of information was given us, leaving the neighborhood for high-level reporting on the Japanese in Shanghai, Beijing, even in Japan itself. I'd read the translations, scratch my head, shrug my shoulders, bundle them up for Camp One. There they'd be sent on to Chungking without comment, unless Charlie Parkin added something. I didn't have the vocabulary then to define what was wrong with these reports. I knew it wasn't only my ignorance of Japanese order of battle. There was no way to judge the reliability of the information, no sourcing, no trail back to where the information came from. I didn't envy Jayne, who didn't have an easy time of it. Miles spoke highly of Jayne's performance, especially later on when Communist troops were massing in our area in the summer of 1945.

In a letter to Miles in September 1944, Parkin threw in a paragraph that must have seemed to him incidental. It made a big difference to us later on. "May I suggest," Parkin wrote, "that you have your recreation officer there in the valley get each succeeding set of books published by the Special Service Division out to us." Soon after, cartons of these cheaply produced pocket versions of good novels and fine nonfiction arrived. While this was by no means Parkin's principal accomplishment, I was always grateful for this thoughtfulness on his part.

In early October, then second lieutenant Jake Siegrist left camp with Marine sergeants Jensen and Hillman, Corporal Boger, and Pharmacist's Mate First Class Wesselink on an expedition to the Zhuji area to destroy a section of the Hangzhou-Jinhua railway. The first part of the trip was by water, our standard route to the Zhuji area from then on. The party went across the nearby provincial border to Chun'an in Zhejiang Province—much of this region has since been flooded by a reservoir—and took a sampan from there for the Qiantang River. In Tunglu, a city on the west bank of the Qiantang River, he made a rendezvous with Colonel Shu, Good Leg, that is. The party walked from there, east of the Qiantang, until settling in a mountain village that would be their operational base.

Jake reported that Colonel Shu willingly discussed methods of operations against the railway, intelligence collection, instruction for his men in the use of clams and fuse-lighters. He refused adamantly to allow Jake and his party to reconnoiter the railway. Shu went on to say that he had been ordered to keep the Americans from taking part in the operation. Shu went over his plan to blow up two bridges and some track and Jake approved it, still arguing for a part. Shu would agree only to take them to a point near the railway where they could observe.

On the night of 30 October, nearly a month after leaving Camp One, Jake and his men split into two parties, one setting up an aid station for casualties, and Jake and Jensen going to a few hundred yards from the railway. There they saw the flashes and heard the detonations as the clams blew up along the railway north of the station at Anhua and heard large explosions when the charges at the two bridges blew. On their way back, Jake and his party heard firing nearby. They did not engage the Japanese who were trying to cut the escape route from the area of the railway. Two Chinese soldiers were wounded and treated by Wesselink. Jake thought the raid to have been "carefully planned, well executed." The Chinese later reported that they'd shut down the railway between Zhuji and Jinhua for four days.

Siegrist led three such raids on the railway during the time I was at Camp One. Boger, who was on all three, remembers celebrating New Year's Day 1945 by opening a can of Vienna sausage. Their February raid on the railway coincided with the Marine invasion of Iwo Jima. The January raid brought Siegrist, Boger, and Hillman, and the Chinese with them, a "well done" from Tai Li and Miles.

They'd blown rails in twenty-two places, burned a supply warehouse in Zhuji, attacked the Japanese barracks at Bingguo. The Chinese claimed eight Japanese killed and three probables there. Demolition charges severely damaged the railroad station at Zhuji. They fired bazookas at Japanese strong points in Zhuji and Bingguo, effect unknown.

Siegrist and company had been alternating with teams led by Peanut Hull. On 2 November 1944, Peanut left the camp for Zhuji with five of the new people Chungking had sent us. Things were backwards. Chungking kept asking the Navy Department to send more people. When they arrived, out they went to the camps whether or not needed. Rather than our personnel needs being tailored to our operational situation, we were having to consider adjusting our little war in Zhejiang to the personnel situation. Peanut and Jake said we couldn't crowd the Zhuji area, but I agreed with Charlie Parkin, we had to give the new people a taste of operations. We couldn't keep them fully employed at Camp One. (In early 1945, I complained to Chungking about the number of men sent to us that summer and fall and about the low caliber of a few of them, so undeveloped that we couldn't have them dealing with the Chinese.)

On 7 November, a message came from Chungking relieving Charlie Parkin of command of the camp. As a result of the feud with the Naval Group, OSS had recalled him. By doing so, OSS presented me with the gift of my first command. I had been planning to follow Peanut to Zhuji, as I had been nowhere since Ximoushi in September. And so I went, saying I needed to know the Zhuji area properly to carry out the new responsibility of command. That was not entirely unjustified. I left George Parker in charge during my absence. With me were two veterans, Sergeant Tawater and Pharmacist's Mate First Class J. K. McCoy, two of our stalwarts, and Ens. Alec Primos, USNR.

There was a warm November sun on the Qiantang River as we moved downriver to the operational area. On the downriver run, the sampan had the current with it. Propulsion was by sail when the wind was right. If not, we were dragged along by a gang of men walking on the bank, each connected by a line to the mast. It was not unheard of, when the crews went around a river bend out of sight of the sampan, for the men to throw their lines on the ground and run off—hilarious if it happened to someone else.

These river sampans were some forty feet long and covered by a cylindrical awning of woven matting. The bilges were inhabited by varieties of beetles, cockroaches, fleas, and bedbugs. We slept in the boat, under the awning, on shelves far too short for misshapen foreigners. At night, the bugs dispatched their raiding parties. On this trip on the Qiantang, McCoy brought along an early aerosol bomb, a squat black canister the size of a pint can. He sent a chemical cloud—DDT, I suppose—into the bilge. Formations of black and brown beetles rushed out of the bilge to march up inside the awning to join us, hanging overhead, twitching and bristling, letting go occasionally to plop on our heads. As they'd taken our quarters, we moved out on deck that night. The experiment was not repeated.

These were pleasure cruises. The wind gusted on the water that November, but the air was dry, so mild that we sat in the sun on top of the awning, eating the tangerines and peanuts we'd buy ashore, reading, and smoking. We'd stuffed our pockets with the books that Parkin had ordered, as soon as finishing one, swapping it for another: "God, we've got some slow readers!" We smoked the cigarettes that came from Shanghai in an orange and green pack. Not bad. The blend was close to an American taste. As we were at the very end of the supply line, we rarely got American cigarettes, and when we did, a case didn't last long.

Lying on the awning, we could look up from our reading to the slowly shifting panorama of mountains back from the shore, covered with low brush, shading from tawny to a hazy blue. The Chinese spared few trees. An occasional specimen had been left for us, the more treasured for being alone, spreading itself gold or flaming red, displayed on the shore like a bonsai.

We debarked, probably at Jiaqi, upriver from the Japanese garrison at Fuyang. The Japanese occupied area was always dark to me. Zhejiang east of the river was dark country, and not only because we moved, nearing the railway, at night. Going in, my excitement was mixed with foreboding. The sunny trail ahead, the cheerful-looking farmstead, the green thicket of bamboo set tastefully next to a cluster of whitewashed walls and black-tiled roofs—each charming prospect hummed a warning of the dark presence, the malevolence ahead.

That is to say, I respected the Japanese. If Jake or Peanut, Tawater or McCoy, ever felt the way I did they showed no sign of it. Of course, I wasn't chattering to them about my forebodings, either.

Usually we walked two nights to a rendezvous in the Zhuji area. This time, we joined Peanut's party early one morning where he waited with Colonel Xu in a schoolhouse. Bad Leg's people, the former puppet troops, were impressive, dressed like bandits, and as friendly as the troops we were used to working with. That morning they were hanging about the schoolyard, cleaning weapons, some of them scooping rice from bowls into their mouths. They stopped what they were doing to greet us with smiles and to ask if we'd eaten—eaten rice yet?—another way of saying good morning: *"Chiguo fan meiyou, ah?"*

Inside, Bad Leg was lying on a litter. Peanut and I sat next to him on stools, discussing the next move. He was a remarkable man. While we talked, his medical aide, lightly trained in Western medicine, bared Bad Leg's thigh. The entrance and exit wounds were still open and draining. (I think we persuaded him later on to go to Pact Doc for treatment.) The aide drew a strip of lint from a bowl of antiseptic and poked it through the wound, slowly drawing it out on the other side. While he could not keep the pain from his face nor prevent the involuntary trembling of his lower body, Colonel Xu went right on talking to us. He kept his mind on the business at hand far better than could I, seeing his agony.

He said the Japanese were on the move, and ominously, they had moved last night. Ordinarily, Japanese patrols sallied forth by day and returned to the safety of pillboxes and barracks at night. Their agents along the river would have tipped them off to the arrival of Peanut's party and of his route into occupied territory. And, said the colonel, they would have clocked in the four of us late arrivals. The Japanese were moving in force, Japanese troops, including cavalry, accompanied by puppet forces. We couldn't work on the railway as long as the Japanese were out. Their aim was not to guard the railway but to destroy his unit and the Americans, at least to drive us back across the river. We were embarrassed that our inconvenient numbers had brought the Japanese down on him. He was too polite to say that, and pointed out our routes of withdrawal on a map. We started off.

Colonel Xu traveled prone, in a litter, bouncing on the shoulders of four of his men. When he wasn't questioning his officers or giving them orders, he'd talk to us as we trotted along the narrow trails beside him. Despite the constant pain from his wound, he was as cool and pleasant as if on a picnic. By dawn the next day, we'd reached the village where we'd planned to sleep that day. Instead, we were told to keep moving, and went back to the steep mountain trails. At noontime, we came down into a village in a narrow valley, bare hills rising sharply around it. Every door was open and people were milling about the streets, giving us worried glances, knowing we were bringing trouble with us.

Peanut and I had switched parties, and all the new people were with me, a hungry, footsore lot, asking if all this was necessary. My knees were creaky from the past months of going up and down mountains and I walked with a stave in either hand. I was as glad as anyone to sit on a stool in a teahouse in the village. We were planning to get something to eat when Peanut, Tawater, and McCoy, traveling with Bad Leg's party, appeared. Peanut said the Japanese, led by cavalry, were coming in on the other side of town. I didn't waste any time getting to my feet. The new men did not grasp our situation, asking why we couldn't stay for lunch. By now, villagers were running past the teahouse, carrying babies, valuables, yanking crying children along by the hand, toting old people on litters. We joined the stream of refugees leaving the village, going out one side as the Japanese paused, cautious, at the other, some two hundred yards down the street.

We ran for the next two days, leaving the villagers to

drop back to rearrange their lives. Bad Leg was jounced along the trail, smiling and encouraging everyone else. We must have stopped to eat, even to sleep, but I can't remember doing it. We kept climbing straight up one side of a mountain, down the other, on up the next. The Japanese took the easy paths around the bottoms, trying to get ahead, cut us off. Colonel Xu had a party guard our rear, waiting at the crest of each mountain we climbed. The Japanese didn't test them. Finally, we stopped running, and one day at dawn, we could look across the ranges to a far valley of clouds, morning mist hanging over the Qiantang River.

The Japanese gave up the chase, too soon, I thought. We were all tired out. Another day, and they might have had us. I dragged myself and the new men back to the river and home, leaving the field to Colonel Xu and his men, to Peanut, McCoy, and Tawater. I told Parkin that Peanut and Jake were right. We'd demonstrated how easily we could saturate the Zhuji area. Just approaching the railway, not even blowing anything up, got the Japanese buzzing like hornets.

The Japanese discouraged guerrilla activity by the reasonable, if cold-blooded, policy of retaliating for guerrilla actions by punishing the innocent. I thought that they could have done more to discourage us this last time by trying harder to run us down, sticking right with us, leapfrogging their forces in aggressive patrolling. But it took a lot of Japanese to do that. As this operation showed, they had to come out in force just to move by night or to stray far from their base into the mountains where the guerrillas might turn on them.

Neither we nor our Chinese comrades could have survived such a chase without the good will of the villages in the occupied areas. We were confident that no matter what happened to us—say one of us Americans were wounded or lost during a night movement—we'd be handed to safety under the noses of the Japanese.

It's nice to make a sentimental picture of it, the Chinese people united against the Japanese oppressor. That's not the way it was. Most Chinese wanted more than anything else to stay out of trouble, avoid the attention of the Japanese and of the guerrillas, too. Our Chinese, the Chinese we worked with, were supported by an underground organization. For every villager in the underground were ten or more who wanted no part of it, lived in fear of the Japanese and in fear of being asked to carry out a task for the guerrillas. In the towns, smuggling between Japanese-occupied China and free China was big business. Guerrillas are bad for business.

Most Chinese were sitting on a fence, trying to keep out of trouble, to accommodate, to get along, waiting to see who would win in the Pacific, the Americans or the Japanese, waiting to see who would win China, Communists or Nationalists. Few of the millions of Chinese stepped forward to risk their property, their families, death or worse, in the course of these struggles. All the more admirable, we thought, were the few who did.

Matching our admiration of our friends was the ignorance that made us so dependent on them. We barely knew where we were much of the time, comparing inaccurate maps with the countryside—we could have remapped our part of China—being led, docile, from one place to another, illiterate and speaking only basic Chinese, dependent on these few others to know what was going on around us. Really, we knew little enough about the people we were working with. Colonel Xu is an example—a former collaborator with the Japanese, for goodness sake! When we offered him weapons and ammunition to encourage him, he'd shake his head, insist that we give him only enough for the next operation. He couldn't handle more than that. When he'd used it up against the Japanese, then he'd ask for more. That was refreshing. We found that Tai Li and Ma and Guo didn't like our working with him, hinting at banditry, communism, and so on. We were dangerously pragmatic and perverse enough—Peanut and Jake and I—to consider it a recommendation that Tai Li and his people did not control Xu.

Chapter 22

Our way of doing things was beginning to take on a pattern. The makeup of Peanut Hull's team that stayed behind in Zhejiang, after I went back to Camp One in November 1944, exemplifies the design. The small size of the team was typical. We didn't need many men for the small raids we were being allowed to carry out by the limited tolerance granted us under the Tai Li/General Ma terms of engagement. The enemy was hardly more generous, arousing himself when raided too frequently or when too many Americans took to strolling through his occupied territory. If Camp One had been made up entirely of Hulls and Siegrists, Raineys and Bogers, others of that skilled and bold ilk, confined to operating in the Zhuji area as we were, we would not have been able to come near deploying them.

A second part of the design was the makeup of the teams. A Marine junior officer with a handful of our men was the American element, with a Chinese interpreter attached. Liang Yuntang, Alfred Liang, was with Peanut this time. A well-educated, young Hong Kong Chinese, Alfred was interpreter by title, more liaison officer in performance. Being neither members of the Loyal Patriotic Army nor of the navy, our interpreters were not required to be loyal to either, having been drafted into the job by Tai Li. Most of our interpreters were overseas Chinese who, voluntarily returning to China for patriotic reasons, were disappointed by what they found. Many were unhappy to be working for Tai Li. All of them found trying to interpret, to mediate, to bridge the cultural gaps between Chinese officials and young Americans, often a graceless task. Like Liang, our interpreters might be better educated, more sophisticated, than the Americans and the Chinese they tried to explain to each other.

With Hull was Maj. C. C. Ho, normally officer in charge of the students at Camp One, who'd come over to our side, in a manner of speaking, taken by our methods of training and certainly as eager as we to get at the Japanese. Major Ho, who enjoyed the nickname, Charley, was a native of Zhejiang with a good combat record. He and Hull were a talkative, gregarious pair who enjoyed each other's company. (Peanut was shaken, on one of these expeditions when Ho discovered a private soldier had stolen a Smith & Wesson .38 navy revolver from supplies the team was carrying to a guerrilla group. Ho pulled out his own pistol and shot the man dead on the spot.)

With the team was 1st Lt. T. F. Wu, a small, neat, soldierly person who'd kept himself close to me and Peanut at Ximoushi. Much to our chagrin, he'd insisted on keeping watch over us when we slept, staying near day and night, assigned to see we came to no harm. I was surprised to learn this mild, courteous person had earlier served as an assassin in Shanghai, the first assassin I'd ever come to know at all well.

The Chinese soldiers were a handful of regulars, handpicked for talent and verve from the Camp One staff by the Americans or Major Ho. The team members shared a bent of enthusiasm, an easiness in working together, an affection for the task, a like-mindedness. That's how to distinguish these people: They were like-minded.

Once across the river, the team would link up with one or another of the Chinese officers with roots in the Zhuji area, Good Leg, an officer of the LPA, or Bad Leg, whose murky politics were not a disqualifying factor, with us Americans, anyway.

Another part of the design was the ambiguous relationship of command between Chinese and Americans. It's easier to say what it wasn't than to describe what it was. It wasn't Tai Li's slippery legalism of "supervision" in our operations in Zhejiang. Ximoushi was the closest to that formula when General Wang, whom we never saw again, presented for our approval his staff's by-the-book plan of attack, which he then did not follow. Stock military terms for us—liaison, advisers, trainers—won't do, either. You have to look at each situation to see how a decision was made.

Hull's report picks up the story after I'd left, saying, tongue-in-cheek, that he, Tawater, McCoy, "were detailed by Lt. Horton to remain in the area to dispose of some explosive materials that were brought from Camp One." He and Major Ho "thought it better to stay in hiding for a while which we did until the Japanese had withdrawn to their bases around Zhuji." Three days later, they were with Colonel Shu, Good Leg, that is, who had been working with Jake Siegrist a few weeks before, and talking about blowing up railway tracks and small bridges. "On this date (21 November)," said Hull, "we drew up an agreement and the following things were decided."

> 1) C.C. Ho, Lt. Hull with a group of eighty of Colonel (Shu's) men will commence operations in destroying railroads between the time 2300/27 and 0100/28 November Shanghai time in the South Zhuji area.
> 2) Col. Shu . . . with Tawater and McCoy with a group of men will commence operations for destroying the railroad between the time 2300/27 and 0100/28 November in the North Zhuji area.
> 3) After operations the two groups will assemble in the vicinity of Machen.

Whether this was a written agreement is not clear. I doubt that it was. According to the after-action accounts of the three Americans, Major Ho and Lieutenant Hull worked together well. Tawater and McCoy found Colonel Shu difficult to work with, reporting that he did not keep his promises, and as their reports showed, they found other reasons for distrusting him.

Hull and Major Ho prepared demolitions materials before moving within ten miles of the portion of railway running from Zhuji to Anhua, a small town less than fifteen miles south of Zhuji. This was on November 25: Here, says Hull,

Maj. Ho pointed out to me the four places in the area he intended to blow. We had eight men each having a clam to place on the railroad. Later on this day Maj. Ho approached me with an idea of blowing a train. I immediately told him it was a simple job but had no Chinese trained to do the job, also adding I could do it with my interpreter, Alfred Liang. He agreed that it could be done and explained to me that the train was expected between 7 and 9 PM; also saying an inspection car came over this route every hour to inspect the track. We made the necessary arrangements for plastic and other materials. . . .

Like-mindedness at work here: Hull's report continues:

We arrived at the railroad at 1900 and were making plans to plant the charge when the train was heard approaching. I at once thought we had arrived too late. After the train had passed Maj. Ho and I decided to plant the charge anyway in hopes of getting the train the next night. We crossed the railroad about one li north of Anhua station. On the east side of the track we entered a Chinese civilian's house where Major Ho sent for the head man of Anhua.

On his arrival we found there was another train expected at 2230. We moved to the railroad again, Alfred Liang, Lt. Wu and two guards and I planted the charge (20 lbs. plastic under each rail) and we returned to the civilian's house which was 200 yards from the track. At 2230 a north-bound train came into Anhua station and after stopping for 5 to 10 minutes departed on its way. The locomotive set off the pressure device which in turn set off the plastic. Flame shot 100 feet into the air and white steam began to shoot out of the locomotive in several different places. From my observation point I could see the locomotive was derailed.

Our eight men had been divided into two groups to fire on the locomotive and the first three cars which (Japanese troops) occupy, also to fire on Anhua station which they did when the explosion went off. Within five minutes the Japanese opened fire on us with an artillery piece, firing 15 to 20 rounds. Our men withdrew to the (command post) and we all left on the run.

Our plan was to hide in occupied China for three or four days and return. The day of the 27th was spent moving around, hiding and covering our tracks. Ho divided the eighty men into four groups to return to the railroad that night and do their job.

It was reported to me later and verified by civilian reports to me that one group got through and blew eighteen rails on the night of the 27th. On the night of the 29th two groups got through and blew thirty more rails; on the night of December 1st the last group got through and blew sixteen rails.

Hull had done the unexpected by fleeing east into Japanese-occupied territory instead of going west toward the river, as was our habit. Hull says that his party spent the next five days

either running from Japanese, puppet troops, communists, or hiding. On the day Nov. 30th our party was 100 li from the coast of China. On Dec 4th we moved closer to the railroad and that night at 1830 we crossed the rails again about 2 li from the spot where we had blown the train. While passing through this area I saw Chinese homes still burning that had been fired by the Japanese three days before. On 10 December I met Tawater and McCoy (and) returned to Camp One 18 December.

Tawater and McCoy, in the meantime, had been assigned to observe operations with Colonel Shu, who split his men into two groups. Shu and McCoy went off with one group, and Tawater went off to observe the other. Both men complained that Colonel Shu kept them from approaching close enough to see the clams put on the rails. The best Tawater could say was that he'd heard intermittent explosions on either side of 2330 on the night of 27 November. Colonel

Shu said later that sixty clams had been used and two culverts blown with the twenty-five–pound boxes of plastic.

Tawater and McCoy did not dispute his claim. They did draw up a bill of particulars against Colonel Shu in the reports they wrote when back at Camp One.

For one thing, before the raids, Shu went off on an errand, borrowing Chinese ten thousand dollars from McCoy, saying he would return it in three days. He never did return it. (At that period of the inflation, that was about United States fifty dollars.)

Unbeknownst to Shu, Tawater saw Shu, before the first raid, take some twenty kits of fuse lighters Tawater had rigged to fuses and detonators. Shu later began talking of a second raid—contrary to the earlier agreement—but then, even later on, said there weren't enough detonator kits for a second raid. There was no second raid, and Tawater and McCoy thought Shu was pretending all along when he spoke of it. And Shu denied having the materials Tawater knew he had taken.

I had told Tawater to be sure to measure the width of the railway track—a requirement Chungking had sent to us. Shu first agreed to let Tawater do this. At the time of the raid, Shu refused and also refused to let Tawater detonate a clam on the railway, something else he had promised Tawater. "Colonel Shu . . . would not listen or explain. He just made a derisive gesture and walked away." Tawater kept at it, again reminding Shu of his promise to let him go in to measure the track.

But my suggestion was laughed at, and no explanation would be given me for the refusal. When I explained that I had been ordered to measure the track I was told the Chinese were ordering me not to. The only way I could have carried out Lt. Hull's orders would have been to defy the Chinese and in view of this organization's policies in the past, I thought this was inadvisable.

Tawater had the only radio, and I'd sent him a message from Camp One asking him to comment on a rumor we'd heard that our team had derailed a troop train. Tawater and

McCoy told Colonel Shu they had to find Hull to answer my inquiry.

> Although we had no interpreter with us, both McCoy and I could speak a little Chinese and because of our past experience and knowledge of this area we felt we could easily find Lt. Hull. We notified Col. Shu that we wanted coolies and as many soldiers as he wanted to send and planned to leave at seven o'clock on the 8th. Col. Shu gave no reason but said we could not leave until eight o'clock.
>
> That night a letter came from Lt. Hull saying that he was waiting for us at Pan Chi Ke. Col. Shu told us that 600 Japs were sleeping that night at Metzu (75 li away) and that they were coming after us and would be there the morning of the 9th.
>
> At 0530 on the morning of the 8th, we woke, hearing rifle shots. Although I had more training and experience on a carbine than any Chinese in the area, McCoy and I were rushed out over the mountains having no chance to protect ourselves or to do our part—only a chance of getting shot in the back as we retreated with the old men, women and children. We heard about 75 shots and some 15 heavy explosions.

Later that morning, they were told that the Chinese had lost ten men killed and four wounded and had killed eighteen Japanese. From then on, they concentrated on treating the casualties and taking three severely wounded men to Pact Doc. Tawater ended his report by saying

> For these reasons I believe that Col. Shu did not give or make any attempt to give any cooperation whatsoever to the Americans. I strongly suggest that if Americans participate with Col. Shu in future operations that the extent of his cooperations be firmly predetermined.

McCoy was similarly distrustful of Shu. He remembered that "Col. Shu promised Lt. Hull and myself that he would give all cooperation in the evacuation of any casualties that might be inflicted. Col. Shu failed in this promise by slowly evacuating three seriously wounded soldiers after the attack of Dec. 8th." McCoy got the wounded men to the hospital at Pact Doc through the force of his own will. He was angry at the end of it. "Chinese cooperation in moving wounded soldiers is very unfavorable," he wrote. "As this log shows many promises that (sic) were not kept."

Peanut Hull concluded his report with four points about work in the Zhuji area:

1. Americans can work in this area.
2. The civilians in this area will cooperate with all the help they can give.
3. I suggest that a few Americans be in this area at all times. It is open to operations but also dangerous. Three Jap assassins were caught on this trip—one, armed with a dagger, within 50 yards of an American.
4. The North Zhuji area is open to operations. It would be wise to work in both areas.

Tawater, despite the problems with Colonel Shu, had similar recommendations.

The area north of Zhuji seems to be unusually good for future operations. The area is richer than most and the soldiers get better treatment and food. The civilian cooperation is unusually good, the Japanese troop concentrations apparently light—consisting of scattered pillboxes with reported personnel of around 20, usually possessing at least one light machine gun. There are many ways to get to the railroad, many escape routes and plenty of mountains to hide in.

I forwarded these reports to Chungking and added my own warm comments in praise of the three authors, and expressing doubts about the behavior, if not the motives, of Colonel Shu. I knew that Shu had been as stubborn with Siegrist, refusing him a direct part in the October raid. I disliked his treating Tawater and McCoy as he did, probably thinking he could deceive and bully them because they were enlisted men.

I singled out some of our like-minded Chinese for praise: Major Ho, Lieutenant Wu, another Chinese officer, Captain Chen, Alfred Liang, and two other interpreters, Colonel Xu (Bad Leg), and an officer named Ho, Colonel Shu's executive officer, with whom we'd had better experiences than with his boss. And I added, "Americans who have operated with Chinese have great respect for the individual Chinese soldier; he is, on the average, brave, simple, loyal to his commanding officer and lacking only in education and training."

Hull, Tawater, and McCoy were exceptional people. So were the Chinese I named. But I had other motives in commenting on Hull's raid and our cadre of like-minded souls. I was becoming uneasy about Chungking, suspecting our headquarters had little appreciation of the situation in which we lived and worked, and no understanding of our local struggles to get operations going.

It is suggested that this operation in which Lt. Hull took part is the first successful and typical guerrilla-sabotage operation in which Americans have taken part. An interesting point is that no generals were concerned in the planning and execution of this operation. This, I consider, is almost a prerequisite of a successful operation. The Chinese generals with whom I have had contact insist upon hamstringing their own personnel and Americans with conditions, orders and counter-orders which seem largely unnecessary and, I believe, symptomatic of the centralization of authority which seems responsible for many of China's ills. It is therefore recommended to work with the "Colonels" on operations if and when the generals give their permission. It is hoped that sooner or later the weak excuse that "it is too dangerous for Americans to work in occupied territory" may cease to be offered by the generals.

Miles was determined that we show respect for the Chinese we worked with and, by and large, we all adhered to the principle as a matter of decency as well as diplomacy. Even under provocation, as Tawater put it above, he did not further argue with Colonel Shu "in view of this organization's policies. . . ." Any other attitude shown by Miles could have led us to slump into the know-nothingism I'd seen among Americans in Kunming, for example, who saw the war at second or third hand. But the policy, as good as it was, was harmful when we pretended that we and the Chinese had the same goals in the war; that the Chinese were fighting now as fiercely as they did in the past; that Chinese claims of damage to the Japanese were all true.

I wanted to cut through this piety. Not all Chinese were equally brave, devoted, patriotic, and so on. The pretense was wrong and caused a problem with the truth when we Americans talked about what we were trying to do. But, indeed, we had found some Chinese who lived up to and exceeded the pious descriptions. That's what I wanted Chungking to understand.

Chapter 23

In a discourse on operations that Peanut Hull put together
at the end of December 1944, he spoke of the suffering our
operations brought down on the heads of the Chinese. He
begins here by recalling the moments leading up to the de-
struction of the locomotive at Anhua back in November.

After dark our own group of seventeen men (who were
to set the charge under the track) moved to a civilian's
house two hundred yards from the railroad and waited
until 2130. During our wait here the commander sent for
the mayor of Anhua village which was about four hundred yards away. On his arrival he made it very clear that
he was glad we were there to harm the Japs. The commanding officer, trying to secure last minute intelligence,
asked the mayor as to the time schedule of the expected
train. He gave a very startling answer, "I will tell you
when the train is coming and will be killed tomorrow for
doing it, but after I am dead the mayor that takes my
place will help you in any way he can."

Thereupon, they proceeded to blow up the locomotive.
Hull continues:

After observing the damage we started running and continued to do so for the following eight days, never staying in one place more than five or six hours. Some days
were spent dodging Japs and some dodging, in addition,

Chinese puppet troops and also Chinese Communists, who, in this area, are about 2000 strong. One occasion we found a village plastered with Communist propaganda bulletins that were left there the night before. The civilians continued to help us immensely, hiding us in their homes, giving us information, etc. I noticed day after day that the civilians all seemed anxious to talk to me. My interpreter told me that these people had not seen an American since the war had started (at one point we were only thirty-five miles from the seacoast) and it was like a shot in the arm to them to see an American again. When passing through the area we had left eight days earlier I saw civilian houses still smoking where they had been burned to the ground. I then realized what the mayor in Anhua had told me was true. Their homes would be burned and the civilians would suffer but they would continue to help China. On questioning some of the civilians I found their spirit was still high and they were still willing to do anything at all to help.

We didn't lightly dismiss this freedom to skip away scot-free while innocent civilians were punished. We used to worry about the answer we'd give if faced with the question put to the mayor of Anhua, grateful that it wasn't our families in the place of the villagers in Anhua. But we didn't let Japanese reprisals stop us, either.

In a report of a raid he led in January of 1945, Jake Siegrist spoke of an attack on a Japanese barracks next to the town of Bingguo in Zhejiang. "After the second attack at Bingguo Japanese soldiers burned the town in retaliation and started plans to build a new barracks and to fortify the hill overlooking their two previous pillboxes." Siegrist added: "I believe that as few Americans as possible should work in this area, as great numbers hamper the work more seriously than ever." We put our effectiveness ahead of our concern for the innocent.

Hull, Chief Boatswain's Mate E. L. Sims, Jr., and Tawater were back on the railway in early March 1945. Bad Leg turned over fifty of his men to Hull, telling him he was to command them. Peanut named Major Ho as his executive officer and detailed Captain Chen Yuhua, another of our like-minded stalwarts, to lead the party blowing up rails. "The biggest snow in years had just fallen in the area which made it too difficult and dangerous for the enemy to operate night trains. Our plan was to wreck a day train, which had never been attempted in this area and would . . . involv(e) the element of surprise.

Alfred Liang, his role, as usual, going far beyond that of interpreter, gives his account of the expedition:

We planned to hide a 20-pound charge underneath a rail on the night of the 7th hoping that a Japanese train would set it off the following day. We set off from Yeh Ya Tang at about 1800 on the 7th and arrived about two hours later at a village at the foot of a mountain. . . . We continued on when everybody drank his fill of water by climbing that mountain, easy going at first, getting more rugged as we ascended the trail. We had to crawl on fours during the last part of the climb. Going down the mountain was yet tougher. . . .

The exact spot where we planted our charge was about 1 li from a Japanese pillbox to one side and not more than 400 yards to the other side was another one. Just opposite to the latter, in the saddle of a small hill called Bingguo was a barrack with about 50 Japanese. The ground was very hard and of a rock foundation. . . . CBM Sims and Sgt. Tawater started digging as soon as we got there with Capt. Chen Yuhua and myself help- ing. . . . Capt. Hull was with us. A Chinese officer who had orders from Capt. Ho came along to enquire about our progress. He added that the Japanese patrol might come by any minute. . . . the Americans worked on it with greater determination and quicker hands, but they were not, in the least, daunted by this report. Their cool- ness was best interpreted by the term 'Sang Froid.' . . . I took one of the coolies we brought with us, told him to shovel the dirt in the baskets we had with us. That done, I took him with me and dumped the dirt in a pond hard by to avoid leaving any trail of up-turned dirt which would, undoubtedly, arouse suspicion.

Once the charge was planted in the hole and further concealed with dirt and gravel, the party retired to a nearby hill to wait. After dawn, they watched a pair of Japanese soldiers patrol the track, inspecting it without detecting where the charge had been laid. Liang continues:

> At about 0930 we heard the noises of an engine coming from our right and everybody jumped to alert again. Seconds later a train was seen coming out of a hill which blocked our view of the track further to our right. Capt. Hull, watching through the binoculars, shouted, "It's a troop train, it's a troop train! See it, it is full of soldiers." At exactly 0934 of the 8th, the locomotive running rockingly on the rails set off the charge, was derailed but still going ahead awhile and immediately afterwards, fell off in the rice paddies on its right pulling two cars down into the rice paddies with it. Two more cars were derailed but stood on the railroad foundation on the other side of the collapsed locomotive. . . . We could see the Japanese soldiers coming out hurriedly of the wrecked and undamaged cars.

They'd killed thirteen Japanese soldiers, wounded thirty-five, and, with clams, destroyed fifty-three sections of rail. Because locomotives could not cross the Qiantang on the damaged bridge at Hangzhou, the Japanese were unable to replace them. Hull and his teams now had destroyed two, leaving one locomotive to serve the Hangzhou-Jinhua line. Peanut said this at the end of his report on that raid:

> American personnel have been operating in this area constantly for seven months with great success. Due to increasing enemy troops in the Zhuji area it is strongly recommended that American personnel find another field of operations. The enemy now have plain clothes agents throughout this area trying to secure advance information on American movements, etc. The possibilities of success have been decreased greatly because of this. Chinese and American casualties have been surprisingly slight in the past but will increase unless this area is

given a rest. Chinese assistance in this area has been wonderful. I am sure that small groups of Americans have come out of the Zhuji area with a better taste in their mouths for our gallant allies than they ever possessed before. They're truthfully an unbeatable race.

We'd been trying right along to open a new operational area to the north, getting the Chinese to agree to the idea, only to have them throw some new obstacle in the way to prevent it. I was away from camp and so missed one of their worst performances. The day before I left on the November trip to the Zhuji area, we'd gotten Guo's agreement for ten students to go with Lieutenant McGaha on the Yangzi expedition. Guo agreed, to our faces, anyway, to the idea that promising students would benefit from going off with us on operations. The next morning, just after I'd left, General Guo presented George Parker with an unnegotiable decision—Guo having made himself unavailable for negotiation by leaving camp before sending a message to Parker. Tai Li, the message said, had forbidden the students to be sent on operations. Parker sent a protest to Chungking, but to no avail. Ordinarily, we got little satisfaction from asking Chungking headquarters to weigh in on our side once Tai Li had spoken.

The day after that, the Chinese command refused to issue orders for an interpreter to go with McGaha's group to the Yangzi, also a matter agreed to earlier. This time Parker suspended training and—Guo still absent—the orders were issued to the interpreter. Each instance was clearly a way of preventing McGaha's team from going to the Yangzi area without being direct about it. Our stubborness was no match for Chinese guile.

In January, I reported to Chungking: "Word was received that Lt. McGaha and group had departed Gen. Ma's headquarters for Jiangyin-Wuxi area. Their mission is sabotage work along the Nanjing-Shanghai Railway and targets of opportunity. Very gratifying as we have been trying to get someone in this area since last June." Surely I should have known better. From the 31 January 1945 monthly report: "Lt. McGaha and group are now returning to Unit One, having been turned back from the Yangzi area as the Chinese maintain it is too dangerous for Americans."

Despite gnashing my teeth because Generals Tai and Ma had won again, probably "the Chinese" were right about that, maybe for the wrong reasons. The flat terrain does not provide the refuge of mountains. Secondly, it was a political hotbed, although perhaps no worse than other Japanese-occupied areas. We didn't know who our friends would be, and we needed to send an officer up to look into that before sending a team. (And I was later on, myself, to go on such an inquiry.) An account of the Yangzi valley in 1941, at the time of the Nationalist clash with the Communist New Fourth Army, was as true in 1944-45.

> The area . . . lacked the mountains and natural cover useful for concealing guerrilla forces, and was a maze of crisscrossing jurisdictions of Guomindang regular units, local militia, gangs of stragglers and deserters from regular units, and members of Green Gang and other criminal organizations. Some of these forces, coordinated by (Tai Li), were particularly resentful when the Communists edged into their zones of operations along the Nanjing-Shanghai railroad.

Units of the New Fourth Army, still strong around the Yangzi, were coming south, infiltrating the LPA area. These were the "bandits" who at least once intercepted a courier going from LPA headquarters to Camp One. Two P-38 pilots shot down in the Yangzi valley in the summer of 1944 were picked up by an element of the New Fourth. They were treated handsomely, given souvenir Japanese flags, passed through no-man's-land to Chinese on our side of the line, brought to Camp One, and were left with an impression of warm friendliness on the part of the Communists.

Passing through the Chinese countryside, we'd meet parties of soldiers and exchange smiles, greetings, and cigarettes, talk until we finished our cigarettes, move off with friendly farewells. Once—I think it was a day or so out of Ma's headquarters—we came on a unit of a dozen men in gray uniforms, who stood unsmiling on our path and acknowledged our greetings with a cold nod. Our Chinese wore frozen expressions as we pushed on by. I gave detached consideration to the odds for getting a bullet in the back. That was the only meeting I remember with Communist troops. Their political officer hadn't gotten the word to flash the Americans a set of toothy Yan'an smiles.

As the Communists began to show themselves, we asked Chungking for guidance and were told to stay neutral—I can't find the words of the instruction in the record. The monthly report for January 1945 noted that "One hundred carbines, with accessories and ammunition, were turned over to General Guo for use in the camp area due to Communist moves in the north." I planned to defend the camp vigorously—Guo said he was worried the Communists were after our guns and ammunition—no matter what the guidance.

Hull's account speaks of two thousand Communists in the area east of the railway. (I don't know the basis for his numbers.) These could have been infiltrators from the New Fourth Army or stay-behinds from one of the Soviets in southeast China. In addition to Mao's Jiangxi Soviet, there had been other enclaves at that time, one south of Camp One in the Zhejiang-Jiangxi border area and one to the west on the Hubei-Anhui border.

When Hull returned from one of his expeditions—it must have been in December 1944 because I'd have left by the time he came back from the March foray—he told me that some people in the Guomindang underground who'd been helping us had disappeared. He'd been told that the Communists were moving through, eliminating the Guomindang structure in Japanese-occupied areas by assassination.

We suspected the Communists of infiltrating Zhejiang to be on hand in case there was an American landing, pretending they held the territory. We never saw any evidence of the Communists fighting the Japanese in our areas or of the Japanese going after them. For that reason, I've always been skeptical of Communist claims of anti-Japanese victories elsewhere in China during this epoch. Our skepticism was unusual. Americans on Stilwell's staff, experts in the embassy, the newspaper correspondents, generally swallowed Communist camels while straining at Nationalist gnats. We were just as tempted to kick over complexity in favor of simplicity, see the world in black-and-white terms: The Nationalists are so difficult to work with, so rigid, the Communists must be better. The Communists missed a chance with us at Camp One. A little flattery from them might have subdued our doubts about them and fanned a spitefulness toward the LPA.

As engrossed as we were in Camp One's war against the forces of His Imperial Japanese Majesty along the Hangzhou-Jinhua railway, we never exaggerated the effect of these pinpricks, no matter how proud we were of Hull's and Siegrist's teams. We didn't think of these attacks as ends in themselves but as steps along the way to more effective operations. We never gave up completely the hope of disrupting the Japanese rear, harrying their communications lines in support of American troops who'd land on the China coast.

Just by looking into the sky, we could see that the tide of war was turning. In early 1944, we saw nothing but Japanese planes in our air. The camp—or our river—was on a flyway, and they were always coming overhead, flying low, formations of bombers usually, not bothering with us, on their way somewhere. By summer, the Americans were beginning to take over the air. The B-24s, the B-25s, the contrails of the high-flying B-29s, moved overhead now. We were picking up information through the Chinese on the effect of fighter sweeps along the Yangzi as well as picking up our aviators who'd been shot down on those strikes.

While our teams were striking blows at the Japanese in Zhejiang, I was brooding in Xiongcun about cases of indiscipline in camp and complaining to Chungking about personnel policies.

Evidently, some persons in Washington have been telling men destined for this duty that on reaching China "you are just the same as officers" as this lame excuse for insolence or negligence in carrying out of orders has been offered too many times. It is difficult for officers and petty officers in the field to expect even the lowest form of disciplinary qualities in young, immature men when irresponsible persons are in a position to hamper this organization.

The Japanese *Ichigo* offensive in the summer of '44 had cut off our land route to west China. Unfortunately, the Japanese did not control the air, and a navy lieutenant from Chungking was able to fly into east China and motor up as far as Camp One on a familiarization and inspection tour to east China. I told him that we had more men than we could use and how poorly prepared for duty in China were many of the recent ones. I may have put it less judiciously. He immediately and brightly suggested we keep them busy by organizing softball games. If he succeeded at forming an East China softball league, we were not part of it. We did train some of the new people in musketry, scouting and patrolling, Chinese language, rousing the interest of some of them, while others clung to their right to remain stoutly ignorant.

Like Masters and Parkin before me, I was trying to get along with the Chinese. That most of the problems were petty didn't mean I didn't have to go see General Guo about them: the supply of charcoal, the cost of gasoline, sleeping sentries, and the like. Sometimes Guo called me in. Entry for 5 January 1945:

General Guo reported the shooting by an American of a Chinese coolie to Lt. Horton. Dr. Tucker was sent to Huichou to treat the man and Lt. Hull to investigate the matter. Reported matter as accident occurring on road from Huichou to Chichi. When Smith (not the man's name) who had left Camp One for General Ma's headquarters this morning fired at a bird, the bullet ricocheted from rock and striking coolie in left leg. General Guo paid visit to officer's wardroom to discuss houseboy problem with Lt. Horton and Lt. Parker.

The "houseboy problem"—whatever it was—had no connection with the wounded coolie, an incident that led me to become an early partisan of gun control.

General Guo had a way of tattling to Chungking about something we'd done—as in the case of the students who he'd agreed would go north with McGaha—or about something he thought we might be going to do. Often, the first we'd hear of it was an angry dispatch from our own headquarters, taking the Chinese word for it before hearing our side.

To be fair about it, I regret to report that I was not always suitably responsive to higher authority. We had a team all set to go—I don't know which one it was—the men selected, weapons and supplies distributed, timetable and targets worked out, substitutes named for training classes, in all respects ready to leave for the river and Zhejiang early the next morning. That night, I deciphered a dispatch telling us to delay their departure. Maybe Ma had said it was too dangerous, or maybe Guo had told Chungking our people couldn't be spared from training classes, or maybe Tai Li didn't want us over there making mischief. I don't remember what the pretext was this time.

I read the dispatch and put it to one side, saying nothing of it to anyone. I walked across to our radio shack and told the radioman to send a routine signal the next day, when he came up to work the Chungking circuit, asking that the message be repeated. The entirely false implication of such a signal was that the message was garbled and indecipherable. I saw to it the team got underway early in the morning before Chungking could repeat the message.

Chapter 24

The Catholics in the camp had the ministrations of Father Alonso, a Spanish priest in Huizhou. Some of the Protestants began holding services in our new mess hall. With Bibles to read from, but a hymnal lacking, the attempts at singing were tentative. Christmas was coming on, and the words to carols were being recalled and put on paper. The bar was decorated. Skits were organized, and we began having pre-Christmas parties, rehearsing carols early in the evening. Carols might bring on attacks of homesickness, a roomful of silent men stunned into gloom.

We'd break out talking and go to the bar for another Shaoxing *jiu* or the homemade spiked citrus juice of the day and revert to secular carols, "Roll Out the Barrel," "There is a Tavern in the Town," "The Souse Family," "Bless 'Em All," "I Don't Want to be a Soldier (I Don't Want to Go to War)." When the last one started, Chief Sims would interrupt by holding up his hand to announce that the number was dedicated to his devotedly civilian brother-in-law. The popular "Salty Dog (Won't You Be My Salty Dog?)" had been introduced to Camp One by Cpl. Snake Hunley.

On New Year's Day, we had a shooting match on the river bank with carbines. The men marking targets across the river announced that I had scored a possible—every shot in the bull's-eye. Despite the care I had devoted to making my weapon accurate, I suspected this to be untrue.

But I pretended to believe it and chided the Marines for being outshot by an amateur.

Winter at Camp One, like our own mid-Atlantic climate, brought clear, sunny days and the chance of light snows before the solstice. The first soft snows were delightful, turning the camp into a landscape by a Brueghel. The voices of children would float from a quiet street on the far side of the village. Two hundred yards away, you could hear the hostler leaning out of his window, mumbling about ghosts with the old sentry. A blue sky could turn to yellow ocher when the wind carried dust from the Gobi Desert a thousand miles to our north. As the winter wore on, the sky would lower, darken, bring cold rain, even a serious snow when we were good and tired of it.

"30 January. . . . Lts. Horton and Siegrist bought a calf for use in the Officer's Mess." Jake knew all about cows and cutting them up, and we walked to a field of brown rice stubble at the edge of the village to stand with a farmer and talk about a calf of his. While Jake appraised the calf, poking various parts of the poor animal, the farmer's small son stood thickly bundled nearby, arms sticking out at the sides, mouth open, nose running, staring at the foreigners. I joked with the farmer: "If you don't want to sell the calf, how about the boy?"—adding something to the effect that he looked plumper than the calf. The farmer laughed, but the boy began to howl and couldn't be comforted. If he'd had doubts before, he had proof now that the foreign devils ate children.

Why I went with Jake to see the calf, I don't know. There may have been something in the regulations requiring the commanding officer to be present at such a transaction. More likely, Jake asked me to come along. Another perquisite, if going to look at a calf was a perquisite, that came with my taking over from Charlie Parkin was a pair of 7x50 navy binoculars that I had long envied and found as useful as I thought they'd be for watching birds up close. Still another was a bedroom of my own. I had fewer chores, but a lot more to worry about.

The gift of command was not diminished for me by its having resulted from OSS politicking. I was surprised and pleased. I doubt that I gave myself airs or got puffed up by it, but I was changed, not in a moment but gradually, much as a cheese cures and sharpens. With the responsibility of command, I took a new interest in what Camp One was doing and in whether we could accomplish it any better. I continued to put guerrilla operations above everything else we did. Nothing wrong with that, except that our ambition to carry the fight to the Japanese—even within the limits of guerrilla warfare—was frustrated by the Chinese command, from Tai Li on down through Generals Ma and Guo.

Despite my putting operations first, training Chinese troops was our major activity. Aside from having earlier on taught demolitions, I'd had little to do with the complicated scheduling of the courses or the substance of the training. With small interest in teaching and no firm opinions on how it should be done, I needed only to satisfy myself that training was being done well. Our American staff was constantly revising the training, and we were encouraged by the bright and sympathetic junior and midlevel Chinese officers who were putting their heads together with ours to make the training better. We'd kept a training cadre of the most responsive students from training classes, some of the same men who served on the teams operating in the Zhuji area. Differences with the senior officers of the Chinese command on the purpose of training never went away. We insisted not only on each student's being qualified to use a weapon but, more than that, trained in small-unit tactics for guerrilla operations. The Chinese senior command kept its eye on the weapons—continuing to put up with the training as the price to be paid for them.

If the war had gone on longer, the training might have been put to good use by the LPA against the Japanese. We might have succeeded finally at what we wanted: to attack the larger garrisons at Ningguo and Guangte and Anji, to our immediate north, and the fortified towns around Ximoushi, target of the "rehearsal" raid. We wanted to make the Japanese pay in lives to continue their hold on the Hangzhou-Jinhua railway corridor. If there was to be landing on the China coast, we'd want to prevent the Japanese from using the roads, the railways, and the rivers. Even without a landing, we thought this to be a good strategy for our region. Always those "ifs"—despite the training and the weapons we handed out, the LPA was never used decisively against the Japanese.

I spent and wasted time fretting about what we were not doing, constantly comparing what we were doing with the ideal mission. This was a benign contrast to Chungking's way of listing Tai Li's promises as accomplishments, pretending that plans are the same as tasks performed. Despite our ambitions, the main accomplishment of Camp One doesn't translate as a statistic—the number of Chinese soldiers trained, Japanese casualties, railroad rails destroyed—but is to be found in the impression we left with the Chinese with whom we served.

Take the clinic run by Dr. Arthur Tucker, clearly a subsidiary function supporting our real mission. So I thought of it. Art and his pharmacist's mates examined new students for fitness, treated the soldiers in training, cared for wounded soldiers and the seriously ill from Xiongcun and nearby villages, as well as looking after American personnel. Routine care of soldiers meant dealing with common ailments, trachoma, relieving the effect of scabies on the skin, dusting leg ulcers with sulfa drugs, treating infected feet—the only medical care most of them ever had. (Peanut Hull was a regular volunteer at the clinic when he was in camp, an eager specialist in cleaning out leg ulcers.)

The soldiers wore the same cheap straw sandals yearround. During the winter, their feet suffered dreadfully, often showing wounds where the flesh had cracked open. Some Chinese junior officers tacitly agreed that we should ask General Guo to allow us to furnish socks—even cheap cotton socks we could buy in Huizhou—to the soldiers. But face was threatened by an American offer to do what the Chinese command itself could not afford. We understood that and tried to take Guo off the hook by getting Tai Li's approval. When we raised the question to Chungking, Tai Li or his staff likewise turned us down. The only way we got around it at all was seeing to it that a few of the Chinese who went with us on expeditions against the Japanese got pieces of our clothing, our hand-me-downs.

The beneficent work of our medical men with ordinary Chinese was an accomplishment in itself, a part of the greater accomplishment of our being there, of our standing with the Chinese as they struggled through this unhappy time. As puny as were our attacks on the Japanese, they were refreshing, even inspiring, to Chinese soldiers impatient for action against the enemy. Civilians in the occupied area felt the same way. The way the Chinese soldier put up with hardship inspired us in turn. Our accomplishment, of an entirely different order than the things on my mind, was a by-product of the daily work of Tucker and his people, of Hull and Siegrist and the men on their operational teams, of our training instructors. What was good about our work in China was as much a part of our failures as of our successes. If anyone had said at the time that the main result of our being in China would be a lasting and favorable memory of the Americans at Camp One, I would have thought him cynical. And how lasting would it be? Within a few years, the Communist holocaust would obliterate our presence and eliminate our deeds with a new version of history. We were never there at all, it turns out, fighting the Japanese at the side of the Chinese. If our memory lives at all, it lies hidden in the heads of the survivors, afraid to think back to those days, even less to admit to having known us.

It looks quixotic, now, the way we kept trying to elbow our way to where city fathers, Nationalist generals, the Communists, and, presumably, the Japanese, did not want us. But, by our own assessment, we needed a place other than the railway to operate. General Ma could have diverted us from the Yangzi by agreeing to another raid on one of the Japanese-held towns above us in Anhui or in northwest Zhejiang Province. He did not choose to do so, and we kept pursuing our illusions.

The Yangzi region remained politically uncharted for us, a white area on our maps, perilous and flat, a disadvantage to small bands on foot in hit-and-run operations. We'd need a base to work from, a sanctuary to run to after the hitting. Even more than the shelter of mountains, we'd need friends on the ground, the kind we had in Zhejiang. You could sympathize with the city fathers and the village elders of the Yangzi delta. The presence of Americans would upset all their fragile arrangements with Japanese and Communists and Tai Li and draw reprisals down on them. The Chinese commander of the Third War Zone was probably as reluctant as Ma to have us working there. We thought both Ma and Guo were evasively uneasy about allowing us to grasp the extent of Communist infiltration of the region between us and the Yangzi River. They could no longer deny that there were such things as Communists, but they didn't want to talk about it.

I took one more journey that winter before I left Camp One for good, one last embassy, as it were, to the unknown powers of the north. What remains of that walk is like a manuscript with key parts missing. I don't know now what occasioned the trip, and I don't know who went with me. I would hardly have gone alone, so where I say "I" it should read "we." One of the interpreters would have gone with me, and along the way, we'd have picked up guides to lead us, and someone at the end to introduce the two parties, vouch for us to the other. I must have written a trip report on my return, but I see nothing of it in the files. What I write now is no more than a description, a catalog of the set of illustrations that could have accompanied whatever I wrote at the time.

I walked north in steely weather on hard ground through a sere countryside, the black pools of rice paddies fringed with ice and frozen mud. The wind blew sleet into my face and swept pellets of snow from the flagstone paths. Villagers were mostly out of sight, trying to keep warm behind closed doors. The white or faded gray walls and black-tile roofs of farmhouses and temples were severe etchings in monotone. What warmth there was came from the browns and russets of last summer's grasses in the fields, from violet patches as rare rays of sun poked through the clouds to touch the flanks of dark mountains.

At the end of one gray day of walking through snow flurries, I stopped in a town where I was taken to the house of one of the village gentry for the night. The master of the house was some seventy years old, with a gaunt, yellowed face and a wispy beard under a black skullcap, a red button on its top. He wore a long gown with a dog-fur collar, grasping with both hands the handle of a small brass-lined basket holding hunks of glowing charcoal. He kept thrusting the basket under his gown for warmth. He looked like a magistrate of the Ch'ing dynasty, as he might well have been some forty years before.

He showed me to a room lighted only by a wick flickering in a rice bowl of oil. Through an open window about two feet square, high in the wall, the wind was gusting flakes of snow into the room. Against the opposite wall was an altar table, unlit red candles spiked onto high, brass candlesticks on either side of the portraits of ancestors. It was popular then to reproduce photographs of the recent dead in black on a white porcelain slab, the more ghoulish for the distortion of the facial features that seemed to be a result of the process.

The room was terribly cold, but no worse than the chamber of a village temple we ordinarily slept in. On a black bedframe, I unrolled my bedroll, a quilt stuffed with raw silk fiber and wrapped in a piece of oilcloth to keep it dry. Before I could crawl into it, the master of the house came back with a candle to see that I was comfortable. We sat opposite each other in a pair of bentwood, black Ming chairs. Despite the cold, I was so tired I could barely hold up my head, and my brain began playing tricks, the magistrate growing small as though seen through the wrong end of a telescope.

He must have gone, taking the candle with him. I must have gotten into the bedroll and the lamp run out of oil. Once I woke during the night to pitch blackness and quiet. The wind had stopped blowing.

The meeting place, a day or two's walk north, was a white pergola sitting in flat paddy land in a wide valley. With the ever-present mountains low on the horizon, I suppose we were somewhere between the Japanese-held cities of Ningguo in Anhui Province and Xiaofeng across the border in Zhejiang, twenty-five or thirty miles north of LPA headquarters, maybe the same distance west of the fortified village we'd attacked on the rehearsal raid in September.

The pergola was raised above ground level, like an elegant small bandstand, standing prominent and incongruous in the paddies. The scene looked as staged as if done by a set designer who'd never seen China but had been able to come up with something suitable and clever that the piece required. I didn't ask why that site was chosen. For whatever it was worth, anyone approaching our meeting place would have been visible a long way off. And could see us from a long way off, too.

We sat around a round, stone table with a tiled top. On the table was a high-sided, ovoid porcelain bowl, and inside that was a slab of pork, bristles in the hide on one side, then a stratum of white fat and a layer of lean meat. Hot water poured over it from a teapot renewed the broth as we huddled around the table. I shivered with the cold at midday, but there was no wind. As we talked, we took turns dipping broth into our small soup bowls. Someone reached in with chopsticks to tear off hunks of pork and place them in our bowls; probably I, as a foreign friend, was given the honor of the first portion. Although I know that someone sat there with me, the only persons I remember are the two Chinese in dark clothing and black overcoats sitting across from me, the three of us being the principals at the meeting. They were from the underground of a city to the north, polite and deferential, as I was with them. There wasn't much circling around the subject—not a lot of small talk—I remember that. The thing is, I can't remember what it was we talked about.

I remember the flavor of the hot broth with the globules of grease on its surface, how the cold made my legs tremble beneath the table, how good the pork tasted, the careful expressions on the faces of the two men across from me, the texture of the material of their black overcoats. But nothing of substance: not who they were, or what we talked about, or what it might have led to—probably nothing. Yet, what remains with me of that meeting is as vivid as last night's dream.

When I got back to camp, I learned it was time to go. In a few weeks, it would be four years since I'd sailed from the States. Miles had a gracious way of writing the families of his men, and I knew he'd written my parents. I don't know now whether I merely suspected or whether I later learned that they'd written back to suggest four years was enough. In February, word came from Chungking that a Marine captain was on the way from the States to relieve me in March, a slight relief. That is, I'd wait for him and spend a day or two introducing him around. Once he'd signed for the official funds and the stock of weapons, I'd turn over command and leave.

I had hardly taken in the first news when a second dispatch came from Chungking telling me not to await my relief but to get myself immediately to the airfield at Changting in Fujian Province, far to our south. They said I had something like three days to get there before transport planes from west China stopped flying into Changting. The field was judged to be untenable and was to be abandoned. I think the Japanese were expected to seize it. As it was, Japanese fighters, less than an hour away, were harrying the aircraft making the run into Changting.

Just about then it began to snow. My farewells were quick. I wasn't as pleased as I should have been about leaving, as overjoyed as most of my companions would have been. I put my mind to small tasks. The custom was to leave behind what you didn't need for the trip home. I passed on the sheepskin flight jacket Masters had given me and left behind a short samurai sword, the kind Japanese noncoms carried. Not having personally taken it from the former owner, I'd have felt foolish showing it off. I left a green, issue jacket, snugly quilted with raw silk, some cotton khakis too big for me. (It didn't occur to me they'd fit again.) I presented Tucker the can of mustache wax Pickerell had given me when he limped off to Huizhou. I left books and a dog-eared pile of the thin airmail versions of *Time* and the *New Yorker*.

After careful thought, I put aside my bedroll and filled a musette bag with a change of long underwear and socks, my good, wool fatigue cap with emblem and silver bars, some skivvy shorts, a razor, soap, a toothbrush, a few packs of Shanghai cigarettes. (Of desirable possessions, I ranked a toothbrush first and cigarettes second. Anything beyond those was luxury.) Even after giving away everything else, I was well dressed in long underwear, a wool khaki shirt over a navy blue wool watch sweater, wool trousers, high paratroop boots—there had been a shipment of those to Camp One early in the winter—and a blue wool watch cap. Another recent acquisition was a waterproof, thigh-length green coat with hood and a synthetic fur lining—known as an advanced-base coat, for some reason. The coat was too long and bulky to walk in all day but just the thing for sitting in a truck grinding through snow drifts on mountain roads. I took my carbine along for the drive to Changting. I'd keep the .45 caliber Colt pistol I'd carried since the Philippines, and put it in my shoulder holster. I so clearly remember everything I wore because it would take me far more than three days to get to Changting. I wore these clothes, with one change of underwear en route, until I got to Kunming.

I left on 9 March, not knowing that Peanut and his team the day before had destroyed a Japanese troop train in the same snow that was falling at Camp One. Jake Siegrist, to whom I'd turned over command, and Art Tucker, I think it was, walked with me through the snow to Huizhou where the truck waited, and we said good-bye.

I don't know how long it took to get to the airfield. The mountain roads were filling with snow, and we were snow-bound in Shangrao in Jiangsi and again in Fujian. The snow stopped, and the sky cleared when I was in a place called Jian'ou in Fujian. I remember smoking a cigarette one midmorning, sitting in a sun trap against the white-washed wall of a compound. I would have been completely content had I felt cleaner, so I decided to bathe and put on clean underwear, something I'd not done since leaving Camp One some days before. With soap and a borrowed towel, I tiptoed on bare feet through melting snow to a swift-running stream at the edge of the compound. I broke the transparent shelf of ice that bordered its edge, stripped, sat down and splashed in the freezing water, leapt out, soaped myself, went under long enough to get the soap out of my hair, stood trembling in the snow to struggle into the clean long johns, made a bundle of my dirty clothes, hastened back to the sun trap. When I'd put the rest of my clothes on, lit another cigarette and managed to stop shaking, I felt purified.

There was no snow in the valley near Changting, and the airfield was still being used. From there, we flew to the field at Zhijiang, and the next afternoon, I was dropped off at the quarters of the navy contingent in Kunming. I lay down in a dark bedroom with my clothes on. I woke in the dark and looked outside. In the living room were half a dozen young American women in long dresses, officers in navy blue and aviation-green uniforms. They were drinking whiskey and gin out of glasses. I was invited to join them at dinner. The tables were covered with linen, set with glasses and silverware. They were all very nice, and after one or two questions about where I'd been, they went back to talking among themselves. I didn't have much to say. I knew that I'd left China back there somewhere.

Chapter 25

People who know what UDT means seem pleased to hear you were in it, that you were in underwater demolitions. Actually, I was in UDT—Navy Combat Demolitions, the forerunner of today's SEAL teams—and, yet, really I wasn't.

By the time I got to Washington, before I went to Indiana on leave that summer of 1945, I'd decided I didn't want to stay in the States. I didn't like it much. The assignments officer in the Navy Department assured me that, after four years, I could have pretty much anything I wanted, assuming I'd want, as the normal person would, to stay in the States as long as I could string it out. He was surprised when I asked him to tell me the quickest way to get out to the Pacific. That's how I ended up in UDT at the amphibious training base at Fort Pierce in Florida. "You go down there, go through the training, pick up your team, and you're on your way."

The base was on a sea island, Atlantic surf on one side, tide running through the inlet between the island and the town of Fort Pierce on the mainland. We were billeted in a screened hut sitting in sand on the edge of a tidal gut. Every evening, a huge school of mullet poked shyly along the bank beneath the windows with soft lapping sounds. The four double-decked bunks on either side of our hut were nearly filled with a good dozen of us, lieutenants and lieutenant commanders. Each had come to Fort Pierce for underwater demolitions training and to take command of a

UDT team. It soon became clear that there were far more of us than there were teams.

Most of my hutmates had commanded landing craft or landing ships or served on attack transports in North Africa, Italy, Normandy, or in Pacific landings. Many of them were older men with families and didn't mind waiting a while for a team. A lieutenant who'd arrived there when I did had been on a destroyer in the Pacific. He confided to me that service in amphibs was not well regarded by the navy and that the two of us had probably made a mistake in volunteering. Once in amphibs you'd have the devil of a time getting back to the real navy—service on a man-of-war, like his destroyer, is what he meant. He doubted we'd ever get teams, being last in line, and we might as well enjoy ourselves. I was revising my opinion of the helpful assignments officer in the Navy Department. I wondered if he had been given a quota to fill—a demand generated by a typographical error, a ten for a one, something like that—packing our hut with superfluous commanding officers of UDT teams, much as Chungking had sent people we didn't need and hadn't asked for to Camp One.

The first day of training consisted of a test. We assembled in swimming trunks at the edge of a concrete pool filled with warm water so murky that sitting on the edge you could hardly see your feet. We took turns diving for a brick, and then for a small rock. Then one of the trainers threw a coin in the pool, and you were told to dive after it and not come up until you'd found it. The water had rarely been changed—Oyster Bay, they called it. Groping blindly around the bottom after the coin was more like a fraternity hazing than military training. "Boy Scouts," spluttered the destroyer officer loudly, when he bobbed up finally to hurl his coin over the edge of the pool. I thought it was more like a required gym class.

The next test was a half-mile swim. I was happy that the crawl, which I'd never learned, was forbidden for its noisy splashing. The breast stroke or sidestroke were the prescribed forms. Many of the young sailors, in the navy tradition, could not swim and were given instruction until they qualified at half a mile.

Once past this stage, training began.

The mission of underwater demolitions teams was to prepare enemy-held beaches for a landing of our forces. We were trained to reconnoiter a beach and to destroy obstacles that could keep men and boats from getting ashore. Beach defenses, in the water and on the beach itself, were clumsy items, oversized blocks of concrete, railroad rails welded together, concertinas of barbed wire. They had to be destroyed by hand, so to speak, as naval gunfire alone didn't clear them out of the way.

Primacord—an explosive that looks like clothesline— was the handiest material as it could be wrapped around metal rails, concrete posts, wire entanglements, to shatter them. We learned to debark from small landing craft and paddle quietly in, by day or by night, towing plastic explosives or blocks of TNT with us, primacord wound around us, blasting caps and fuse waterproofed and wrapped around our middles, and blow the beach. In one night operation, we swam ashore in fatigues and helmet liners, the sandflies were so bad. They came biting right through the fabric. We all swore that night we'd never come back to Florida once we got away.

Reconnaissance was the most fun. We'd come in a boat to a point a few hundred yards offshore and, one by one, roll over the side, clad in trunks, face mask, and flippers, carrying a slate and a stylus. Dropped a hundred or two hundred feet apart, we'd swim in close to shore, treading water as we sketched the portions of beach defenses assigned to us.

Then we'd swim back out and tread water, lined up to be retrieved by the boat. In combat, the operation by this time might have been noticed. If the forces ashore had come awake to what was going on, they might be firing on swimmers and on the boat recovering them. So the swimmers were picked up at high speed. Our technique for pickup used a rubber boat fastened to the seaward side of a small fast landing craft, an LCVP, meaning Landing Craft, Vehicle, Personnel. The heaviest or strongest man on the team laid on his back in the rubber boat, with his feet forward. He crooked one arm out over the water as the boat roared down on a swimmer. As the boat closed on him, the swimmer crooked his own arm. If done properly, as the two elbows locked the velocity of the boat swung the swimmer through the air, like a gymnast, into the rubber boat. You were one moment tense in the water, then upside down in the air, flopping like a gaffed fish into the rubber boat, often with the wind knocked out of you. You had quickly to climb over the gunwale into the LCVP to make way for the next swimmer or have him slamming down on top of you.

Doctrine held that a swimmer might have only one chance to be picked up, so we were well drilled in the routine. Surprisingly, the heads of swimmers are not easily seen from shore, and the success of the operation depended heavily on that. We were being trained by veterans of Pacific landings and of Normandy—UDT casualties had been particularly heavy at Normandy. In the early Pacific landings, when the mother ship—a fast destroyer transport—approached an island, screened by other vessels, lowered boats that came toward the beach and then withdrew to the mother ship, the Japanese thought an initial attempt at landing had been foiled. By now, the Japanese had grasped the point of the maneuver. We were warned that when we swam ashore in the invasion of the Japanese home islands, beach defenses would be peppered with booby traps—antipersonnel mines—and we'd be confronted underwater by Japanese offensive swimmers.

We trained along with UDT units finishing their team training. When your time came to be assigned a team, you'd shake down your team by training as a unit at Fort Pierce before moving to Coronado in California for cold-water training. There you'd learn to use scuba gear and to wear wet suits. So far we'd only snorkeled around in mask and flippers.

After we'd finished training, there was still no sign of when we'd get our teams. One version had it that we were waiting for drafts of men to make up the new teams—a full team would have about a hundred men. There was talk of lieutenants being assigned as executive officers of new teams, rather than being given command—entirely reasonable, if you were matched with an experienced commander.

But all this remained indefinite. The destroyer fellow suspected that the UDT establishment preferred to give command assignments to their own people rather than to the interlopers in our hut.

There was no one to give you any idea of the future. There was the training staff, and then there were the teams. Then there was us who didn't belong to anybody. "Relax," was the advice from the old hands. We helped out in training from time to time, but the training staff didn't give us much to do. You got the idea you were in the way. An army engineer officer—there had been army UDT teams as well—the destroyer lieutenant, and I would borrow an LCVP to go fishing, running along slowly just outside the surf line. Or we'd fish from the beach, taking time off from that to body surf. It seemed most everyone on the base pushed aboard the train from New York when it stopped at Fort Pierce on Friday night. We'd walk through the train to the club car and crowd out the civilian drinkers, usually getting off in Palm Beach. A couple of times we went as far as Miami. A tired, disheveled crowd caught the last Cannonball back up the line to Fort Pierce on Sunday night. As hedonism began to displace militarism, we were finding it convenient to come back to base on Monday, then stay over into Tuesday. Some of the married officers in the hut went off to visit their families. We took flying lessons at the airport. No one seemed to care, as long as you stood your duty as officer of the day for the base command, and that didn't come up often. The navy seemed to be made up of new kinds of people, mess officers, public affairs officers, assignments officers, welfare officers, physical training officers, swimming coaches—specialties I'd never known of or ever suspected to be necessary, particularly in wartime.

I fulfilled the vow made by so many of our generation and read *War and Peace* through to the end in the quiet of the hut, much of it over one weekend when others were away. When found out, I was amiably accused by my hutmates of harboring intellectual pretensions. My attitude wasn't particularly good. Nor was my morale. I missed China, but it wasn't only that. I didn't belong to anything. What makes war attractive is being a part of a team, whether a team blowing up rails in Zhejiang, or a demolitions team, or being a watch stander aboard a four-piper. I wonder how the UDT establishment—if there was such a thing—regarded us. Who might I have asked? What would he have said?

In July, I was promoted to lieutenant commander. I couldn't help being pleased, at the same time deciding that it finished me for the navy. Had I been still an ensign or even a jg, my lack of experience at sea would not have mattered. The rise in rank starkly illuminated my professional incompetence. Guerrilla warfare, UDT, were fine in wartime, but the real navy was in ships.

That summer of 1945, no matter how differently we regarded the navy and our place in it, no matter how desperate our experiences, no matter what had happened to us or to comrades, not one of us ever doubted that we'd win the war. That was one assumption we all held without question. We could lose ships and men and campaigns, but I never heard anyone seriously discuss the possibility of our losing—not that we could define how we'd win. But losing was inconceivable.

Another certainty was that the Japanese would never give up. In the summer of 1945 our submarines—it was mostly their work—had cut the Japanese homeland off from the the China mainland and from the Japanese empire in Southeast Asia. But none of us thought that Japan could be starved into submission. We all knew we'd have to land under fire on the home islands and kill every last man in uniform—the way it had been in the Pacific islands—to defeat Japan.

So it was a shock when suddenly the war ended, an anticlimax. Everything had changed so abruptly that we couldn't grasp the meaning of peace, and in the pleasure of it, we didn't try. We said nothing of the morality of the atomic bombs, although we barely understood what they were. We were grateful. The only dissenters I saw at Fort Pierce were ensigns from one of the UDT teams standing together, some with tears in their eyes, cheated of their chance to see action.

The end of the war was the big anticlimax. Landing on

Japan might have been the last great adventure of them all. I think I'd have missed Tai Li and General Ma and the Third War Zone Commander saying it was too dangerous, that we'd better put off the landing until a more propitious time.

"How did China get such a grip on you?" my wife asked us years later when we went back to visit Camp One. I can't give an easy answer, but China has never let go.

Postscript

In the course of writing this account of wartime years, I have been careful to try to put down what I did and thought at the time. Intensity of feeling is less faithfully reproduced. I do not care to pretend to emotions I may remember but no longer feel, whether sadness, excitement, fear, or ardor.

I have forgotten neither the bitterness I felt at the time about the treatment of comrades the Japanese took prisoner in the Philippines nor my feelings of guilt for escaping their fate. Over the years, I decided that, having escaped being tested by the harshness of captivity, I have no grounds for judging fellow Americans who behaved less than honorably while in captivity. Friends of mine who survived the camps, the brutal treatment from their jailers, the sinkings of prison ships, while they never felt kindly toward Japan, refused to let bitterness consume them. It would be false of me to cherish a secondhand bitterness, as it were, out of loyalty to them and for what I never suffered.

About the early days of the war, far more competent witnesses than I have spoken, and their testimony has been refined by the work of serious historians. The record still suffers from Douglas MacArthur's being treated with a generosity he does not deserve. Washington tolerated his misjudgments from the first days of the Pacific War right on through the unnecessary campaign of Philippine liberation. His later accomplishments as viceroy in Japan should not color his wartime record.

Where I was one of few foreign observers on the ground

in China, I speak with more assurance. Admiral Miles gave me good jobs to do and praised me far too highly in fitness reports for doing them. Yet, I criticize some of his decisions rather than to return his generous treatment of me. Between his fellow Americans undermining him and the Chinese determined to limit his actions, he had an unusually difficult task.

While I was impatient with the Chinese command, I could see then, as well as now, why they were incapable of agreeing to our demands for energetic joint action against the Japanese. I can see how they got to be the way they were. But I don't excuse them. Camp One alone, and our cadres drawn from the ranks of the Loyal Patriotic Army along with Chinese irregulars, could have made it hot for the Japanese in their occupation of Zhejiang Province, maybe led them to withdraw into the city of Hangzhou itself. We kept hoping for a landing on the China coast. I still wonder whether General Ma would have been willing to commit the LPA to cutting the Japanese lines of communication. In the end, the devious games played by Tai Li and his subordinate generals did little for them and nothing for China.

The veracity of Chinese claims of damage and casualties inflicted on the Japanese is shaky. I've questioned the sweeping claims made by SACO—our joint organization with Tai Li—and by the LPA with which we worked at Camp One. I admit the practical impossibility of assessing these claims. Even though my memoir is not a history of the Navy Group, I won't avoid briefly discussing the claims.

In the Records of the U.S. Naval Group China is a twenty-one paragraph memorandum addressed to Miles and dated 4 June 1945. Neither the author of it nor its purpose are shown, but I assume it was put together by the Naval Group staff in Chungking. The typed title is "LPA and Guerrilla Actions in Which Americans Participated." The words "LPA and Guerrilla" are struck out and replaced by the inked-in word, "SACO." A third of the actions described were those of Camp One which, at that time anyway, had carried out more raids than any other navy unit.

The report shows the extent of direct American participation in guerrilla actions. It is useful for establishing which claims could be verified by American witnesses. The report lists a 20 March 1945 raid on Zhuji by Captain Hull which took place after I'd left Camp One, and therefore didn't know about, in which a Japanese officer was killed and another captured. There is no reference to our "rehearsal" raid at Ximoushi, leading me to question how thorough the report is. Combat being what it is, in even these verified actions, the claims of enemy casualties cannot be taken as certain.

For research into the veracity of the SACO claims, the archives of the Republic of China in Taipei might be helpful, unless they simply duplicate old SACO records. I doubt that other elements of the Chinese government had independent methods of evaluating SACO claims. (Who would go checking up on Tai Li?) Even less reliable would be the archives of the People's Republic. The Communists would not have known in detail what the Nationalists—including SACO and the LPA—did against the Japanese. Their demonstrated interest has been the denigrating of actions of the Nationalists (and of the Americans) against the Japanese and the puffing up of their own exploits, the latter beyond the credulity of even the most ardent foreign sympathizer. Nevertheless, I'm sure many Chinese today accept without question the official version that the Pacific War was won by the Communist's Eighth Route Army alone.

Other American commands in China lacked an independent way of judging SACO claims. The opinions of our embassy, of journalists, and of Stilwell's staff, were generalized antipathy to SACO and the Navy Group because of our relation with Tai Li. Envying it as a competitor, the OSS tried to eliminate the Navy Group or steal its charter for guerrilla operations. Many Americans who were skeptical of Tai Li and the Nationalists generally accepted without question the military claims of the Chinese Communists.

At Camp One, we learned that the Chinese who reported accurately were exceptions. Our finicky interest in exact numbers of men or miles was more amusing to the Chinese than exemplary. To express the idea of a large number of

Japanese troops, the Chinese used the word, *wan*, which means "a great number." It also means "ten thousand." We Americans preferred to transcribe the latter, that exact-seeming meaning. Having converted a wild estimate into a finite number, we might later charge the source with fabricating the figure.

We can be sure that the LPA reported to Chungking incidents that did not happen. In the same way, authorities in the Chinese countryside made false claims to Beijing during the time of the Communists' Great Leap Forward. In both cases, an arbitrary central Chinese authority demands results, and subordinate units dutifully respond with fabricated figures to please. Tai Li showed the same respect for the truth as shown by the Chinese Communists today.

I suggest that the archives of the Japanese Army, Navy, and the civil occupation authorities, are the places to go for research on Japanese combat casualties in China, rather than to Chinese or American sources. Take, for example, the microcosm of the Hangzhou-Jinhua railway. If Japanese reports closely resemble what Peanut Hull and Jake Siegrist reported—which we know to be truthful—we'd have a beginning on an index of the reliability of Japanese numbers.

The least generous, the most unjust evaluation, would dismiss Chinese claims in the manner of loudmouth Americans in Kunming in 1943. "Ever see a wounded Chinese soldier?" they'd ask each other with a loud guffaw. How could you possibly see such a thing sitting around Kunming? Brave Chinese men and women did noble things during the resistance. Some of their deeds were accurately recorded. Many died nameless in combat or under Japanese torture. In the pursuit of accuracy, let's never forget that truth.

China's grip on me had as much to do with youth and the excitements of war as with the charm of China and her people. My sentimental feelings for the Chinese were pretty well quenched by the actions of the Communists on their coming to power. Their eagerness to rid China of foreign influence, a popular move with most Chinese, was understandable. Their falsification of their own past—never mind what they said of us Americans—their elimination of their own history, was only one of their intellectual offenses, as criminal as it was ungenerous. Far worse was the organized viciousness which they turned on their own people, on themselves. Two years in China had taught me something of cruelty and callousness in a country at war. Who could have expected that the new Chinese rulers would wage war against their own people?

Notes

Chapter 6

p. 50 Admiral Dennison's remarks on leadership were made in an interview for his oral history. Page 70, Chapter V, *Reminiscences of Admiral Robert Lee Dennison, U.S. Navy (Retired)* Annapolis: United States Naval Institute, 1975.

Chapter 8

p. 71 Those first fatalities were Ens. Robert Tills in Davao and Ens. Robert White in Guam.

p. 72 "Inexplicable" is the word used twice by Ronald H. Spector in discussing the loss of aircraft at Clark Field. See pp. 107-8 of Spector's *Eagle Against the Sun*, New York: Random House, 1985. The shock and the size of the disaster at Pearl Harbor did much to save General MacArthur's skin. Spector's is a lively, readable, and accurate general history of the Pacific War.

p. 79 Admiral Robert Dennison, in his reminiscences, op. cit., tells of attending MacArthur's staff meeting on Christmas Eve and learning there of MacArthur's deciding to declare Manila an open city. He says this was the first that MacArthur's own staff had heard of his decision. I suppose Dennison and I must have returned to the Marsman Building from Fort Santiago at about the same time and that he would have gone straight to Admiral Hart while I was passing the word to officers lower down the command ladder.

Chapter 9

p. 81 The word, *pidgin*, as used here means, "my responsibility, my business." It comes out of pidgin English, a lingua franca in the Far East made up of mostly English words in a Chinese/English syntax. As amusing to hear as it was convenient, it had an undesirable colonial taint and has long ago passed out of use as a means of communication between Chinese and foreigners. The word *pidgin* itself is allegedly an approximation of a Chinese pronunciation of the word *business*. Asiatic Fleet slang had a number of pidgin words, "pidgin" being the most popular.

p. 81 I was staying Topside Christmas night with members of the Field Radio Unit, Station Cast, the navy communications intelligence detachment on Corregidor, my hosts at Christmas dinner. My bad reaction to tunnel living was normal, although the tunnel was a welcome haven after the heavy bombardment of Corregidor began in 1942. When Lt. Comdr. Charles Adair was serving as Hart's flag lieutenant in the summer of 1941, he accompanied Hart on an inspection tour of Corregidor, during which they had visited Malinta, the big army tunnel. That convinced Adair that tunnel life was not for him. When it was clear that the staff would be leaving Manila, Adair made arrangements to get aboard the *Lanikai*, commanded by then-lieutenant Kemp Tolley, USN, and it was Adair who got permission for her to sail south. *The Reminiscences of Rear Admiral Charles Adair,* Annapolis: The United States Naval Institute, 1977.

See the account of *Lanikai's* voyage south in Kemp Tolley, Rear Admiral, USN, (Retired) *Cruise of the Lanikai, Incitement to War,* Annapolis, Naval Institute Press, 1973. Tolley dedicated the book to Charles Adair.

My roommate Topside that night was Lt. Paul Nygh of the Royal Netherlands Navy. He was also a passenger on the *Lanikai*, he and Adair joining the *Lanikai* before she sailed south on the twenty-sixth. Tolley, Ibid., says Nygh was killed in 1943 in an attempted infiltration of the island of Flores in the Indies chain.

p. 82 *Pillsbury* was typical of the ships in the squadron, a flush-deck, four-stacker destroyer, commissioned in 1920, displacing 1190 tons, 310 feet at the waterline with a beam of 31 feet, and drawing 9 1/2 feet, she carried four 4-inch, 50-caliber deck guns, a 3-inch, 23-caliber antiaircraft gun, two .50-caliber machine guns, and .30-caliber Lewis guns. These ships had little effective defense against attack by aircraft. Their main offensive capability was concentrated in twelve torpedo tubes. The normal complement is given as 122 men, and she was supposed to be capable of 35 knots. Ref. *Dictionary of American Fighting Ships,* Washington, D.C.: Naval Historical Division, Office of the Chief of Naval Operations.

p. 83 In the course of recording Admiral Dennison's oral history, the interviewer asked him to comment on this statement: "Admiral Hart, in his report, laments the fact that if he had taken earlier action, he could have ordered out and saved approximately a thousand naval personnel who eventually went to Corregidor and most of them became prisoners."

Dennison answered, "Well, this was really an inexcusable thing. We'd taken over (the French-flag *Maréchal Joffre*) put a prize crew aboard it and she sailed with a naval captain and a few naval officers without anybody in her. Why? There were a lot of navy people who had no way that they could be of assistance to the defense of Corregidor or Bataan or anything else. They were mechanics or enginemen, storekeepers, some of the personnel from Cavite and all they were doing was drinking water and eating food because their skills weren't needed, and I don't wonder that Hart laments the fine officers that were left behind. . . ." Dennison, op. cit. p. 29. The *Maréchal Joffre* did get safely through. The number of naval personnel taken in the Philippines was more than two thousand. Needless to say, we four ensigns who left would not have ranked high on a list of valuable personnel, whereas the radiomen with us did.

Of those who remained on Corregidor, the 4th Marines were not used until the last day on Corregidor. They could have made a difference in resistance had they been committed as early as Lingayen Gulf or at any time later on Bataan. MacArthur kept them on Corregidor, refusing to use them apparently for no better reason than that they were part of the navy.

Of our classmates from midshipmen's school, some commanded boats during the fighting at Bataan and Corregidor. Others were platoon leaders in the naval battalion assigned with the 4th Marines to beach defense on Corregidor, commanding some of the sailors Dennison referred to whose expertise was hardly infantry warfare. My roommate, Bill Long, for instance, was wounded commanding his platoon on 6 May, the day of the Japanese landing on Corregidor, and was cited, that day, among a dozen others in the naval battalion, for "conducting themselves as soldiers and veterans." After liberation in 1945, he was awarded the Silver Star for his gallantry. The only one of our group to be assigned to the Yangzi Patrol, Bill Lloyd, had come down to the Philippines with his gunboat. An officer in T Company of the naval battalion, on the 6th Bill was "killed leading an attempt to wipe out a (Japanese) machine-gun nest" the same day. These last quotations are taken from a piece by Hanson W. Baldwin, "Last Stand of the 4th Marines," in S. S. Smith, *The United States Marine Corps in World War II*, New York: Random House, 1969. This epic battle is little known. Our people, greatly outnumbered by the Japanese invaders who preceded the attack on the small island with months of artillery fire and bombing, had no chance at all. Their morale was such that they refused to take their obvious defeat easily. They fought a hopeless battle with skill and valor, making the Japanese pay heavily for every inch of ground they seized.

p. 84 In addition to Captain Pound, *Pillsbury* officers were the executive officer, Lt. Robert Germany, Lt. Theodore Hilger, Lt. A. H. Vorpahl, Lt. (jg) Edmundo Gandia, Lt. (jg) Howard Fisher, Ens. Leonard T. Sulkis, and the division doctor, Lt. Alton Bookout. All except Len Sulkis were regular navy, the doctor being of the medical corps.

Chapter 10

pp. 92–93 Never mind the names of the command from week to week during this period. Admiral Glassford had commanded the Yangzi Patrol, coming south with it to the Philippines in December 1941, going then immediately south in command of Task Force 5, mostly ships Hart had sent south before the war started.

Chapter 11

p. 101 The air force officer was named Frank Kurtz, and his experiences as a B-17 pilot in the early days of the war appeared in the collection by William S. White, *Queens Die Proudly*, New York: Harcourt, Brace and Company, 1943.

p. 108 We didn't know at the time—I bet anything Jack Payne did—that the "decision had been predicated on the assumption that the *Isabel* was of no particular military value, and her loss would make little difference in the war against Japan." W. G. Winslow, *The Fleet the Gods Forgot, the U.S. Asiatic Fleet in World War II*, Annapolis: Naval Institute Press, 1982, p. 274. Winslow goes on to tell of the voyage of *Isabel* to Fremantle.

p. 108 Lieutenant—later Admiral—Dempsey was awarded the Navy Cross for his aggressive work on combat patrol in 1941 and 1942.

p. 109 In Java, ABDACOM was no more. The Dutch took control, with the result that a number of our warships were soon lost, along with British and Dutch men-of-war, in an "effort that probably postponed the invasion of Java by one day." *Encyclopaedia Britannica*, 1959, op cit., p. 792X.

p. 109 "The *Isabel* was at the refueling pier that afternoon when twenty-one officers and enlisted men reported on board for transportation," notes Winslow, Ibid., p. 279. That was Dempsey, Lawrence, and I, plus the radiomen.

pp. 109–110 Winslow, Ibid., mentions the torpedo that missed us but says nothing of either the beer or the exchange of messages with *Seawitch* concerning the Japanese plane, probably as a result of Payne's discretion. Payne himself or the ship's log must have been the source of Winslow's account. Payne may not have entered his praiseworthy indiscretions in the log.

p. 111 The Japanese picked up one crew member of the *Asheville* and him only to identify the ship, leaving the other survivors to die in the water. He died later in prison camp. *Cruise of the Lanikai*, op. cit., p. 224.

p. 111 Len Sulkis was lost on the *Pillsbury*. She'd been sunk with all hands by the Japanese at night south of Java after she left Tjilatjap. After the war (see his *Reminiscences*, op. cit.) Charles Adair asked that Japanese naval officers be interrogated about the fate of Asiatic Fleet ships south of Java from 1 to 4 March 1942. The Japanese forces that sank our ships were made up of four battleships, five cruisers, a number of destroyers, and an aircraft carrier, the *Soryu*. The Japanese didn't try to save anyone, saying that: "They retired hastily—no survivors rescued."

This force also sank the destroyer, *Edsall*, with all hands, including her passengers, P-40 pilots who had lost their planes, again without looking for survivors, as well as the *Asheville* and the *Pecos* with survivors of the *Langley* aboard. These Japanese ships sank many of the merchant ships with the families we'd put aboard at Tjilatjap.

Chapter 13

The reader interested in putting this epoch into a wider historical context is directed to Jonathan D. Spence, *The Search for Modern China*, New York: W.W. Norton and Company, 1990. It covers the years 1644 to the present.

p. 123 For convenience, I refer to Miles as an admiral throughout. In 1943, he was a captain, later on a commodore, even later an admiral.

p. 124 It's seriously misleading to compare Tai Li to two such different men of widely different cultures. See Barbara Tuchman on Tai Li in *Stilwell and the American Experience in China, 1911–45*, New York: The Macmillan Company, 1970. p. 261. Tuchman writes well, and the book is worth reading despite her indiscriminate agreement with Gen. Joseph Stilwell's views of the world and of the Chinese Nationalist government in particular.

p. 124 See Milton E. Miles, *A Different Kind of War*, Taipei: Caves Books, Ltd., 1967, p. 18, concerning the navy's mission. I shall refer to this book often, simply as Miles, op. cit. When I quote him from another source I'll make that clear.

p. 125 Miles, op. cit., discusses the importance of weather on p. 11.

p. 125 Miles complains about the army's peanut butter on p. 126 of Miles, Ibid.

Chapter 14

p. 129 It was the luck of the war that led some of us to be drawn to China, others of us to Japan. These two cultures, enrapturing so many foreigners yet both notably antiforeign, were finally penetrated by foreign influence in the nineteenth century. Despite their exclusiveness, even fierce disdain of the outside world—or partly because of that—the fascination continues. See "Going Back to Camp One", in *Naval History*, Vol. 3 No. 4, Fall 1989, U.S. Naval Insitute, Annapolis, a piece I wrote about a trip to China in 1986.

p. 130 The Flying Tigers were a colorful lot who fought the Japanese in the air and by being there raised Chinese morale. A former navy chief who'd been a member of the American Volunteer Group was still in Kunming when I got there. Before he left he told me yarns about the AVG that left me uncomfortably impressed by the seamy side of that outfit, black-marketing being more than a sideline of some personnel.

The 14th Air Force had an air of organization and discipline that was lacking in the AVG.

p. 132 Anti-Japanese feeling had been particularly strong among intellectuals for a quarter century, but it was the exceptional one of them who showed his patriotism by joining the Chinese Army. Many of the interpreters who worked with us were overseas Chinese inspired to come home to join in the anti-Japanese struggle. A few of them were or had been army officers. Some were unhappy at having been drafted into Tai Li's organization. Some of them showed a Chinese scorn for foreign ways and resented foreign advice. A few particularly disliked Westerners, finding us as arrogant in our way as we found them. Accepting our help against the Japanese was a compromise a lot of Chinese disliked.

p. 134 The sound of my name allowed a number of variations in the characters phonetically expressing it. The meaning of the characters on the carved chop I was ceremonially presented, I think by General Li in Kunming, was "climbing lotus," a name I accepted out of politeness. I was not much happier with a chop given me later on, where I came out as "affable and peaceful."

p. 134 Traveling in China in 1986, I was using "comrade" freely, assuming that Chinese under a Communist regime would surely be as free with that salutation. Our American tour guide quietly drew me aside to tell me, "They don't use *tongzhi* any more. Just say '*duibuqi*— excuse me,' if you want someone's attention"—exactly as we had back in the bad Guomindang days!

p. 136 Miles, op. cit., p. 128.

Chapter 15

p. 142 Miles did postgraduate work at the Naval Academy in electrical engineering and later earned a master's degree from Columbia University in the subject. Much of his navy duty had involved technical matters. His previous assignment as recorder to the Interior Control Board, before he was sent to China, dealt with new technical equipment for navy ships.

p. 142 See Miles, op. cit., Chapter 8, "The SACO Agreement and O.S.S. Disagreement," pp. 159-174. It was our old friend, Admiral Purnell, who frustrated OSS scheming in Washington. In fairness, let me say that on the working level there were some fine OSS officers in Chungking that summer who were as put off by OSS politicking as the rest of us. Members of the OSS contingent added style to our Chungking headquarters, Saul Steinberg being the leading example. Our view of ourselves and of the Chungking valley were forever defined by his talented pen. Steinberg's work became widely known after the war, particularly through his engaging drawings that appeared regularly in *The New Yorker*.

p. 143 His remarks on "old China hands" appear in a letter Miles wrote to the Navy Department in 1942. Miles, op. cit., p. 93.

p. 145 The two letters I wrote Miles from Calcutta are in a collection in the National Archives entitled Record Group 38, Records of U.S. Naval Group China, Vice Admiral Milton E. Miles, 1927–1957. Miles had these pulled together for writing his memoir, *A Different Kind of War*. The collection is not indexed to facilitate finding a particular document or place or subject. Mrs. Kathleen Lloyd of the Naval Historical Center told me the contents of the chapters of Miles's book are the best guide to the files, as indeed they are. The papers are often segregated in the files according to the chapter subjects. When I cite this collection, as I shall be doing from here on, I'll refer to it simply as Records of the U.S. Naval Group. Richard Von Doenhoff and Barry Zerby of Military Reference at the National Archives helped me locate the proper files.

p. 146 Records of the discussions at these meetings on 12 and 19 December were kept by Lt. S. I. Morris and are found in the Records of U.S. Naval Group, op. cit. Joe Champe and Ted Cathey distinguished themselves during the summer of 1944. Their adventures with Chinese troops along the Yangzi are reported by Miles, op. cit. and in the collection on SACO by Roy Stratton. Roy Olin Stratton, *SACO—The Rice Paddy Navy*, C.S. Palmer Publishing Company, Pleasantville, New York, 1950. Stratton's work, out of print, repeats claims of successes against the Japanese by SACO in a collection of anecdotes gathered soon after the war. Stratton's statement on p. vii, quoted below, cannot be substantiated by operations witnessed or otherwise verified by American participants. I don't mean to say that all Chinese claims should be dismissed. I do suggest that only research in Chinese and Japanese files, as well as ours, can lead to a sound assessment of the accomplishments of SACO.

From June 1, 1944 to July 1, 1945, SACO guerrillas, at times led by Navy and Marine Corps personnel, killed 23,540 Japanese, wounded 9,166, captured 291 and destroyed 209 bridges, 84 locomotives and 141 ships and river craft, besides many depots and warehouses.

p. 147 Miles, op. cit., p. 214.

p. 147 Miles, Ibid., p. 217.

p. 148 From a dispatch dated 2 May 1944, Records of U.S. Naval Group, op. cit.

Chapter 17

p. 163 The Camp One monthly report for September 1943 is contained in Records Group 38, Records of the U. S. Naval Group, op. cit.

p. 164–165 The mechanics of Japanese reprisal were based on the traditional Chinese system of *bao jia*, a hundred families being organized into a *jia* and ten of those making a *bao*. In practice a village or several small villages would make up a *bao*. The head man of the *bao* was called the *baozhang*. It was with the *baozhang* or village headman that we often dealt on coming to a Chinese village.

Chapter 18

p. 171 The missions Miles outlined are contained in a memorandum he wrote Tai Li on 26 August 1943. Records of U.S. Naval Group, op. cit. He listed also motor roads and five airfields in Zhejiang Province for reconnaissance and possible sabotage missions, sections of railway from Nanking to Shanghai to Hangzhou to Ningpo, and Yangzi River traffic near Wuhu and Nanjing.

p. 173–174 Miles reported his conversations with Tai Li in a letter to Washington of 8 June 1944, Ibid. For some reason, Miles decided that the departure of a few of us for operations would cause a shortage of people. He asked for an unnecessary three officers and twelve sergeants to be sent to Camp One so we could be released.

p. 175 Miles, op. cit., p. 254 and p. 258.

p. 175 The memo on the "Philippine Express" or "Marianas Express" to the China coast was written by Cap. J. C. Metzel in November 1944. Records of U. S. Naval Group, op. cit.

p. 175–176 The remark by Miles about the capture of Iwo Jima appears in Miles, op. cit., p. 467. Spector, op. cit., p. 420, says the loss of the Chinese airfields in the summer of 1944 "rendered the seizure of a port on the China coast less than urgent." The landing in the Philippines, beginning at Leyte in October 1944, with consequent huge loss of life— American and Japanese troops, Philippine civilians—hardly seems to have been urgent either, but General MacArthur's political skills were irresistible.

p. 176 Shaoxing, near Hangzhou, is famous for its light yellow wine. The town was in Japanese hands, but we arranged to get wine out to Camp One. It came in a handsome beige pottery crock that it took two men to carry. We drank it soon, as cold as we could get it, some of us pretending it was a martini—requiring a forceful imagination—others, a sherry, and it was more like that. It oxidized and went sour fast.

p. 178 Parkin in a letter of 14 October 1944 and one written on 27 September. Records of U.S. Naval Group, op. cit.

Chapter 19

p. 180 1959 edition of the Britannica, Volume 11, p. 151.

p. 180 The reports on the Qiantang River bridge that Parkin sent to Chungking are found in the Records of U.S. Naval Group, op. cit.

p. 187 *Laobaixing*—literally, "old hundred names." A friendly term for a farmer or villager, like paisano in Spanish. A Chinese *li*, used as a measurement of distance, is usually considered about a third of a mile. In practice the *li* was measured by the mood of your informant of the moment.

p. 187 Bob Boger, one of the group of us that went back to Camp One in 1986, wrote me this in a letter in 1991.

p. 187 Records of U.S. Naval Group, op. cit.

Chapter 20

p. 190 The account of the 20 September raid on Ximoushi is based on the test of a report I wrote to Chungking on return to General Ma's. Records of U.S. Naval Group, op. cit.

p. 196 The accounts of the Zhuji raid are taken from Camp One correspondence reporting the action. Ibid. I am indebted also to conversations with Jacob Siegrist, Robert Boger, and James Rainey, who took part in the raid. Letters Boger and Rainey wrote in 1991 are quoted in the test. The quotation on p. 260 from Parkin's memorandum as well as later quotations are found in the Records of the U. S. Naval Group, op. cit.

Chapter 21

p. 200 Clams are a metal container with magnets attached and shaped to fit under the flange of a railroad rail. Packed with explosive, the clam destroys the rail on being detonated. Siegrist's and the reports of the expedition I went on in November are in the Records of the U.S. Naval Group, op. cit.

In the text I have changed the phonetic spellings we Americans gave place names to the current pinyin renditions of Chinese where I can. Lacking Chinese characters, some of my versions may be off, but certainly as close as some of our wild approximations at the time.

p. 201 Miles's remarks about Jayne are found in Miles, op. cit., pp. 419, 483, 485-6, 516-18.

p. 200, 202 Parkin's remarks are found in the Records of the U.S. Naval Group, op. cit.

p. 203 Siegrist's operational reports are in Ibid.

Chapter 22

p. 212–217 The report of Hull's raid at Zhuji, the comments of Tawater and McCoy, and my forwarding letter, all at some greater length than repeated here, are to be found in Records of U. S. Naval Group, op. cit.

Chapter 23

p. 220–221 Hull's full report, a discourse on his observation of guerrilla operations, is dated 28 December 1944 and is included in the Records of U.S. Naval Group, op. cit.

p. 221 Siegrist's "Report of Sabotage Action on Hangzhou-Jinhua Railway Area 5-6-7 January 1945 is included in Ibid.

p. 222 From Hull's "REPORT OF TROOP TRAIN WRECKING IN ZHUJI AREA MARCH 1945, Ibid.

p. 222–223 The full account by Alfred Liang is included in "STATEMENT OF EVENTS HAPPENED 6TH–8TH MARCH 1944." Ibid.

p. 223–224 From Hull's "REPORT OF TROOP TRAIN WRECKING IN ZHUJI AREA MARCH 1945, Ibid.

p. 225 From Camp One correspondence, Ibid.

p. 225 The remarks on the Yangzi valley are from Spence, op. cit., p. 464. On Communists in the LPA area in the summer of 1945. See Miles, op. cit., Chapter 21, where he quotes Lieutenant Hilton Jayne's information on Communist pressure on the LPA.

p. 225 On the friendly Communists north of the Yangzi. According to the June 1944 Camp One monthly report, Lt. F. A. Roll, and Lt. J. W. Bartlett Jr., both of the 449th Fighter Squadron, were shot down during a raid on Anjing on 18 June and got to Camp One on 28 June. I think these were the two who were delivered by the New Fourth to LPA elements along the Yangzi. Their names, for some reason, are not shown on the list of pilots picked up by Navy Group or passed into Navy Group hands, a number of whom passed through Camp One on their way back to west China. Ibid.

p. 226 On the carbines, Ibid.

p. 226 Re Soviets, see Spence, op. cit., pp. 377–8.

p. 227–228 The remarks about the unschooled men appear in an imprudent letter that George Parker and I composed sometime in late 1944 or even early 1945, the date being illegible. Records of U. S. Naval Group, op. cit.

Chapter 24

p. 231 The Camp One monthly report for 31 January 1945, Records of U.S. Naval Group, op. cit.